The Absent Father Effect on Daughters

The Absent Father Effect on Daughters investigates the impact of absent – physically or emotionally – and inadequate fathers on the lives and psyches of their daughters through the perspective of Jungian analytical psychology. This book tells the stories of daughters who describe the insecurity of self, the splintering and disintegration of the personality and the silencing of voice.

Issues of fathers and daughters reach to the intra-psychic depths and archetypal roots, to issues of self and culture, both personal and collective. Susan E. Schwartz illustrates the maladies and disappointments of daughters who lack a father figure and incorporates clinical examples describing how daughters can break out of idealizations, betrayals, abandonments and losses to move towards repair and renewal. The book takes an interdisciplinary approach, expanding and elucidating Jungian concepts through dreams, personal stories, fairy tales and the poetry of Sylvia Plath, along with psychoanalytic theory, including André Green's 'dead father effect' and Julia Kristeva's theories on women and the body as abject.

Examining daughters both personally and collectively affected by the lack of a father, *The Absent Father Effect on Daughters* is highly relevant for those wanting to understand the complex dynamics of daughters and fathers to become their authentic selves. It will be essential reading for anyone seeking understanding, analytical and depth psychologists, other therapy professionals, academics and students with Jungian and post-Jungian interests.

Susan E. Schwartz is a Jungian analyst and clinical psychologist in Arizona, USA. As a member of the International Association of Analytical Psychology she has taught and presented at conferences and workshops in the United States and worldwide. She has several articles and book chapters on these aspects of Jungian psychology. Her website is www.susanschwartzphd.com.

'Truly something new and original on the daughter–father connection. Schwartz explains how and why daughters remain enmeshed with fathers whom, for whatever reason, have been less than good-enough. There is no demonization; rather, an exquisite compassion shines through. Whilst she writes as a clinician – and a really good one, as her account of working with dreams shows – Schwartz offers something that, by definition really, applies to every woman and the majority of men who will read it.'

– **Andrew Samuels**, author of *The Plural Psyche: Personality, Morality and the Father* and editor of *The Father: Contemporary Jungian Perspectives*

'How do you have an incest fantasy about someone who isn't there; or if they are, they terrify? How do you mourn the loss of someone you never knew, of a relationship you never had? Drawing on her life's work as a clinician, the author deftly goes to the heart of trauma in the father-daughter relationship: showing how connecting to the archetypal father and collective experience a healing can begin.'

– **Dale Mathers**, Jungian analyst, UK

'Susan Schwartz has written a much-needed book about fathers and daughters, one that addresses the psychic damage of the "emotionally absent and deadened father", which "affects a daughter's body, mind and soul". With compassion, wisdom and a Jungian theoretical and clinical understanding of the psyche, Schwartz places this psychological dilemma in a wider context of psychoanalysis and the depth psychologies. Her clinical examples are apt and her passionate encouragement for us to understand this issue is inspiring.'

– **Margaret Klenck**, MDiv, LP, Jungian analyst and past president of the Jungian Psychoanalytic Association, New York, USA

The Absent Father Effect on Daughters

Father Desire, Father Wounds

Susan E. Schwartz

Routledge
Taylor & Francis Group

LONDON AND NEW YORK

First published 2021
by Routledge
2 Park Square, Milton Park, Abingdon, Oxon OX14 4RN

and by Routledge
52 Vanderbilt Avenue, New York, NY 10017

Routledge is an imprint of the Taylor & Francis Group, an informa business

British Library Cataloguing-in-Publication Data
A catalogue record for this book is available from the British Library

Library of Congress Cataloging-in-Publication Data
Names: Schwartz, Susan E., 1946- author.
Title: The absent father effect on daughters: father desire, father
wounds / Susan E. Schwartz.
Description: 1 Edition. | New York: Routledge, 2020. |
Includes bibliographical references and index.
Identifiers: LCCN 2020026956 (print) | LCCN 2020026957 (ebook) |
ISBN 9780367360856 (paperback) | ISBN 9780367360818 (hardback) |
ISBN 9780429343728 (ebook)
Subjects: LCSH: Fathers and daughters. | Absentee fathers. |
Fatherhood–Psychological aspects. | Daughters–Psychology. |
Child development. | Jungian psychology.
Classification: LCC HQ755.85 S387 2020 (print) |
LCC HQ755.85 (ebook) | DDC 306.874/2–dc23
LC record available at https://lccn.loc.gov/2020026956
LC ebook record available at https://lccn.loc.gov/2020026957

ISBN: 978-0-367-36081-8 (hbk)
ISBN: 978-0-367-36085-6 (pbk)
ISBN: 978-0-429-34372-8 (ebk)

Typeset in Times
by Deanta Global Publishing Services, Chennai, India

Sublime and severe, the rock is supremely dangerous; for it takes whatever it wants and offers no explanation. It is power and might without love and grace; the god of an old testament, the Ancient of Days.

Gillian Rose, *Love's Work* (1996, pp. 48–49)

To Frederic for his sensitive support and care

Contents

Acknowledgements

I want to convey thanks to my colleague Pui Harvey who over the years has always been there in truth; Daniela Roher for reading and commenting on some of the chapters; and Barbara Aliza for the cover design. Acknowledgement goes to all the friends who have supported and encouraged me along the way. Also to LeeAnn Pickrell, who edited with a fine eye for style. Of course, I am indebted to those who have shared their life stories in Jungian analysis, clarifying the development of these ideas for both of us on this journey.

Credits

Introduction

This is a love story, but an unrequited one. It is about the needs a daughter has for a father figure, made more prominent and painful when he is absent. A daughter is left to cope in countless ways with the difficulties encountered when her father is not there. The presence of the father's absence affects a daughter's body, mind and soul. I contend it is *this presence of absence* that is most harmful. Additionally, absence is accentuated because it implies a space to be filled and the need to attend to the lack. Absence is also significantly 'a call for the potential of the positive to emerge ... it allows for new thought and fresh experience' (Kohon, 1999, pp. 114–15). For the many reasons detailed throughout this book, the father is an important aspect of the psyche and significant for development of a daughter's psychological and physical life expressed personally and culturally. 'The father is decisive in the destiny of the individual' (Jung, 1961, p. 303). Jung's quote reminds us of the value of a loving father for a daughter's growth.

This book develops the idea that overidentification with or ignorance of the absent father has serious ramifications. A daughter can become unconscious and inwardly empty, without connection to herself. Here, I pay specific attention to the absent father–daughter dynamics, even though other factors affect her development, such as her mother, culture and learned gender roles and styles. Of note is that when there is no father, a daughter is left wondering if she is valued and worthy of love from herself and others. When her father cannot see, regard or be with her, she has a hole in her heart; the threads of her personality rupture. She is placed on the journey to repair and join the missing pieces together. Consider Sarah Kofman's words on the 'pathos of distance':

> which separates two types of life that have always already been in existence: the one flourishing and superabundant, projecting its own excess into things and embellishing them; the other degenerate, able only to impoverish the world by reducing it to the narrow and ugly measure of the concept, in order to spite itself and out of resentment toward life.
>
> (Kofman, 1994, p. 20)

The situation of a father's absence implies the question of how a father dreams of his daughter. What does he wish for her? When absent, he has not realized her needs for good attachment or how he might damage her by his withdrawal. This lack of regard creates delicate areas within the daughter punctuated with various psychological impasses. Because she does not appear in his vision, she receives no reflection from him, impeding her self-development.

I explore this topic from the perspective of Jungian analytical psychology with its particular in-depth approach to the personality. This includes the unconscious made apparent in father complexes, archetypes and symbols appearing in a daughter's life and dreams. Each of these aspects reveals the origins of fathers and daughters, the potentials and paradoxes, the issues and problems and their release and resolution. How the father is imagined and perceived comes to us through books, media of all kinds, mythology, fairy tales, movies and literature. Depending on each culture and era, the father takes on somewhat different roles and images that reflect his presence in our collective and personal psyches.

This book evolved from being privy to the numerous stories told in Jungian analytical psychotherapy by daughters with absent fathers. It derived from colleagues, friends and personal experiences of the deprivation suffered without a father's love and care. These daughters emoted the needs, longings and wishes for the presence of a good father. This common and necessary desire has sadly gone unmet through generations. The need for the love of a father is made more painful and apparent by its absence and loss. The accompanying melancholy and the residual lack remain palpable. Here I trace the array of feelings and the effects on women bonded to the father not there.

The topics range from the negative father complex, to the daddy's girl or the puella archetype and narcissism, as interpreted in Jungian analytical psychology. The book also explores other approaches to the absent father, including the perspectives of French psychoanalyst André Green on the dead father effect, British Jungian analyst Hester Solomon on the 'as-if' personality and the body collapse in autoimmune disease applied to the theory of abjection from French psychoanalyst Julia Kristeva. Of interest to therapy professionals is a chapter addressing issues of transference/countertransference and the reflective, symbolic and transcendent functions providing healing.

The book has relevance for those wanting to understand the complex dynamics of daughters and fathers affecting personality development and the capacity to be authentically true to one's self. Each of the chapters addresses multiple responses to a father's absence, and each personal story has collective repercussions. The focus is on daughters and fathers to help shed light not only on the symptoms and problems but also on the treatment and hope. The chapters contain composite examples of daughter narratives and their subsequent journey through dreams, interior reflections and relationships. This book is composed of their stories and the emotional events encountered in therapy along the way to self-discovery. The narrations allow readers to identify with the private and intimate examples of the obstacles expressing life tensions and challenges and the possibilities for development. Interspersed are quotes from a variety of writers. As Adam Phillips reminds us: 'Our passionate selves are our best selves: and a passionate life is only possible, by definition, if we can make our passions known: to ourselves ... There can be no passion – without representation. ... Passion entails circulation and exchange' (Phillips, 1999, p. 166).

References

Jung, C.G. (1961). *Freud and Psychoanalysis*, Vol. 4. Princeton, NJ: Princeton University Press.

Kofman, S. (1994). *Nietzsche and Metaphor*. D. Large (Trans.). Stanford, CA: Stanford University Press.

Kohon, G. (Ed.) (1999). *The Dead Mother: The Work of André Green*. London, England: Routledge.

Phillips, A. (1999). Taking aims: André Green and the pragmatics of passion. In: G. Kohon (Ed.), *The Dead Mother: The Work of André Green* (pp. 165–74). London, England: Routledge.

Chapter 1

The parallax

> We hear endlessly all around us that unvarying sound which is not an echo
> from without, but the resonance of a vibration from within.
>
> Marcel Proust, *Swann's Way* (1922, p. 93)

A *parallax*, according to the *Oxford English Dictionary*, is a word referring to the apparent displacement and change in the position of an object relative to other objects. What changes is the observer's sight directed towards the object. The word originates from the Greek and the French meaning to change, exchange and also to include other viewpoints. This exploration is a window through which to perceive the father absence, a parallax focusing on the grimmer perspectives. These narrations are meant to evoke, to escape the fetters and the devitalizing depression, and subsequently to bring out self-assertion and creation. They illustrate and reveal the complicated map of the psyche. The dynamics form a kaleidoscope of images revealing disturbances of the soul, the misalignments and the repair.

To find her centre a daughter has to turn inwards to find her life story. The parallax of her perspectives alters by recognizing the disturbances from the absent father. Sifting through and peeling off the layers of time, learned responses, the wishes covering reality takes a long time. Through all this the daughter begins to feel, think, reflect and discover herself.

Personal and collective reflections open the wounds to reveal damages and patterns, allowing the daughter to discover what can be transformed. My emphasis in this book is on the exploration of psychological life affected by the absent father personally and collectively. Focus on the daughter herself is a parallax, a twist and a purposeful change of emphasis. The daughter is one of the female archetypes in need of exploration (Porterfield, Polette, & Baumlin, 2009, p. 4) to foster individual and collective healing. To unravel the issues caused by father absence, the daughter recollects what was lost and damaged. Personally, culturally and psychologically a daughter finds her way through the generations of cumulative wounds, losses and absences, and, in the process, diverges from her father's way onto her own way.

A myth of betrayal

In the ancient Greek myth of Iphigenia, her father, Agamemnon, in essence sacrificed her to get a good wind to sail to the Trojan War. While the Greek army was preparing to set sail for Troy, Agamemnon killed a sacred deer, angering the goddess Artemis. Artemis calmed all winds, so the ships could not set sail. The seer Calchas informed Agamemnon that to appease the goddess he had to sacrifice Iphigenia. Reluctant at first, Agamemnon was forced in the end to agree. He lied to his daughter and his wife, saying that Iphigenia was to marry Achilles before they left. The mother and daughter happily went to the port of Aulis, only to discover the horrible truth. Achilles, unaware his name had been used in this lie, tried to prevent the sacrifice. Iphigenia then decided to sacrifice herself in honour and of her own volition. The most popular version of what happened afterwards is that at the moment of sacrifice Artemis substituted a deer for Iphigenia and the seer Calchas, who was the only witness, remained silent. Artemis brought Iphigenia to the city of Tauris where she then became the goddess's priestess.

This myth brings forth the archetypal story of betrayal by a father using his daughter for his benefit, resulting in her demise. She is damaged by her father's personal greed and need for glory. Like so many stories and realities, it reveals one of the many iterations of the daughter betrayed, abandoned and killed, be it physically, as in this story, or psychologically.

From childhood we create complex, ongoing narratives from words, body language, emotions, images, rituals and interactions to articulate our life. Psychic growth occurs in relation to a father and a daughter's experiences with him. When a father is absent, he neglects the relationship with his daughter. He becomes associated with yearning, sadness, frustrated love, anger and rage, oppression and desire. These contradictory feelings cause stress to body and soul, and from this comes the urgent need for the daughter to find herself.

The emphasis here is on the father's betrayal, his breaking of the good paternal promise, the deprivation of support and love and its effects on the daughter's mind, body and love for self and other. 'The primary context in which betrayal is experienced is the family, for it is there that the first love pact is sealed, a pact that menaces and at the same time makes possible individual psychological birth' (Carotenuto, 2015, p. 43). An absent father oppresses to the extent he is and is not there. His absence contributes to a self-image as inadequate, infantile and dutiful. The daughter might also be ambivalent about her life, angry and depressed.

The father is supposed to foster emotional life and value but does not. What the daughter gets instead of love is emptiness which she can neither securely attach to nor separate from. This is often accompanied by masochistic and unloving attitudes, mostly turned onto herself. The result is confusion and denial of autonomy. She is, in effect, imprisoned with the absent father and in this place remains unconscious. The disturbance caused by an absent father early in life can set up a daughter to hate and distance herself not only from him but also from other males and be unable to access the range of the masculine and the feminine within herself.

Many daughters are raised on the myth of the daughter–father romance. But is this myth really true? Why has this story been accepted as true even when a father has rarely been present? Remaining faithful to the myth of the father who rules and has authority has ramifications as the daughter renounces the meaning for her existence (Carotenuto, 2015, p. 52). The absence of a father sets a daughter up for anguish and disappointment, often killing her creativity and life force. Her endeavours are stamped with depression, anxiety and disturbed relationships.

Aurora dreamt there was a line of men in hats and suits. Her father was with them at a distance from her. The men had cameras from her father's era. She could go with them. However, she noticed another man dressed in modern clothes, sitting on the side of the road at a table full of lovely things from the father's era. He suggested she sit down, and as she did so he gave her an iPhone filled with photos of her current home, the area across the street and one of her favourite women poets.

As we discussed the dream, Aurora did not think to associate the men with her father. Although this might be an obvious association, she had been so hurt by him and cruelly rejected she had erased all else but the dull reaction of duty.

The dream brought up memories of his emotional stoicism and lack of love or kindness. Her father was absent in quite radical ways, even bordering on the perverse in his lack of attention. Out in the world he was lauded and the centre of attention, a quite charismatic man. At home, however, he was mean and selfish, a patriarchal presence, stern, demanding, forbidding, rarely present, filled with rules of how to be, pointing out how she fell short. The contrast was confusing, and she could tell no one how she suffered his lack of love. Who would believe her? Moreover, he ignored her or his comments to her were derisive. Nothing she did gained any good recognition. Yet she anticipated his coming home when he did. He had an extensive library, and she snuck out the books she loved to read. She did not tell him because she knew she would be punished or put down. Yet he was better than her mother who ignored her altogether.

In the dream the man by the roadside, although sitting down with a cane and seemingly tired, had lovely things from the father's era. She could take a picture with the iPhone, a modern camera, and see the surroundings from her viewpoint. She did not have to go the father's way, although the dream paradoxically recognized some value there. Perhaps she had yet to discover the value as it had been obstructed by his abrupt, cold and dismissive manner towards her. Currently she was at a crossroads: a relationship had ended, her career was in question, physical issues needed attention. The dream and her associations illustrated the divergence from the father, his rules and authoritarianism. Had she, however, retained an unconscious identification with him although she had determined to be otherwise?

Her primary relationship for many years was with someone equally distant and unemotional, someone who wanted things done but who expressed little warmth and connection. She had to keep proving her worth. She did not get her needs met, but then she was not in touch with them. She had no place to get care. Long ago she had learned not to go to her father for anything as he would just be cold and forbidding and accuse her of wanting too much. Even as a child she could not ask for his attention. She avoided him so much she had few memories and did not ever question the situation, as there were no answers. Over the years, at each upsetting or shocking event, she kept emotions locked up inside herself, never sharing them as she felt rejected and shut off. She defied her father with her ambition and intellect, needing to prove her worth and him wrong. All her energy went into her career as a high-level executive, and she often worked 100 hours a week.

After her father died, she recognized the emptiness of her emotional life and left the relationship with the woman who felt like her family. Although the relationship had been emotionally empty, it was all she knew. When we began meeting, she was in her mid-forties and this was her first therapeutic venture into her interior self. Over time she began to value what proved to be her rich inner world, looking forward to the feelings she now noticed, the dreams she recorded and the thoughts she had. She became eager to learn more and to put the pieces of her life together. From her father's absence and his lack of emotionality and putting her needs down, she had learned self-avoidance. This had repeated itself in her primary relationship for 15 years, until after her father's death when the emotions came pouring out. As she said, she had blown apart her life and was eagerly exploring what she had formerly ignored.

Catastrophe of absence

When absent, a father cannot reflect to a daughter a separate and individual self. Instead, he represents a locus of distress, and she searches anxiously and in vain for connection. She is disappointed in the shattering of wishes while retaining an attitude of denial concerning what has happened. The catastrophe of absence takes time to recognize. 'The only paradises cannot be those that are lost, but those that are unlocked as a result of coercion, reluctance, cajolery and humiliation, their thresholds crossed without calm prescience, or any preliminary perspicacity' (Rose, 1996, p. 35). Digesting reality slowly brings the demise of the pretend fantasy father. In order to make sense of what is not understandable, a daughter often accepts blame for their lack of relationship. As Jung commented, 'Until you make the unconscious conscious, it will direct your life and you will call it fate' (Jung, 1968, para. 126).

The absence of father love includes his enactment of ambivalent, inconsistent or downright hostile behaviours with and around the daughter. The world becomes rejecting, and she is static, refusing it all – passion, love, feeling, emotion, being. She needs help out of this incomprehensible catastrophe, help to not take it in and re-create the loss internally and in other relationships. The absence is 'an intermediary situation between presence … and loss' (Urribarri, 2017). In other words, and from a perspective seeking personality expansion, absence stands in the centre of the experiences of presence and loss.

The absence of a personal father impacts the way a daughter internalizes the collective psychological and social norms influencing her identity. Frustration and anger turn not outwards to the father, as he is not there, but inwards towards herself. For many daughters to face this means confronting the unacceptable, the disillusions, betrayals and lies, which are also promulgated by society and culture.

The father's distance can be measured in the psychic space created by his absence. Facing this, she can no longer deny what it is to be without love, regard and importance. Behind hate for the father absence is the desire for love, which can become a fascination that can rivet the daughter to the father. Curiously this lure becomes stronger when a father has not offered himself for identification and does not welcome the daughter into his life. Nevertheless, and even more so because he is absent, he remains significant in her mind.

The lost, absent father demands attention at the same time he has been withholding it. Given all this, how curious it is that there has been such a scarcity of reflection on the father as a significant member of the family; how unconscious he has remained yet how prominent. Coming to terms with this history – both personal and cultural, conscious and unconscious – is a complex process. The stories included here are narrated to undo the accumulated repressions. The process requires entering this labyrinth, through the desire, anxiety, pain, mourning and unconsciousness to open other experiences. In confronting the father issues the daughter trespasses the former idealized father, absent in so many ways, to access what is real. This situation reflects the impoverishment that is attributed to the early traumatizing experiences with the longed for and idealized other (Solomon, 2004, p. 639).

According to the *Oxford English Dictionary* the word *absent* means 'the state of being away from a place or person … the nonexistence or lack'. Absence includes the father's emotional absence, even if he is physically present. The explication of these dynamics and their effects is underlaid with the hope that fathers and daughters emerge out of old entrenched positions into conscious and fulfilling relationships. In relation to this Jung said:

> We are confronted, at every new stage in the differentiation of consciousness to which civilization attains, with the task of finding a new interpretation appropriate to this stage, in order to connect the life of the past that still exists in us with the life of the present, which threatens to slip away from it.
>
> (Jung, 1959, p. 267)

The agonies of absence do not fade away. The conflicts, confusion, self-doubt and depression are strongly felt. Until relatively recently, a rather strangely unexplored and pervasive conspiracy of silence surrounded the daughter–father relationship. It was not discussed or addressed, and it was assiduously ignored. Past child-rearing practices obfuscated the effects of the father not being there or, conversely, being there but not there at the same time. Still, despite the widespread and almost collective character of these experiences, Western culture has tended to underestimate the necessity for a father's strong involvement from the beginning of a daughter's life.

Historically, the daughter was considered to be of little value and was property for barter. She belonged to the father and his way so thoroughly that his absence or how he acted, especially in regard to her, went unquestioned. The untouched space around fathers culturally, personally and psychologically submerged his influence into the unconscious. We might think this more prevalent in the past, but it is still notable in the current family dynamics of Western culture. Although written years ago, the following is applicable. Donald Winnicott, British psychoanalyst and paediatrician, said, 'the little depth or detail about the role of the father was also because he had such a small definition in the family and was not significant as a male person there' (1995, p. 142). Too many fathers still assume the needed emotion and care will come from the mother, thereby cheating themselves and their daughters.

In their meagre offerings and without the experiences of loving fathers, daughters are left with a gaping hole where father love should be. He has contagious effects when present in an absent way. The daughter might try to please or save the father to obtain a semblance of parenting. Some choose to be different from him whereas others are compliant and unconsciously remain prisoners to the past. French psychoanalyst Julia Kristeva commented:

> The self – wounded, incomplete, empty, is felt to have a fundamental flaw, a congenital deficiency. Such logic presupposes a severe super-ego and a complex dialectic of idealization and devalorization, both of self and other. It is an identification with the loved/hated other – through incorporation, introjection, projection – that is effected by the taking into oneself of an ideal, sublime, part or trait of the other and that becomes the tyrannical inner judge.
>
> (1992, p. 6)

The previous description applies to a daughter emptied of self, not knowing how to find herself as she has taken in an empty father.

Fathering has to do with past and future relations, events and emotions. What follows from this is a progressive identification of difference. Its process and message originate with the father as other (Perelberg, 2018, p. 24). In this position the presence of a father is important for finding reflection, knowledge and separation. It is also through father as other that a daughter comes to experience herself. This is the very experience replicated and repaired through the therapeutic relationship.

Diverse psychoanalytic and cultural concepts have portrayed the father figure as powerful, idolized, an impervious entity promising protection and guidance but remaining the ultimate authority. When it comes to the daughter, traditional Freudian psychoanalytic thinking has addressed the myth of the Oedipal father and son, but that of the daughter and father has not garnered so much attention. In Greek mythology, the focus is not on the female but more on the father and son as primary, the daughter as secondary and rather insignificant, typically depicted with lack. Jung himself was a father with four daughters, and he hardly addressed the daughter–father relationship. He wrote one essay on the father.

What has been ignored or given insufficient attention creates upset. '[B]efore we can ... face the future ... we have ... to remember the needs of our instinctive, intuitive, natural self' (Meier, 1985, p. 56). This means a recognition of that which has never left and remains within the psyche, just waiting for attention. Admittedly, the dynamics depicted here are slanted on the bleaker side to emphasize the effects of father absence and lack on daughters. However, the appeal is to fathers who also benefit from experiencing their daughters in healthy ways.

Absence overshadows

> To climb steep hills requires slow pace at first.
>> William Shakespeare, *Henry VIII* (1613), Act I,
>> scene 1, line 131

This situation of absence references the shadow in Jungian analytical psychology, referring to those aspects remaining undeveloped, unseen and ignored with repercussions for both daughters and fathers. The father attachment made of his absence can negatively manifest in the daughter's restless anxiety or depression; her spirit may be desperate, squashed and bereft. Because of father absence, parts of her psyche remain inaccessible, untouched and unconscious. The gaps connote disjunction between conscious and unconscious, distorting reality. From the absent father, she has learned to not want too much, not say too much, not climb too high.

The more consciousness is taken over by ignoring the effect of the absent father, the more absence creates a blank space and she is lost in a maze. This passes on the 'rhetoric of pain, with bearing witness to that which has never been witnessed: with absence; and with the melancholy that arises from failed or faulted communication' (Kalinich & Taylor, 2009, p. 163). The daughter passively does not question, or she might choose to turn away from the father and all he represents. In either case, she remains unknown, the dynamics unexamined, and she is distant and also absent from her own knowledge of self.

Jung described this as an unrecognized shadow, something within that is quite close but unknown. 'The shadow is a living part of the personality and therefore wants to live with it in some form. It cannot be argued out of existence or rationalized into harmlessness' (Jung, 1959, p. 44). When a father is emotionally distant and absent, a daughter's early experiences of love come packaged with deprivation. Anxiety is connected with the anticipation of re-experiencing the father loss and his separation with its effects on her personality.

Without the foundation of a father, the daughter feels on edge, as if she's falling into a crevasse, without security, and this feeling only hardens in adulthood. There is inner desperation and lack of self-acceptance. She cannot find fidelity to her rhythm, and she feels she does not really exist. There is a kind of barrier within herself and the world can become pointless.

The responsible father

An emotionally related and present father facilitates a daughter's healthy energy and builds self-esteem. He is the other besides the mother figure with whom she establishes individuality. His consistency and support give a solid rhythm for life. He knows how to hug her, to attend to her emotions, to support her mind and foster self-care. Obviously, an adequate relationship with him provides acceptance, love, stability, discipline and self-strength and, when sufficient, gives her the confidence to express creative potential (Kavaler-Adler, 2000, p. 187). He is a doorway to the world and integral to developing identity. The increasing realization is that a father's involvement throughout life affects the daughter and also the father. He is now recognized as important in children developing self-feeling, body connection, respect, care and an inner reflective, thoughtful and secure existence.

There is no question that fathers play an important part in their daughter's lives. An involved father is crucial for psychological, behavioural and general health and wellbeing. Having a related father figure helps a daughter, as she needs his wisdom, experience, imparting of skills and kindly guidance. When fathers are actively present in a loving, nurturing relationship, daughters have greater self-confidence, perform better in school and are able to avoid risky behaviours.

A good father facilitates his daughter's attempts to explore the environment and freely actualize herself. A father provides many possibilities for her being and supports the overthrow of restrictions that could be placed upon her or divert her individual originality. Her movement into the world is facilitated with his nurturance. Meaning-making comes with relationship to the father and depends on 'the self-organizing emergent properties of the human mind but also on the daughter's introduction to the world of social meanings through interpersonal relationship' (Knox, 2004, p. 6).

Currently changing family structures and the loss of his former position opens the possibility of aliveness in the paternal function (Kalinich & Taylor, 2009, p. 192). The twenty-first-century father is in flux as by now he has acquired some societal and psychological expectations for his participation and emotional expressivity. Although receiving little attention in the past, the effect of the father figure has come to the forefront. Incrementally and more apparent in the current era, a father has become increasingly involved, emotional and active in the heart of the family rather than outside it.

His/story of lack

And still the figure of the father remains associated with repressions, misalignments and lack of development. This is a current story with a long history of lack. In the past, the importance of the father for his daughter was forgotten or denied. The deleterious effect on daughters, until relatively recently, remained insufficiently explored and generally ignored. In the father's absence, the daughter becomes dominated by destructive impulses, cut off from her instincts. Her personality is rooted in his lack.

From this she learns self-doubts, her truthfulness waylaid in nameless disjunctions. When a daughter cannot exist safely and independently in the eyes of the father, it can bring about a dissociative denial of self-agency, a denial of self in relationship and fear of love (Knox, 2010, p. 137). Relationships feel like they have to be controlled; she becomes watchful of the other and loses touch with herself. Without sufficient emotional connection, a daughter's subsequent attachments are shaped with distance, lack of trust and personal anxiety. Satisfaction in life is limited, adulthood feigned rather than fulfilled. Just as secure attachment shows the positive impact on daughters' development, insecure attachment impacts development of the negative father complex. Girls whose early childhood is characterized by father absence can grow up on either extreme of demeaning or lauding the paternal.

Deprived of the alchemy of engagement with a father, even in therapy the daughter frequently does not quickly bring up or focus on him. He has been a blank space she can't get close to. Or, the efforts to forget or ignore her feelings mask the effects of his absence, creating yet more absence. Perhaps he told her she was fine without him, or he was interested in her but not able to be there. She had to accept his absence but that did not mean he did not love her. So what did his absence mean? And in his absence how can she find love?

Being a father is not just a biological fact but has psychological and cultural implications. This chapter and the following ones are meant to graphically and tragically convey the deleterious effects on a daughter. 'The repressed and neglected insist on being known. It means addressing the deficits that have neglected parts of the personality so the self-regulation of the psyche can begin to attend for healing' (Stein, 1983, p. 68).

Consciousness is not linear but loops back to foster the imaginative in newly emergent ways. It takes the work and rewards from self-examination. Therapeutic work is an effort at broadening and deepening, a going towards inner reflection. It means realizing the complexity and wealth of what lies in the psyche and the richness possible between father and daughter. These stories describe, rather than rigidly define, the absent father problem with the aim of broadening possibilities, so consciousness increases and the situation alters to benefit both. They describe daughters working with the loss and absence to fill in themselves. 'Man is nothing else than his plan; he exists only to the extent that he fulfils himself; he is therefore nothing else than the ensemble of his acts, nothing else than his life' (Sartre, 2000, p. 32; quoted in Sahakian & Sahakian, 1966, p. 167). This lack propels the search through inner discoveries and is linked to society and culture, personal along with collective transformation, in the hope of creating her expansion.

References

Carotenuto, A. (2015). *To Love, to Betray*. Asheville, NC: Chiron Publications.
Jung, C.G. (1959). *The Archetypes and the Collective Unconscious*. New York, NY: Pantheon Books.

Jung, C.G. (1968). *Aion*. New York, NY: Pantheon Books.

Kalinich, L. & Taylor, S.W. (2009). *The Dead Father*. London, England: Routledge.

Kavaler-Adler, S. (2000). *The Compulsion to Create*. New York, NY: Other Press Professional.

Knox, J. (2004). From archetypes to reflective function. *Journal of Analytical Psychology*, *49*(1): 1–19.

Knox, J. (2010). *Self-Agency in Psychotherapy*. New York, NY: W.W. Norton & Co.

Kristeva, J. (1991). *Strangers to Ourselves*. Leon Roudiez (Trans.). London, England: Harvester Wheatsheaf.

Kristeva, J. (1992). *Strangers to Ourselves*. New York, NY: Columbia University Press.

Meier, C.A. (1985). *Testament to the Wilderness*. Culver City, CA: Lapis Press.

Perelberg, R. (Ed.) (2018). *The Psychic Bisexuality: A British-French Dialogue*. London, England: Routledge.

Porterfield, S., Polette, K. & Baumlin, T.F. (Eds.) (2009). *Perpetual Adolescence*. Albany: State University of New York Press.

Proust, M. (1922). *Swann's Way: Remembrance of Things Past* [Ebook 7178]. Retrieved from https://www.gutenberg.org/files/7178/7178-h/7178-h.htm.

Rose, G. (1996). *Love's Work*. New York, NY: Schocken Books.

Sahakian, W.S., Mabel, L. & Sahakian, M.L. (1966). *Ideas of the Great Philosophers*. New York, NY: Barnes & Noble.

Sartre, J.-P. (2000). *Existentialism and Human Emotions*. New York, NY: Citadel.

Solomon, H. (2004). Self creation and the limitless void of dissociation: The 'as if' personality. *Journal of Analytical Psychology*, *49*(5): 635–56.

Stein, M. (1983). *In Midlife: A Jungian Perspective*. Woodstock, CT: Spring Publications.

Urribarri, F. (2017). An interview with Andre Green: On a psychoanalytic journal from 1960 to 2011. In: R.J. Perelberg & G. Kohon (Ed.), *The Greening of Psychoanalysis: Andre Green's New Paradigm in Contemporary Therapy and Practice* (pp. 115–32). London, England: Routledge Books.

Winnicott, D.W. (1995). Ego distortion in terms of true and false self. In: *The Maturational Process and the Facilitating Environment*. London, England: Karnac Books.

Chapter 2

Loss and longing

Something I don't understand was happening. What did she want, that woman who is me? What was happening ... How can I explain it to you: suddenly the whole world that was me shriveled up in fatigue, I could no longer bear on my shoulders – what? – and was succumbing to a tension that I didn't know had always been mine ... the first signs of a landslide, of underground limestone caves, collapsing beneath the weight of stratified archeological layers ... There must be someone who understands. And it's inside myself that I must create that someone who will understand.

Clarise Lispector, *The Passion According to G.H.* (2012, p. 39)

How do we heal the father who is absent and has left holes in his daughter's heart? A daughter may turn from her power or creativity, potential wasted, voice unheard. The desire for the father's love becomes more insistent when listening to its residual of melancholy. Hailey, a patient, noted in therapy when talking about her father:

Not wanting to admit my father's distance and lack of attention is really a fear of it being my issue not his. I fear judgment for the isolated life I've created and can't seem to shake. Judgement I actually deserve. I hope I did not appear to blame my father today in therapy. I have just wanted to ignore distress, power through it and feel stronger for getting through on my own. Made me more self-reliant. The numbness was organic, only affecting me and so harmless to others. But, have I waited too late for help to really make an impact on me or the world?

This father was obviously not there to recognize her psychic aliveness. She was without his confirmation. Her grounding sunk and was never addressed. As she grows, the daughter needs connection with her father followed by his encouragement for timely separation and acknowledgement of their similarities and differences. The psychological interest shifts from similarity to difference and is a basis for meaningful relationships without the fear of loss of self (Knox, 2003, p. 181).

Hailey, always wishing for a father, *dreamt of a father–daughter day*. In the dream, she was happy but, upon awakening, found herself in tears. She remembered with a start how much he was not in her life and how little he knew her or she knew him. She recalled feeling nervous around him and fearful she would displease him, anticipating he would retaliate. She worried she had to be perfect so he would like her and come back. But, whenever she saw him, he took the limelight and she felt diminished. She could say nothing about her feelings and believed that verbalizing her wishes would anger him. Although hurt and disappointed she never addressed this or asked for anything. Through the years she relived the dream during daytime, and at night-time dreamed the dream over and over again, wishing for a father.

The father need encounters the lost foundations and experiences in a daughter's memory. The longing for a father, for good attention and support, are never met and can prevent her from receiving and expressing pleasure. She internalizes failure, and any good is followed by bad. In other words, the good feeling does not last, and she does not know why. Should she give up her longings and desires, uncertain about wanting and wishing? The impotence and loss of direction or control of her life pains her, but she feels helpless against the physical pull of it (Hauke, 1995, p. 520).

The search for the father is connected to the search for herself. It resides in the places she does not yet know. At each stage of a daughter's development the relationship with her father affects her sense of self. She re-experiences the loss of a father, the premature separation he imposed when he was not there, and she's left with the anguish of unmet needs. The following quote relates to how Hailey, mentioned earlier, dealt with the depression and loss:

> I love that [father] ... but even more so I hate it; because I love it, and in order not to lose it, I imbed it in myself; but because I hate it, that other within myself is a bad self, I am bad, I am non-existent ...
>
> (Kristeva, 1988, p. 11)

This loss of self-orientation is reflected in a lack in the self and a lack in connections with others.

The father is ideally an anchor, giving the daughter a foundation, a solid point of reference. Yet when absent, her experiences of self are achieved against the background of loss. This influences how she does or does not cope with the inevitable vicissitudes experienced throughout life. When the father is absent, she is susceptible to the invasion of negative images and behaviours. She adopts various mechanisms to cope with what feels like an amorphous yet intolerable loss.

Perceiving and interpreting events is impossible without the lens of past experiences – that is how we function. The past contextualizes the present day and shapes perceptions, interpretations and emotional reactions. Some women say they felt loved by their father, especially when young. He might have been attentive then and idealized. Often he was projected onto due to his vacancy, emptiness and his just not being there. To compensate, the daughter created images of what she wanted him to be.

The magnitude of unravelling this comes out in the following quote. 'The more extreme traumatically engendered condition is that in which any capacity to represent self-experience is ruptured: a state of paralysis in which even the blank impress is lost within a void' (Connolly, 2011, p. 5). This describes the many-layered and wounded places to be unlocked. Often the loss of father is so distressing the daughter just has to forget. The chronic loss of the father can be accompanied by a constant hum of anxiety. The stories of so many daughters swim in troubled waters. Their background is loaded with rifts, inconsistencies and uncertainties punctuating self-representation with internal injury and emotional destitution.

Disentangling these psychological knots is not easy, nor is the analysis smooth. It includes struggling through the impasses with their divisions, distortions and dissociations, the obfuscated but unresolved conflicts and longings. Those who just became dutiful daughters obliterate themselves, becoming ghosts, playing roles, just getting by.

An example

> What wound did ever heal but by degrees
>
> William Shakespeare, *Othello* (c. 1603),
> Act II, scene 3, line 377

Jade, a composite of many women, came to our initial therapy session outwardly well arranged, competent and polished. She revealed rather quickly and even flippantly she had no one close in her life; no one really knew her. Her partner was unemotional, distant and inaccessible. She knew he did not really see her. Friends knew her but distantly. Her family was what she called a 'mess'. Specifically, she did not know her father as he left when she was three years old, an age when events and feelings can be recalled. Her parents divorced; she stayed with her mother; and her father rarely visited – until she again met him in her teens. And then all the repressed longing and needs, the emotionally distressing desires for a father over all the years of absence overwhelmed her. At that moment she just *knew* he felt the same; she *knew* they were simpatico. But he did *not* reciprocate her enthusiasm, and she recalled immense disappointment.

She never told him or anyone else about this. Rather, she threw herself into achieving. Ill-equipped to face the huge disappointment and loss of him yet again, she busied herself with school, activities and sports, striving to be the best at everything. She never stopped to feel or examine whether she did this in an attempt to be noticed by him or to divert her sorrow. Sheltered deeply within her, there remained a secret core no one could know. Jade made sure no one entered and was by herself there. Even when others perceived her as extremely competent, she needed someone to give her a sense of security, as she felt all was not solid within. She held many secrets behind the competent façade, hiding her frantic and anxious emotions, the shadows carefully managed and all neatly compartmentalized. Jade learned to draw a curtain over private moments, as her life became more of a story than a statement, never quite landing on the actual. In her mind she made her absent father into a father she excused because he said he cared. Now she was in knots wishing it – feelings, emotions, the whole situation – was not so bad, but then she had a hunch it was worse than she was willing to admit.

Within this, Jade lost her self, inch by inch. There is a treachery, a secret psychic death that begins in childhood when a child is unloved and unseen, the 'I' unnoticed. A centre of gravity that should be internalized becomes loosened and damaged. The residue leaves the absence of affirmation undermining the roots of her system.

The fantasy absent father impacted all areas of Jade's life. To face another reality would change her world and she was not sure what this would mean. Meanwhile, the relationship with her partner was devoid of emotion. Work no longer satisfied her. The world felt uneven and she was frequently close to tears, an emotional state unfamiliar and hidden until now. She felt it was time to examine the issues she had put into a box and locked away years ago. She chose Jungian analytical therapy as a way to proceed on this journey.

It gradually became clear that the absent father experience repeated itself generation after generation in her family. Her father's father died young. Her mother's father just worked and made money. These fathers were bent on status, position and money, not home or family. No one paid attention to children who were raised to be seen, not heard; the stoic attitude prevailed. In adulthood Jade found herself drawn to those who were also emotionally unresponsive, replicating the fathers not there. Jung likened this repetition of the family pattern to psychological sin, or the curse of Atreus running through the generations. It reflected a lack of consciousness, an observant ego or assertion of choice (Jung, 1963, p. 192).

Jade is a portrait of the many women walking through these pages, sobbing in emotional tatters or numb to the reality of their father's absence, uncertain how to emerge from the pool of sorrow into themselves. They are not to see and no one else is either. Their insides are under lock and key.

> Through fantasies of introjection and identification, the 'lost object' is taken into the psyche, where it takes up a new intrapsychic life. This is the irony of human development: The 'acceptance of loss' in the external world is met with a corresponding recreation of the object in the internal world.
>
> (Lear, 2014, p. 473–74)

The internalized loss seeks conscious recognition if it is to encounter and then work to transform the repressed and undeveloped needs.

Longing, as defined by the *Oxford English Dictionary*, is a strong persistent desire, especially for something unattainable or distant. It is related to hunger, wish, yearning, pining. From the early emotional and relational wounds with the absent father, dependency is thwarted and there is no point in hoping and nothing that can be imagined. With little knowledge of a personal father, Jade coped with her longing by adopting collective standards and ideas. She is a daughter of the overarching father/patriarchal ruler made stronger without a personal father being present. In similar instances, some women protect themselves by withdrawing. Or some adopt the father way in a hyper-power attitude. Or, like Jade, through their intellect and achievement, they build successful professional lives but cut off all emotion or intimacy.

Jade *dreamt she was in a mechanistic painting with gears and gadgets. She was unable to reach the man she loved.* The dream recurred for years. It represented her search for self, other and father. A colourless dream, it left her with much frustration and longing and the feeling of being loveless. Longing is often accompanied by emotions of shame, wrath, terror and aloneness. Longing expresses the pain from wanting love so much it can seem like an ache in the soul. The loss felt immense and had to be denied while the intensity of the emotion paradoxically descended to her core. The loss of the father fundamentally affects the structuring of the human psyche (Kohon, 1999, p. 143). Longing is a primal need that arises from the depths of the unconscious to the conscious. When we long, we search for inclusion, acceptance and love. This emotion is like an alchemical fire burning the superfluities to ash. Longing is a spark and impetus to get through the fire.

The father's qualities populate a daughter's interior world and affect her exterior world, socially and culturally. That is why each personal journey, like those described here, has collective ramifications. The early limbic-system contact with parents shapes character, laying down the wiring for emotional habits and patterns of connecting, greatly influencing the nature of what we bring to all subsequent relationships, depending on how nurturing or toxic these formative relationships have been. 'The outcome of a woman's struggle to feel psychologically and socially whole and integrated and diversified is, to a great extent, fashioned with the father/daughter relationship' (Samuels, 1993, p. 151). Yet, in example after example, the daughter is left with a blank space where a father should be. Sometimes she has nothing to say about him, emotions are so deadened, and for so long, there has been no response.

Daughters go through much twisting and turning to find themselves. Fathers are responsible for the emotional wellbeing of their daughters, and without their emotional interplay, the loss and absence beg to be filled, creating the energy needed to move the ponderous weight of lack (Samuels, 1985, p. 10). The father's absence impacts the daughter's personality and affects the subjective inner representational world. A daughter might deny her needs by providing for her father as he coaxes sympathy from her, wanting to be doted on and obeyed. Or she might identify with him as a way of attaching to him, but this might mean she takes on his failures and anxieties as well. In essence, her desires have been too narrowly framed or replaced with seeds of refusal. In analysis, the process calls for deactivating and untangling enigmatic, often disturbing and sometimes more terrifying, experiences than the daughter would like to recall. The issue is particularly complex as father absence overrides everything else; she becomes too diminished and the father power given too much authority, especially when unknown.

Examining loss leads to a recapitulation of early experiences, activating feelings and emotions. Father absence is a psychological, emotional, physical and cultural loss. Hardly mourned, it has been taken for granted. How does the daughter mourn what she never had and what generally went unacknowledged? She might find herself hating the absent father, the attachment that was no attachment at all. She might sink into a bitter depression. A sadness permeates and points to the wounded areas where she feels unacceptable and afflicted with fundamental flaws. For her, the paternal presence and experience of being seen or having good resonance remains barren. 'For an individual to come to be, she needs freedom from certain internal and external tyrannies' (Lear, 1990, p. 23).

The conflict between needs for closeness and also for differentiation require the self to struggle with itself and with the other (Solomon, 2007, p. 245). But this is difficult when a true and vital part of herself was not reflected in a father's eyes. Generations of fathers who had trouble developing and maintaining loving relationships with their daughters also never had affectionate relationships with their own fathers. The fatherless fathers whose fathers showed them little love are unconsciously repeating these experiences. This loss is what many identify, as it is sadly a common story. The father is still not recognized as a definite figure of relatedness, although he is often glorified, with the rationale he did his best and so is blameless. Keeping this picture intact, whether accurate or not, a daughter has to deny the problems and accept the disappointments, losses and longings.

Insufficient father nurturance creates guilt, sorrow and betrayal. The father absence brings a shattering of essential experiences. The daughter faces obstacles to accessing either aggression or desire – two components necessary for knowing herself and for developing her talents, thereby denying her creative impetus and creating various psychological fallout.

The pursuit of a father with its attendant emotions and feelings illustrates how much has been missing. This is starkly replicated when looking for information about fathers and daughters. Relatively little in the popular literature contains an internal or thoughtful perspective. Sometimes there is a surface or behavioural focus, but no acknowledgement of the intricacies and complexities of the dynamics between daughters and fathers. Often there are references to what a daughter can do to make it better. The simplified attitudes reflect a neglect of the complex layers composing the daughter–father relationship.

Collective lack

As British Jungian analyst Andrew Samuels contends, paternal deficits affect generational, cultural and psychological expansion and limit movement from narrowed roles (1993, p. 153). When the father figure remains a blank space, in this tunnel of darkness living communication with him is blocked. The daughter is denied a vital link for her separate identity and equality with a father. When as an adult, he apologizes for not being present, but makes it all about himself as he could do nothing else, he still remains absent. This leaves a daughter to deal with the residual emotions of anger and dismay, feeling betrayed and abandoned, hesitant, without sufficient care or attention. Most of all, she lacked a father who knew how to model connection to her own self. In such a scenario she carries a ponderous residue from his absence while the father remains unconscious.

Psychological literature on father absence, although increasing, has still given the role of the father short shrift. This represents a collective failure with unfortunate consequences. To add to the pervasive denial of attention to the father–daughter conundrum, psychological analytical theorists have been limited because of their own and their fathers' shadows. Freudian thought assigned the father a major role, although Freud as well as Jung noted difficulties in relationships with their fathers. The ideology and cultural overlay concentrating on women-centred child-rearing and absent fathers has also unconsciously biased and strengthened the patriarchal status quo of father absence.

For example, Jung wrote one essay in *Collected Works*, which appears in Volume 4 (1961) and is entitled 'The significance of the father in the destiny of the individual', with only small mention of the daughter. There are symbolic and mythological references throughout Jung's writings and references to the archetypes of the father and the daughter. However, little attention is paid specifically to the daughter with an emotionally met and fulfilling relationship to the father. This is all the more surprising as Jung had four daughters yet wrote so little about this relationship. We could excuse this, saying he had other issues to focus on, but this is the usual reason daughters are relegated to the background. Likewise, this fact reveals the predominant focus of Western society and its history, leaving the daughter and the absent father largely unaddressed.

The absence of his own father is one of the significant aspects said to have propelled Jung into his deeper researches into the unconscious. His story parallels the many daughters experiencing the absent father. From an early age, Jung reported a feeling of hollowness from his father who was a minister but without spiritual belief. This left him with questions both unexpressed and unanswered, an empty space the father could not fill for Jung or himself. Religious discussions between them were reported as unsatisfactory as Jung's father advised him to not think and just believe. In contrast to this dictum and from the lack of guidance and feeling, Jung recognized he must find his own experiences (Dunne, 2015, p. 18). The absence of his father later fuelled the search, resulting in Jung's theories of the archetypes, the collective unconscious and the prolific symbolism of the psyche contained in religion, history, myth and fairy tales. There he found the deeper answers his father could not provide. In fact, Jung took the unresolved lack of belief from his father and made the reality of the psyche the goal of his life (Nagy, 1991, p. 12). In essence, the absence of his father emotionally and spiritually fuelled Jung's deeper searches into the psyche, with effects both personal and collective.

A complex set of dynamics arises from father absence. The detriments from his absence throughout the generations set up patterns that have not been fully realized. Collective history and personal narratives contain complex wounds, internal splits, fractured selves and the psychological journey arrested. Examining what is problematic can lead to the possible, much like the alchemical phoenix rising from the *nigredo* or decomposition, creating the ashes.

Here I emphasize the importance of the father as both an outer and an inner object in the daughter's development (Samuels, 1989, pp. 66ff). His absence creates confusion. What is expected to be there is not. The avoidance of loss and longing occludes awareness of what a daughter wants and needs. Only through an intricate process can she sort out the truth from the fiction, the real from the imaginary.

By engaging with the absence, the position of the father no longer cuts off her identity, limiting feelings and actions. Healing requires dealing with the longings, sorrows and losses. Although the wounds from the absence of father scar, once understood and integrated, gradually they become a source for development. The process changes the daughter's identity from one of being without to being with, from lack to fulfilment, from unconscious to conscious.

> Unhappy that I am, I cannot heave
> My heart into my mouth. I love your majesty
> According to my bond, no more nor less.

Cordelia from *King Lear* (Act I, Scene I)

References

Connolly, A. (2011). Healing the wounds of our fathers: Intergenerational trauma, memory, symbolization and narrative. *Journal of Analytical Psychology, 56*(5), 607–26.

Dunne, C. (2015). *Carl Jung: Wounded Healer of the Soul*. London, England: Watkins Publishing.

Hauke, C. (1995). Fragmentation and narcissism: A revaluation. *Journal of Analytical Psychology, 40*(4), 497–522.

Jung, C.G. (1961). *Freud and Psychoanalysis*, Vol. 4. Princeton, NJ: Princeton University Press.

Jung, C.G. (1963). *Memories, Dreams, Reflections*. New York, NY: Vintage.

Knox, J. (2003). *Archetype, Attachment, Analysis*. London, England: Routledge.

Kohon, G. (Ed.) (1999). *The Dead Mother: The Work of André Green*. London, England: Routledge.

Kristeva, J. (1988). *In the Beginning Was Love*. New York, NY: Columbia University Press.

Lear, J. (1990). *Love and Its Place in Nature*. New York, NY: Farrar, Straus & Giroux.

Lear, J. (2014). Mourning and moral psychology. *Psychoanalytic Psychology, 31*(4), 470–81.

Lispector, C. (2012). *The Passion According to G.H.* New York, NY: New Directions.

Nagy, M. (1991). *Philosophical Issues in the Psychology of C.G. Jung*. Albany: State University of New York Press.

Samuels, A. (Ed.) (1985). *The Father*. New York, NY: New York University Press.

Samuels, A. (1989). *The Plural Psyche*. London, England: Routledge.

Samuels, A. (1993). *The Political Psyche*. London, England: Routledge.

Solomon, H. (2007). *The Self in Transformation*. London, England: Karnac Books.

Chapter 3

Father desire, father wounds

> I am not what I seem. Seeming is but a garment I wear – a care-woven garment that protects me from thy questionings and thee from my negligence. The 'I' in me, my friend, dwells in the house of silence, and therein it shall remain for ever more, unperceived, unapproachable.
>
> Kahlil Gibran, *The Madman: His Parables and Poems*

A woman dreamt she was to take care of her father. The meaning of this one line depends on the dreamer and can connote many things about the relationship to her father. Why is she to take care of him? What does the dreamer desire and what are the implied wounds? Why is the dream so succinct and without embellishment? The dream implies the question of which father – the internalized father, the personal father, the father complex or archetype?

Myth of father wounding

The father figure is innate in the psyche and is also made up of introjected experiences with the personal father and cultural ideology. As in the following story from the Old Testament (Judges 11:37–40), it is obvious fathers harm their daughters by being unconscious.

Jephthah, a leader in Israel, had vowed to sacrifice whoever 'comes forth from the doors of my house to meet me', if the Lord would deliver the Ammonites to him to smote. Having defeated them, he returned home and his daughter came out to greet him. When Jephthah saw her and realized what he had done, he was distraught with grief, but immediately 'blamed the victim', reproaching his daughter for being the one whom he saw first, rather than blaming himself for the vow he had made:

> She was his only child; he had no son or daughter except her. When he saw her, he tore his clothes and said 'Alas, my daughter! You have brought me very low; you have become the cause of great trouble to me. For I have opened my mouth to the Lord, and I cannot take back my vow'.

It seems again the father was unaware of his daughter, unable or unwilling to see or perceive her or her whereabouts, quite like in the fairytales I later cite. When Jephthah's daughter heard of her father's vow, she responded with dignity and restrained anger. She accepted her fate, but on her own terms:

> She said to him, 'My father, if you have opened your mouth to the Lord, do to me according to what has gone out of your mouth, now that the Lord has given you vengeance against your enemies, the Ammonites'.

Modern writers object to the daughter's passive acceptance of her death, wishing she had objected to her father's vow. In the context of the times, however, Jephthah had to sacrifice her and she had to accept her fate. Her father made a promise on behalf of his people, and he believed God had accepted the promise, giving him victory in return. Now the promise had to be honoured despite the terrible cost, and the daughter knew and accepted this.

But is it possible she knew in advance about her father's vow and deliberately came out of the house first? Could the daughter have taken the place intended for someone else in order to show her father the terrible injustice of his action? The daughter's reaction to her fate is shown by what she did. 'And she said to her father "Let this thing be done for me: grant me two months, so that I may go and wander on the mountains, and bewail my virginity, my companions and I"'. She preferred to spend the last days of her life with her friends, not with the father whose ambition and foolish vow caused her death. In her last days, she wanted the company of those she could trust.

This poignant story reflects the tragedy of another father who put himself and his needs first. The promise to God, the Father, is more important than the life of the daughter. The sad and cruel story reflects a father unaware, for so many reasons, of the value of his daughter. And in the story, she is given no name but that of her father's daughter.

The story of daughters and fathers is one of desire, and like all desires, it is powerful and evocative. The desire for love is basic. Is it a need? An instinct? A lifeforce? Spirit? Love is all of these and more. The daughter's wishes and their fulfilment relate directly to the release of desire to facilitate the unconscious as it acts upon consciousness (Stein, 1983, p. 79). Desire moves us, as its lack does not disappear. When a father is not there, the daughter might have little focus or direction, her foundation might be shaken, and her life energy depleted. She learns to take what little is offered and then remains hostage to the father and his perspectives whether or not they fit. Sadly, many daughters remain trapped, no matter how outstanding their achievements or recognition. With little sense of personal constancy or cohesiveness, female desire becomes narrowly framed without a full enough picture for her life.

The relationship with the father is a crucible where individuation can occur, including conscious awareness of longing and desire. However, an absent father ignores, and the daughter learns to ignore herself as well. Father remains a hazy dream, an absence, not a presence, and like a breeze through a vacant home, he vanishes, a shadow. Glimpses of him seemingly there, but not. He eludes, unable to catch up with him, she finds him gone. These are the scenarios occurring day after day, year after year, dream after dream with daughter after daughter. The intimacy with father means encountering these parts formerly split, denied or disowned.

The father gaze

> Why, what is to live? Not to eat and drink and breathe, – but to feel the life in you down all the fibres of being, passionately and joyfully.
>
> Elizabeth Barrett Browning, *The Letters of Robert Browning and Elizabeth Barrett Browning 1845–1846, Vol. I*

Desire comes with an image, but what if a father doesn't provide one? A woman said:

> I know fatherlessness. I know the emptiness it creates, the years searching for something to help fill the void, looking for a substitute to make me whole. I know the insecurity; the endless battles with doubts that are re-created with each new relationship – battles that are never won; the pain that resurfaces after each departure of a relationship … the distinct patterns of sadness, insecurity, confusion, and unresolved pain of those who experience father loss either through death, divorce, or abandonment.
>
> (Barras, 2000, p. 5)

The absence of the father tenaciously occupies the daughter's psyche. A father who remains unknown affects her functioning physically, socially and psychologically. By his absence he shows neglect, a man who has not been responsible to his inner life, forgotten his dreams, refused to explore his psychology because either it was too painful or he was just ill equipped. Or it was not encouraged. Is a daughter a threat to him? Why did he not keep her in his mind?

A relational setup of needs and desires is triggered by the devotedness a father has to his daughter. The sense of who we are arises from the ways our early experiences with caregivers are met or fail to be met. The influence of the father figure is what the infant takes in emotionally and leads to 'an embodied sense of a psychological self' (Mizen, 2014, p. 315). This is a developmental and relational patterning evolving from experiencing father as a love object conveying relatedness and support.

Human infants need secure physical and emotional attachments for developing trust and love from a father figure. A father validates a daughter through his facial and bodily expressions; by holding her in his arms he allows her to develop a private integrity (Sherwood, 1994, p. 65). Although the mirror of the father's face does not reflect a daughter's self-same face, it can reflect emotions, affects, approval, liking and love. His gaze determines how she will interpret others from his cherishment and presence for her. When a daughter is uncertain of who she is because she is uncertain of how she is seen, she experiences anxiety. The father's mental representation is internalized, allowing the child and then the adult to find herself in the other (Knox, 2003, p. 156). When this is not available, protest, despair and detachment eventually become the responses. Because self-realization is embedded in all psychological processes and the psyche, like the body, strives to keep balance, a daughter learns to compensate, resorting to persona formation. This becomes her façade, hiding the problems so she remains unseen. The persona is a carapace or shell, disconnected from the inside; it becomes a deceptive pseudo-covering to compensate for discontinuous emotions, acting to fill a role (Mizen, 2014, p. 316).

Desire brings the daughter to the clash between the satisfaction of appetites and the fear that they might be unmet and that she might be left with the old longings, disappointments and uncertainty. When desire is thwarted, it can be followed by misdirected attempts to fill the pool of lost feelings, the daughter's hungers frustrated and connections wounded. She suffers the agony of displaced needs, not knowing how to live or feel differently. Perceiving other options becomes difficult.

Socially, personally and relationally a daughter learns denial, avoidance of feeling while her desires and self-expression are dampened. When there are unwanted and/or bad aspects, a self-protective and self-immunization process begins, and the daughter becomes separated and walled off in a singular and unconnected position (Solomon, 2007, p. 232). In the face of injuries from the father absence, she can become an embittered soul, hardened and chronically defensive. A destructive psychological pact is made with the father not there, unavailable for catharsis or to work it though. Yet in a convoluted way she is connected to the father and needs him. She becomes insecure, distrustful of self and others and sceptical of love. The wound continues to bleed.

When her desires are unmet and he is emotionally absent, the space he should occupy is empty, sapping her strength and diminishing her lifeforce. Her unmet disappointments and expectations affect biological, physical, spiritual and moral realms. Being thwarted in the desire for him, she's left with terrifying emptiness and aimlessness born from his absence, making her desire also absent (Knox, 2003, p. 150). She does not know what she wants, reaching for anything, mindless, with no focus or intent. Deprived of father care, a schism occurs within, and coping with life's vicissitudes becomes difficult.

The absence of father energy creates problems, longing, unfulfilled desires, while the needs and rage turn inward. Rayelyn asked, 'How do I learn to take care of myself when I am already in my late forties? I do not know how to do it or where to begin'. At times she was enraged, but she took it out on herself by assessing she was not enough. She might deceive herself to avoid the frustration of being let down by her father. If the situation is not understood in its complexity, the daughter is doomed to repeat the lack. 'The fear of psychic separateness, of having a mind of one's own, can lead to various forms of destructive activity' (Knox, 2003, p. 157). Her life comes to mean nothing and she regards it as futile. Each day she wakes up filled with vicious self-hate. She cannot stop this commentary, as she believes it, leaving her without potency.

Rayelyn dreamt she agreed to marry a man from St. Louis who was younger and not very attractive. He was immature and wanted her to move to St. Louis with him as he began his career. He expressed no thought about her preferences or needs. Although established in her career in another city, she agreed to go with him. Then she realized, no, she did not want this and would not marry or go with him.

As she awoke, she remembered she had gone to school in St. Louis and Louis was also the name of her now-dead father. She recalled that he never listened to her pleas to be present and did little that signified he cared. He was always this way. Startled, she recognized he was the man in the dream who still inhabited her psyche. The dream warned she was close to a personality like him inside herself, as her tie with the absent and dead father was so present psychologically.

Rayelyn's dream showed her just going along; she was not yet conscious of the inner collusion against her. How could she exist with this type of internalized male representing her self-centred and emotionally absent and disinterested father? This psychologically incestuous marriage would have her erased. The dream man supposedly wanted her, but his lack of consideration, love or care was like her father. In him she recognized the self-negating cycle demolishing her, creating self-doubt and the continual low-level depression. St. Louis is also in the centre of the United States and could represent her centre, quite a prominent position for an inner father figure. The occurrence of the dream showed she must understand this dynamic vociferously working against her.

Culture

Throughout history the surname of the father has been the identifiable marking taken on by his children (Zoja, 2001, p. 27). Sometimes this is the only identifiable marking. When the father leaves the family for whatever reasons, it is usually the mother who takes care of the children. In fact, the children often do not see their father or are with him less and less over time. In many instances he was missing following conception. The cultural coordinates he could impart and pass on are vacant. The distance between the father and his family conveys emptiness. Rather than having a guide, these daughters are deprived of the collective rules and symbolic rituals beyond the father position of authoritarianism (Zoja, 2001, p. 241). In other words, the father as the rule maker, providing structure as keeper of law and order, retained his power, but not as someone related or emotionally available. The silence around this father absence continues to reverberate loudly.

Fatherlessness impacts at the personal, social, psychological and societal levels (Krampe, 2003, p. 131). The shards from the past exist in the present as unrequited desires and sorrows. The decline in the relationship with the father began long ago, but it is now recognized as a more pervasive collapse. Healing requires a deep inner process so the breadth of the wounds can be recognized and repaired. But only an accurate diagnosis of the wounds offers conditions for healing. Luigi Zoja, an Italian Jungian analyst, said the father has disappeared and died, not in war or in work, but mostly at home (2001, p. 234).

Rayelyn described her father as a man wounded in masculinity, lacking relatedness to her and without support. From a young age, she knew to not ask too much, to not expect anything, as he did not impart useful knowledge. He refused her. She could not challenge him, and she sensed his attitudes were phony and immature, but he had to dominate. Her father gave more allegiance to his mother than to his own family. Rayelyn knew he was not acting like an adult but what could she do? An unconscious generational pattern repeated itself, becoming a re-enactment of the merged relationship with his mother and distance from his father. The father remained the son and placed Rayelyn in the mother competency role. He relied on her to care for him, although she was the child. He harmed her with the unconscious needs she had to meet. This mother–son structure formed the basis of their relationship for as long as she could remember. Depriving his daughter of correct care, she could learn neither how to cope nor the basics of development. Even when absent, the role of the father is still present and unconsciously conveyed through the daughter's interiorly felt expectations. How much this has been transmitted can be recognized as the extent to which the father remains an invisible object in therapeutic work (Perelberg, 2009, p. 723). In fact, Rayelyn did not know what to say about her father. On the one hand she knew he was pathetic, and on the other she wanted a father to love. To completely negate him would mean she had nothing. 'Wishes! Desires! What does life know about them? Life urges and pushes forward and it has its mighty nature into which we stare with our wanting eyes' (Rilke, 2005, p. 98).

Mother

Ideally, fatherhood emerges in the sensitively attuned interactions between each daughter and father, evolving in the course of their relationship. Development moves the daughter from the beginning enclosure with the mother figure to include the father figure. This is an evolving path for discovering the other and how the various feelings and reactions can be integrated.

With the focus on the father here, I am addressing the mother figure less. Much has been written on the mother, and although she is not to be ignored, she has been the centre of many prior discussions, though often in a blaming way. Even in therapy, the mother becomes a primary issue as if the father figure did not exist. This slanted focus on him as absent might create some distortion and seem one-sided. It is meant to compensate, however, for the lack of attention paid to the father, pointing out the serious and cumulative effects caused by the missed father connection.

Together, both mother and father figures form and model union and differences in the psychological, personal and cultural spheres. The father is to embrace and hold in the right way the daughter and the mother as well. The father as other includes how he is interpreted in the culture and how he personally relates to the mother and the daughter. From the archetypal configuration of father, mother and daughter, a secure foundation can be established. Both parental figures inhabit the psyche and their symbolic identifications shape the continuum, foundation and range from feminine to masculine within the daughter.

The father figure brings otherness, a quality that can apply to the inner unassimilated object, foreign or worshipped, but when it remains impoverished the daughter is left without value (Britton, 1998, p. 45). The current flux of roles and gender also means the father can no longer remain merely a distant or domineering figure. The father, coming from another generation and the other sex, has the potential to stimulate expansion and deepening of her personality (Samuels, 1985, p. 31). The father as the valuable and influential other and as different from mother has not yet been fully released from being kept in the bottle of repression and denial with many dynamics unacknowledged.

When the absent father does not connect with the mother, he maintains emotional distance, modelling disunion and disjointedness. The triangular situation remains even when father is absent and becomes a factor in the structure of the mother–daughter relationship. The father's absence impacts the place he occupies in the mother's mind, and this too affects the daughter (Perelberg, 2009, p. 727). The absence of father means there is no balance or union, no modelling of coming together and then separating, enacting the process of development. When the father is not there to unite with the mother and the sense of their pairing is absent, a daughter experiences separation, empty spaces, anger and unmet desires. She might comprehend the father in his absence through the eyes of mother as an incompetent figure who is disappointing and subsequently denigrated (Kohon, 1999, p. 44).

The presence of the father figure affects how she learns about and enacts maleness and femaleness (Samuels, 1985, p. 32). Father introduces a daughter to himself as other in body, emotions and way of being. Obviously, his absence impacts what the daughter learns about other male figures, their position to themselves and to females according to differing cultural, social and psychological patterns. The loss of the object, here referring to the father, is at the origin of pain, anxiety and desire (Perelberg, 2009, p. 723). Without inner ballast, one woman said:

> I had to bring myself up, without a father, having never known the daily moments with him, the sharing and interest or what might have been. I had to grow alone and find my own truth, to try to live without these roots.

The capacity for intention is linked to desire and appetites (Knox, 2003, p. 150), and how these are encouraged is affected by the way the personal father is introjected or taken in. When a daughter only has blank perceptions, the masculine can become distorted, and she creates a contrived, idealized or fantasy father. His distance and absence make the range of paternal images, both inner and outer, complex to decipher.

The legacy

The lack of depth or detail about the role of the father has left him in the shadows. From the first moments of her life, too many fathers are absent from their daughter's care. Rather, the father is described in terms of later more developed aspects, perhaps because men did not engage in childcare in past generations (Greenfield, 1985, p. 189). These shadow areas refer to a woman's sense of herself as a presence and as an assertive, intelligent and sexual agent. They all remain compromised. When daughters are successful high achievers, the effect of the absent father can wreak havoc in her health, sexuality, creativity, reflection and ability to acquire or sustain intimate relationships.

When the father has emotionally disappeared or is a stranger, the daughter is left with a gap where the kind and loving father should be. His absence is a haunting presence as daughters report bleak, tonally inert, intimately blank relationships. The influence of absence can create unreal, mechanical reactions.

For generations a daughter was suppressed, regarded as the least important member in the family. The daughter–father issues remained a dark terrain, and their relationship was relegated to the shadows. Daughters were to be docile and fathers untouched, as if they were not essential to their children's lives. In fact, a father wielded so much influence a daughter did not question her role with him and instead projected her disappointments and difficulties onto her mother in another diminishment to herself and the feminine.

Too few opportunities for good experiences between a father and daughter pass on a legacy of non-involvement and personal detachment. Her actions become inhibited, emotional development arrested and adult maturity faked. Without sufficient emotional connection, attachment becomes disjointed and inhibited. Without a solid sense of self, she cannot handle the separateness of the other. Although the self, in the Jungian sense, cannot be destroyed, it can be isolated from the impact of all experience through the creation of impenetrable defences (Knox, 2007, p. 547). The daughter wards off anything discrepant to her self-image so the other cannot be much different, as she needs the control (Bromberg, 1983, p. 372). Internally alone, she might be sexually frozen, unconsciously preserved in a childish way, appearing helpless, dependent or, at times, inappropriately aggressive. Psychologically she is affectively deadened and unable to move out of the internalized isolation. She is either so self-focused the other is not included or so other-focused she is eliminated. This is what she picks up from the father not there for reciprocity of interaction.

Individuation requires a response from caregivers early in life, allowing the child and later the adult to realize that desires are communicated, responded to and reflected back (Knox, 2003, p. 141). Harm lies in the message the absence of a father conveys. He is not there to recognize her emotional needs or respond to her love in a way that fosters individuation and the development of self-agency (Knox, 2007, p. 544). Self-concept and self-esteem are affected. Typically, the daughter comes to therapy saying her father was not there and she was mostly with mother or maybe alone. One woman said she never talked to her father, as he was so introverted, showing no emotional reactions. She never asked why.

These daughters live in a reflection of father dominance. The father absent, unemotional, neglectful might be physically present but unrelated, unloving, unpredictable, weak, abandoning, useless or even violent and dangerous (Seligman, 1985, p. 82). A vacuum of bewilderment forms, a void filling with various adversities she tends to turn on herself. This is how the father figure can become malicious and malignant to the feminine, and the daughter internalizes his sadomasochistic enactments (p. 85).

To continue with Rayelyn's therapeutic process, *she dreamt a father tortured a child. Images flash of three or four red wolf-like animals that almost devour her. Now he is a grandfather and telling his granddaughter about the awful frightening father he escaped and has written a book about it. He is telling this to emphasize not just surviving but also the possibility of creating from the torture and violence of the past.* As she thought about the dream, Rayelyn realized the wolves were the devouring harm felt from her father, like the dream father representing a legacy of torturing the child. She previously was convinced her father was not so awful, but this submerged the actual reality. Now the dream says she has to tell the story. Upon more reflection, she said her father did not listen or ask about her, nor did she interact with him much. She suffered from his ignored, vulgar or brutal silence. He was just that way; no one could get through. You had to take it, or it would get worse. Her father was emotionally absent and unkind, yet she had to accept his lack of attachment or interest. He was very much an absent presence, a blank space, leaving a residue of apprehension with a shield around himself, preoccupied, distant and also immature. These are also marks of absence.

In reaction, a daughter might become defensive, the complexes rigid and persona over- or under-developed, her natural self absent. The internalization of this form of the absent father threatens the daughter's separate identity. 'Defenses are forms of narratives, created in imagination and fantasy to support a positive sense of identity and personal worth when these are threatened by cruelty, hostility or indifference from those on whom we are most dependent' (Knox, 2003, p. 130). The repressions, misalignments and lacks from the past take up her internal space and her suffering deepens, taking up even more space. Some daughters will be able to integrate the absence and others are too ripped apart by it.

Then Rayelyn *dreamt of a serial killer. In the dream she felt guilty because she did not warn the dream woman about him and she could have.* In discussing the dream, she said the serial killer was like her father. The dream revealed the unconscious memories she would rather not unearth. Yet, the dream also erupted, as now she must become aware of this situation for her very life. She had internalized a dangerous father figure, terrorizing her inner world, obstructing inspiration and arresting self-development.

Around these patterns and behaviours, she grew more and more lost. Rayelyn did not realize the damage, as she had not allowed herself to feel. From her emotionally absent father she learned forced adaptability, vigilant and watching behaviour and to quell her desires. Jung called this 'gross [parental] negligence, slothfulness, neurotic anxiety or soulless conventionality' (1959, p. 161). By soulless conventionality, Jung meant that parents developed their personas to conform to the expectations of the social group and therefore were living inauthentically.

The absent father abandoned Rayelyn, leaving no inner holding place. She created a secret interior zone to protect, but it kept her often hidden from her self. Hers was a story of lack, and in Rayelyn's case the disconnection from self and others was minimized. The search for the father, the lost love object and feelings about him, were dominant psychological themes. The desire to know him was linked to the desire to know and understand herself. The process of opening the wounds was part of her path for self-discovery. Rayelyn's relationship or its lack constituted both a context and an entry gate to her transformation psychologically and culturally. Liberation from the loss and absence loosens the ability to take pleasure in the world and enjoy being alive. Rayelyn's dream showed how much she remained unaware and had compromised.

> Those who have never lost the slightest root seem to you unable to understand any word liable to temper their point of view ... the ear is receptive to conflict only if the body loses its footing. A certain imbalance is necessary, a swaying over some abyss, for a conflict to be heard.
>
> (Kristeva, 1991, p. 17)

Rayelyn needed to know the truth and its harsh reality to find her way through it and into her self. 'I said: It's not the book that's ending. It's a new life beginning … It's all up to you now' (Cixous, 1983, p. 210).

References

Barras, J.R. (2000). *Whatever Happened to Daddy's Little Girl? The Impact of Fatherlessness on Black Women*. London, England: Ballentine Publishing Group.

Britton, R. (1998). *Belief and Imagination*. London, England: Routledge.

Bromberg, P. (1983). The mirror and the mask – On narcissism and psychoanalytic growth. *Contemporary Psychoanalysis, 19*(2), 359–87. doi:10.1080/00107530.1983.10746614.

Cixous, H. (1983). *The Book of Prometheus*. Lincoln, NE: University of Nebraska Press.

Gibran, K. (1918). *The Madman: His Parables and Poems* [Etext 0500601h]. Retrieved from http://gutenberg.net.au/ebooks05/0500601h.html.

Greenfield, B. (1985). The archetypal masculine: Its manifestation in myth and its significance for women. In: A. Samuels (Ed.), *The Father* (pp. 187–210). New York, NY: New York University Press.

Jung, C.G. (1959). *The Archetypes and the Collective Unconscious*. New York, NY: Pantheon Books.

Knox, J. (2003). *Archetype, Attachment, Analysis*. London, England: Routledge.

Knox, J. (2007). The fear of love: The denial of self in relationship. *Journal of Analytical Psychology*, *52*(5), 543–63.

Kohon, G. (Ed.) (1999). *The Dead Mother: The Work of André Green*. London, England: Routledge.

Krampe, E.M. (2003). The inner father. *Fathering*, *1*(2), 131–48.

Kristeva, J. (1991) *Strangers to Ourselves*. Leon Roudiez (Trans.). London, England: Harvester Wheatsheaf.

Mizen, R. (2014). On the capacity to suffer one's self. *Journal of Analytical Psychology*, *59*(3), 314–32.

Perelberg, R. (2009). Murdered father, dead father: Revisiting the Oedipus complex. *International Journal of Psycho-Analysis*, *90*(4), 713–32.

Rilke, R.M. (2005). *The Poet's Guide to Life: The Wisdom of Rilke*. Ulrich Baer (Ed. and Trans.). New York, NY: Random House.

Samuels, A. (Ed.) (1985). *The Father*. New York, NY: New York University Press.

Seligman, E. (1985). The half-alive ones. In: A. Samuels (Ed.), *The Father* (pp. 69–94). New York, NY: New York University Press.

Sherwood, V. (1994). *Psychotherapy of the Quiet Borderline Patient: The As-If Personality Revisited*. Lanham, MD: Jason Aronson.

Solomon, H. (2007). *The Self in Transformation*. London, England: Karnac Books.

Stein, M. (1983). *In Midlife: A Jungian Perspective*. Woodstock, CT: Spring Publications.

Zoja, L. (2001). *The Father: Historical, Psychological and Cultural Perspectives*. Abingdon, Oxon, England: Brunner-Routledge.

Chapter 4

Mirroring in the dead father effect

The *dead father effect* derives from the theories of André Green, the French psychoanalyst of the mid-twentieth to early twenty-first centuries. Although he originally used the phrase 'the dead mother', André Green and his followers also applied this to the absent, depressed and internally deadened father (Kohon, 1999, p. 54). Deadness refers to the father's unconscious and unknown wounds, emotional disconnections and psychological lack, disturbing paternal care and relatedness. The father's preoccupations, his withdrawal, lack of presence and depression are transferred to the daughter. When she internalizes the deadened father, the daughter deadens her own self. Rather than being *in* life she becomes tied to the blank and depleted father, effecting her body and psyche. He remains alive in his absence and present with deleterious consequences.

André Green's concepts are explained and elucidated here by the example of Shiloh, a composite of women, and by her dreams and obsession with self-harm and looking in the mirror. She was trapped by the deadened eyes of the vacant father in a gap, a blank space reflecting nothing. A dead father looks at the daughter but does not see her. His blank gaze gives no lively image to the daughter because there is no self to find in his eyes. André Green commented: 'It is not so much the absence which comes into play, but really the presence with an absent father' (Kohon, 1999, p. 55). Absent physically and emotionally, he contributed to Shiloh's inner dysfunctional environment, negativity and despair. The psychological embrace with this father left her with only lack.

André Green's concept of paternal deadness was also associated with the idea that classical psychoanalysis was founded on the question of mourning. His themes, emerging out of French culture, reflected absence, negation, negativity and nothingness (Kohon, 1999, p. 5). Mourning is part of personality separation and its reintegration, but this is more difficult without a father presence. By early childhood, Shiloh's father seemed to lose interest in her. Not knowing why, she only registered his withdrawal of love. Her father entrapped and encompassed her in his deadness (Sekoff, 1999, p. 121). As Shiloh ignored her feelings, her life repeated the deadening pattern.

Shiloh's process of mourning her father and what she did not receive was carried out at a visceral and symbolic level. The memories were made conscious by how her life was affected and interpreted by her. To heal, she had to recognize the wounded places, her regrets, the abandonments and betrayals, both big and small. The experience of having an absent father provokes a troubling, deeply challenging loss of meaning. André Green described the lack:

> absence of memory, absence in the mind, absence of contact, absence of feeling all – all these absences can be condensed in the idea of a gap ... instead of referring to a simple void or to something which is missing, becomes the substratum of what is real.
>
> (Kohon, 1999, p. 8)

The investment in self is dismantled while the void occupies the mind, leaving behind psychic holes.

> The crisis in the paternal function that led to the deficiency of psychic space is in fact an erosion of the loving father. The function of the father is dead, insofar as his function is giving and loving with his whole heart.
>
> (Green, 1986, p. 151)

The daughter becomes distant from her lively self and aligns her existence with the dead father. André Green went on to name the suffering in which all seems to have ended like 'a psychic ruin that seizes hold of the subject in such a way that all vitality and life becomes frozen, where "in fact it becomes forbidden . . . to be"' (p. 152). As with Shiloh, the inner discourse often becomes critical, demanding or passively empty. If she continues the unconscious identification with the father, her world can translate into 'No, I can't; it won't work; no, no, no'. The effect can be like an internal monster who finds her insufficient, demolishing her energy. She might adopt perfectionistic attitudes, her life seemingly unimportant as she never does anything right. These are her daily judgements, the self-erasure, the thoughts and feelings that preoccupy and take her over.

This father, 'psychically dead meaning he does not acknowledge his moods or the effect and his dissociation from the affects[,] has killed off his inner life' (Bollas, 1999, p. 100). André Green described the daughter mutated by the father loss, lack of presence or aliveness causing fractured attachments and internal discontinuity. In addition, 'The child's life and the father's relationship with the living child have been negated' (Parsons, 1999).

The deadened father perpetuates psychic impotence. The daughter operates in a fog, under the pall of endless boredom, waiting for events to stir her into life. The absence of the father connection impacts a daughter's life direction, internal resourcefulness, body image and ability to think. The thing that endures is 'an essentially conflictual, ambiguous nature of desire, which is conceivable as the desire of the desire of the Other' (Green, 1979, p. 69). As mentioned, her internal narrative illustrates the despoiling of the self-feeling. Emptied of energy or enthusiasm, an emotional morass develops. From this space a daughter has to fashion a father. But how can she do this? 'The father cannot be put to death, only embalmed. The lost father has to be constructed from remaining destroyed fragments ... He is lost' (Kohon, 1999, p. 45). She is tired, without interest, wastes away or just exists in survival mode. She adopts guises and disguises, one after the other, layer after layer, making it impossible to be fully present to herself or others. The presence of his absence extends to all her relationships as the price is her inability to love as love becomes compromised (Green, 1986, p. 153).

To add to the complexity, the daughter longs for a father who might not have ever existed (Kohon, 1999, p. 42). The dead father is not linked to representation, as he is ghostlike, ungraspable. Representation means the possibility of an inner reworking, giving shape and form to the father. But when the father is essentially unavailable, the daughter tries to bring him into presence, to make him responsive, and, of course, she cannot. Her identification with this father fails, leaving her without the experience.

André Green referred to the dead father, noting paternal depression as a death transferred from the father to the daughter (1986, p. 168). In a May 1912 letter to Karl Abraham, Freud also referenced the dead father: 'It is correct to identify the father with death, for the father is a dead man, and death himself ... is only a dead man' (Falzeder, 2015, p. 151). A debilitating insecurity comes from exposure to this dead yet still idealized father (Lussier, 1999, p. 161). The daughter takes on his wounded places as a way to 'reconstitute the lost unity by creating an internal complementarity' (Green, 2001, p. 109). This means that although he is dead – whether literally or figuratively or both – he stays alive through her adoption of a similar approach to herself in her attempts to link with him.

The mirror and the dream

Guarding against hurts and disappointments, Shiloh was tired and discouraged. Her husband lied and cheated on her with pornography. She had been single for many years and struggled financially after her divorce. She went to school and worked, and a string of subsequent partners all cheated on her as well. She felt bewildered, taking drugs to sleep and becoming socially isolated. She began Jungian analysis to find out what was happening to her world. As André Green said, 'Between you and me there seems to be a glass wall, a transparent mirror, separating us' (2001, p. 121).

Shiloh described relationships as betrayals. She was suspicious, checking the texts of those she dated, their cell phones, Facebook, Instagram and emails quite compulsively. Fearing object loss, betrayal and abandonment, as happened with her father, she despaired of ever finding anyone for more than sex. Although she tried to remain emotionally uninvolved, she was seduced into seeking value from these serial partners. Highly critical, much like she described her father, Shiloh was compulsive about many things, mostly her self-image, and worried about being enough and if her performance in life, whether work, relationship or just being, was adequate. Since high school she had been insecure about her weight and her skin. She didn't feel smart enough. She was wrapped in a thick layer of self-doubt. She spoke derisively about her father who left when she was three and did not express interest in her until her teens. She contended she did not need him now but asserted he needed her.

As therapy progressed she seemed engaged but cautious, distrustful, often-times defensive. She had trouble organizing thoughts or letting in new information. Rigidity and one-sidedness reigned, as if she had to be right and no one could influence her otherwise. Early on it became apparent that her self needed the mir-roring with her father but he took it away with his absence. How could ever she make sense of a father who was absent so early in her life? Shiloh remained angry with him and upset that he didn't respect her ways or her mind. She was offended when he told her what to eat; in her mind he was not there earlier so should not impose now. She described him as vain, self-absorbed, hard to reach and self-destructive, similar to how she acted towards herself.

Shiloh dreamt a woman walked into a room with no windows and only one door. After sitting in the room for a while she decided to leave. Stepping up to the door she left the room and entered another. This room had only one window that looked into the last room and also two doors. Anxious to move on, she went through one door without thinking and found herself in a dark hole with no win-dows and a rope. Using this rope, she climbed out of the hole and into a box with no top. She could see straight up but she couldn't see beyond the edges. A ladder gave her an exit out of the box but when she had climbed out she found herself within another box. Momentarily a trap door opened, revealing the contents of the box outside of the one she was in, and then it quickly shut. A slide appeared in the floor so she decided to use it to escape. She slid for a long time, winding around and around until she was dropped back into the same box. Only this time there were mirrors everywhere and all she could see was herself, looking at herself.

Associating with the dream she described feeling inferior and cynical in the dream mirrors. For a long time she seemed unable or resistant to get in touch with, as André Green noted, 'the reality of these interior places distinguished by their lack of structure or organization' (1986, p. 37). The dream reflected the alone-ness, the circularity of being stuck in a box, getting out and returning to it, going nowhere, over and over again. Yet, this was also the act of *circumambulatio*, the psychological and alchemical stage of mixing and circling, much like the way one interprets dreams. The box symbolically is a container and will take time and energy to explore and understand. The dream illustrated the self in the mirror Shiloh could not escape.

The dream also posed the question about what she perceived in the mirrors that she obsessively looked into, day after day, even though she was always upset at what she saw; the obsession deflected her from the underlying issues, as each morning she went to the mirror to check on what was wrong. She searched her face for flaws, covered the self-inflicted skin wounds created while trying make her skin smooth, getting rid of what felt wrong, so no one saw the hurts, the raw and exposed places. She unconsciously took on her father's language of internal destruction and self-hate, failure and inadequacy, self-involvement, the tender ego, the not-being-good-enough attitudes. The validation she sought remained elusive. Eventually she might give up trying and, like many daughters without fathers, become progressively more self-alienated and alone.

Recoiling from herself, Shiloh re-enacted the rejection felt from her father. The mirror reflected not just vanity, but also something defective, a mistake, imperfect skin, too much weight, not enough intelligence, clothes that never looked right, and on it went. She banished all mirrors from her home except a small hand mirror in which she daily examined her face searching for flaws, unable to shake the need to be alone and, ultimately, after hours had passed, often staying home. She enacted an endless mirroring, but negatively and critically, in the small mirror reflecting the image of her face without a body, impersonal, as if not attached.

The dream illustrated a defence of the self, one that protected but would not lead to self-knowledge (Schwartz-Salant, 1982, p. 107). As in the dream, her compulsively looking at herself in the mirror described this defence erected against letting anyone in. This scenario represented the dissociations growing all the more tenacious without a father. Her centre did not sustain her. The ground gave way and she was falling. The order of things was overturned. She stood outside her body and watched, a lonely woman in the mirror, accentuating the cavernous terror of intimacy, vulnerability and feared loss of control.

She was alone, unconnected to the outer world. Perhaps she had to be alone to find her self. This accentuated how much attunement she had lacked from her father. In the mirror her face and skin replicated the face of no father, with its internalized betrayal, melancholia and doubt. Looking in the mirror is a metaphor not only of searching for the self but also of being lost and unable to access the self.

To perceive one's self in a reflecting surface like a mirror is also to recognize the shadow, or dark underside, that opposes yet is part of the shine on the surface. Shiloh considered the shadow her flaws, but her reflection included the positive and unused aspects she could not see. Trying to escape the shadow leads to a life without feeling alive, divorced from the body, accompanied by a sense of depersonalization. To become conscious of the shadow presents the conundrum and tension of being real. The mirror revealed Shiloh's narcissistic needs and the ideals of how she thought she should look. Perfection rather than wholeness became the goal; the person in the mirror was a mask, not truly revealed but orchestrated to obtain approval. Perfection-seeking is marked by recklessness, even cruelty towards the self. A daughter in this situation tends to become passive, inert, dependent, without initiative and aggression (Lussier, 1999, p. 160).

Intimacy and knowledge of the self depend on loving experiences with a father. Deprived of these, many women like Shiloh are looking in mirrors demanding impossible perfection but seeing only disillusionment and disappointment. While the mind may divide the self when not liking what it sees, it can also project a false self, one devised to protect but that actually disallows the real self from being known. The reliance on false images dams access to the natural instincts and keeps the real self walled off and silenced. Such a woman does not feel at the centre of her life; she is stuck between the mirror and the mask (Bromberg, 1983, p. 360).

In therapy sessions Shiloh appeared pleasant, hardly shed any tears, explored feelings but without much emotion. Daughters like her are searching and restless, trying to make up for the dead father who lives in their reactions, memory, mind and personality. She was absorbed not only in his conscious attributes but even more in his unconscious ones. For example, her father appeared to others as generous, present and giving, yet she described him filled with negativity, judgement and condemnation at home. Shiloh identified with this aspect of the father, and also like her father similarly put on the appearance of being generous outwardly but was hateful and distressed underneath, mostly to herself (Modell, 1999, p. 78).

The internal representation of this father is what André Green related as 'a representation of the absence of representation', which psychologically expresses itself in terms of a void, emptiness, futility, meaninglessness (Green, 1986, p. 290). The father and his image becomes a non-represented and unspoken figure from which she has to surmise the information. In this convoluted and intricate process, there is little understanding of self or other because she does not know them (Bollas, 1999, p. 101). Or a daughter might become the opposite of what she perceives about her father. Sometimes she believes only a part of him is dead, and she keeps this part preserved and separate to deny the extent of his lack. The non-representation leaves space for the destructive inner figures to inhabit.

Shiloh stayed with therapy for a period of time. She gradually felt more centred and became more discerning of her partners. She held a responsible job and took herself more seriously. She also had the energy to continue with school. Feeling increasingly solid she even, to her surprise, began to want a lasting relationship. The fixation with the mirror remained but it was lessened, and she used fewer drugs. Shiloh became more open and honest with herself and her father, as she wanted to develop their relationship.

The mechanism

[W]hen you are lost, beside yourself, and you continue getting lost, when you become the panicky movement of getting lost … inundated with otherness, it's in these breathless times that writing traverses you … these are the cries that death and life hurl in their combat.

Helene Cixous, *Inside* (1991, p. 38)

Grace dreamt there was a claw-like machine dunking dummies into the water. They came out shrunken and ghoulish looking. She jumped into the line and was being dunked when she realized she did not know what was happening or how to get out. She had no advance preparations and found herself at the mercy of the machine.

She associated the dream to having little guidance from an emotionally vacant father whom she learned to please, although she did not realize what she was doing. Grace was sensitive to feelings while her father was mechanical like the machine in the dream. She complied with him in spite of his always being preoccupied, distant, a man who did not relate.

Anything but mechanical, her husband was not quiet, and his psychological depressions and mercurial emotions were threatening and without stability. Grace feared for his life, tried desperately to rescue him and, in the process of devotion to him, became diminished. She made herself small, and he became the centre of life, in fact larger than life. Grace tried to manage his despair and addictions but with no thought of what was happening to herself. With her husband Grace replicated how she had been with her father – with the same result. No matter what she did they neither saw nor considered her.

The water in the dream could be aligned with the unconscious as she associated the dream with her marriage, which was now under water. Only in the process of getting a divorce did Grace realize she could have drowned in the deadness underneath her husband's chaos and depression. Her efforts towards him left nothing for her as he sucked her dry. The dream machine was taking her into the line of compliance, unconscious and mechanical, deadening like her father. The machine was also like her marriage, as she tried against all odds to make it work, in the grips of a situation she described as phantom-like. She realized she was replicating her parents, a sad relating where neither person knew the other – all remained on the surface with their mutual passive acceptance of non-communication.

André Green 'charts the psychic reverberations of a child attempting to enliven a depressed, bereft, or absent father. This resuscitation becomes the life task' (Sekoff, 1999, p. 113). Grace did not realize it at the time, but she was unable to either repair or mourn her father as the lost object or awaken the desire located within him. As a child she tried to reanimate her father, interest him and give him a taste for life in the hope that if she healed him she could get something – maybe attention, maybe love, maybe he would see her, maybe she would be valued. Her desiring a father led to many manoeuvres designed, often desperately, to find some link to him. Like many daughters, Grace taught the father how to love. She learned early to unconsciously assess and satisfy his needs. He gave little while she protected and nourished him. Sadly such a father does not realize his daughter has an inner life, separate and distinct from his. Nor does he support her developmental need for appropriate dependency, mirroring or nurturing. Meanwhile, he does not register the toll giving to him takes both emotionally and psychologically.

Because she knew this role from such a young age, Grace replicated it with her husband. She had been consumed with her father and then her husband's sorrows took precedence. For many years she put her career on hold for him, listened to his commentary on her work that was less than encouraging and believed him. She spent much time trying to heal him at the cost of her creative development. Her husband was in rivalry with her; the unspoken truth: he feared she was more talented. They had a pact: she was to save him and then do her work. He did little for her, as he needed the help. This lopsided arrangement continued for years.

Through many ups and downs, from hope to disappointments, her life began to take another turn. In therapy she explored the journey of her marriage and her life for what fit and what did not. Grace began to realize there was no more hope in the marriage and she was tired and needed more emotional support. Dreams and outer life events, advancement in her career, her needs for recognition and not getting it, brought divorce from not only her marriage but also the old way of living.

In therapy what is felt as the bad parts are inevitably resurrected and the emptiness is signalled by overt self-hatred (Green, 1986, p. 55). Faced with the woman with a dead father complex, the therapist might experience, like the daughter herself, times of deadness and an inability to think. André Green noted that adults, like Grace, with a dead father complex come into therapy not with depression but with

> acute conflicts with [those] who are close … [an] [i]mpotence to withdraw from a conflictual situation, impotence to love, to make the most of one's talents, to multiply one's assets, or when this does take place, a profound dissatisfaction with the results.
>
> (1986, p. 149)

In compensation for the loss and absence, Grace could be inwardly frantic, running as fast as she could. Internally, nothing made sense although outwardly she appeared together. Even to herself, she put up a wall against the pain, lack and absence. She fought, pushing, compelled by the sharp-edged sense there was something more to achieve or do and this became a driving force. She tried to nullify the deadness. André Green noted:

> The absence of all meaningful reference points cannot be too strongly emphasized. In all, the subject's objects remain constantly at the limit of the ego, not wholly within, and not quite without … for the place is occupied, in its center, by the dead father.
>
> (1986, pp. 153–54)

If the object of life is outer achievement and ambition, attaining it only leaves an empty space, replicating the experiences with the absent father. It is this space the daughter needs to learn to fill or else she remains absent like the dead father.

The boundaries Grace had to erect around the emotionally absent father restricted her personality from functioning, a rampart against desire, emotion and change. As portrayed in her dead marriage, love was not possible when unconsciously mortgaged to the dead father. The freedom of psychic space shut down. She anticipated demise. No life was possible beyond the boundary of the deadened father and certainly no peace of mind within his embrace (Sekoff, 1999, p. 118). The psychological wounds splintered the solidity of her inner world. She was rudderless, disillusioned. 'Absence can only be borne if it is recognized as such' (Phillips, 1999, p. 165). The recognition of this absence opened the struggle within to be herself, yet she often feared she could not find herself.

Her father's detritus dragged on her as the memories returned. Wounding events are not linear and are often forgotten due to the pain and hurt. The daughter deadens herself and her psyche due to the deadened object within (Schwartz & Bollas, 1976, p. 74). In short, the emotional disruption erases self-care and relatedness owing to the intrusive inner presence of an absent father. Attachment has formed, not to the father, but to the gap, the presence of absence that contains desire, mourning and longing. This is a powerful metaphor both of the father's empty circle, that magnetic core of mindlessness and non-representation, and the destructive pull such a representation exerts on the psyche that is a threat to the daughter's psychic integrity (Connolly, 2011, p. 623). Existence becomes a mere waiting for the moment, not yet here, when real life and love will begin.

Through Jungian analysis Grace began to integrate the sacrifices she had made. They brought her to care for herself through advancing in her work and getting divorced. *Grace dreamt she was offered tea by an older man with mandala-shaped tattoos on various parts of his body. They were beautiful and shimmered. He said to her, 'Finally! Someone who doesn't forget. I have given my tea to many people, and you are the first who doesn't forget'.* Grace was awed by the dream and took it as a sign of her emerging; she felt free to express rather than being tightly bound inside. She began to contemplate how she wanted her life to evolve. Her creativity began to flourish.

Depression

> Lazy and indifferent the heron returns; the sky veils her stars; then bares them.
>
> Virginia Woolf, *Monday or Tuesday* (1921, p. 43)

Too few opportunities for good experiences with a father pass on a legacy of non-involvement and personal detachment. The devotion to the deadened father sets up feelings of depersonalization and distancing associated with the failure to connect. The daughter focuses on him, on males, the masculine or the myriad cultural forms of the powerful father. She waits for him, his approval and for her life. But there is nothing. These are the psychological holes that create an inability to love or make the most of one's talents (Green, 2001, p. 176).

Depressive behaviour, corporeal fragmentation and a failure of narration develops. The hole of paternal absence leaves an internal culture of self-contempt, destructive withdrawal and self-depreciation with a predominant masochistic quality (Green, 2002, p. 644). From the internal defeat a woman is anxious and nervous about life. There might be a subtle but strong death wish against herself. The father is a dead figure, and the daughter a puppet manipulated by this deadness. What can arise in a daughter is unconscious guilt, obsessive manifestations, tormenting feelings, unease with authority (Kohon, 1999, p. 42). However unsatisfactory, she avoids encountering what feels like both the deadness and the terrifying aliveness. The bond composed of her pain, yearning and desire keeps her psychologically shackled. She lacks an understanding of self and other because she does not experientially know it (Bollas, 1999, p. 101). She cannot find her passion, seeking but not getting, frustrated and lonely.

Yet all is not hopeless. As André Green reminded us: 'The mind has the capacity to bring something back again which has been related to an object, without the object being there' (1979, p. 30). To make a conscious place for the feelings and emotions is a way of recognizing and transforming them. It means acknowledging the grief and distinguishing what is alive from what is dead and re-establishing her separate being. André Green described the psychic life founded on loss: 'the absent other marks a place of moving forward but also has become the graveyard where … the absence is nuanced, complex and paradoxical' (Sekoff, 1999, p. 114).

On the one hand, when absence is associated with the unknown and blank father, the ego can shatter, receiving no support. On the other hand, absence can also be a space for revitalizing psychic life. The process adds memory and links ideas not always based on the real so as to ensure they are not completely lost (Kalinich & Taylor, 2009, p. 30). Although the dead father is never absent, that absence can also mean potential presence. The space for psychological growth is implied here, as it is also a necessary condition for a vital psychic life (Sekoff, 1999, p.114). In this sense, absence makes room for new thought and experience. It is a space to open and fill with the authentic expression of a daughter's self. In this, the daughter will move beyond the drag of the deadened father.

The dead father effect leaves the daughter with the task of looking within. While stirring up mourning, at the same time it spurs the reclaiming of herself. Again, André Green associated creativity and intellectual development as possible outcomes from this dead father complex (1986, p. 153). In the words of Elizabeth Barrett Browning, 'Why, what is to live? Not to eat and drink and breathe, – but to feel the life in you down all the fibres of being, passionately and joyfully' (Browning & Browning, 1900).

References

Bollas, C. (1999). Dead mother, dead child. In: G. Kohon (Ed.), *The Dead Mother: The Work of André Green* (pp. 87–108). London, England: Routledge.

Bromberg, P. (1983). The mirror and the mask – On narcissism and psychoanalytic growth. *Contemporary Psychoanalysis*, *19*(2), 359–87. doi:10.1080/00107530.1983.10746614.

Browning, R. & Browning, E.B. (1900). *The Letters of Robert Browning and Elizabeth Barrett Browning 1845–1846*, Vol. 1 [Etext #16182]. Retrieved from https://www.gutenberg.org/files/16182/16182-h/16182-h.htm.

Cixous, H. (1991). *Inside*. Berlin, Germany: Schocken.

Connolly, A. (2011). Healing the wounds of our fathers: Intergenerational trauma, memory, symbolization and narrative. *Journal of Analytical Psychology*, *56*(5), 607–26.

Falzeder, E. (2015). *Psychoanalytic Filiations: Mapping the Psychoanalytic Movement*. London, England: Karnac Books.

Green, A. (1979). *The Tragic Effect*. Cambridge, England: Cambridge University Press.

Green, A. (1986). *On Private Madness*. London, England: The Hogarth Press.
Green, A. (2001). *Life Narcissism, Death Narcissism*. London, England: Free Association Books.
Green, A. (2002). A dual conception of narcissism: Positive and negative organizations. *The Psychoanalytic Quarterly, LXXI*(4), 631–49.
Kalinich, L. & Taylor, S.W. (2009). *The Dead Father*. London, England: Routledge.
Kohon, G. (Ed.) (1999). *The Dead Mother: The Work of André Green*. London, England: Routledge.
Lussier, A. (1999). The dead mother: Variation on a theme. In: G. Kohon (Ed.), *The Dead Mother: The Work of André Green* (pp. 149–62). London, England: Routledge.
Modell, A. (1999). The dead mother syndrome and the reconstruction of trauma. In: G. Kohon (Ed.), *The Dead Mother: The Work of André Green* (pp. 76–86). London, England: Routledge.
Parsons, M. (1999). Psychic reality, negation and the analytic setting. In: G. Kohon (Ed.), *The Dead Mother: The Work of André Green* (pp. 59–75). London, England: Routledge.
Phillips, A. (1999). Taking aims: André Green and the pragmatics of passion. In: G. Kohon (Ed.), *The Dead Mother: The Work of André Green* (pp. 165–74). London, England: Routledge.
Schwartz, M. & Bollas, C. (1976). The absence at the center: Sylvia Plath and suicide. *Criticism, 18*(2). https://digitalcommons.wayne.edu/criticism/vol18/iss2/3.
Schwartz-Salant, N. (1982). *On Narcissism*. Toronto, Canada: Inner City Books.
Sekoff, J. (1999). The undead: Necromancy and the inner world. In: G. Kohon (Ed.), *The Dead Mother: The Work of André Green* (pp. 109–28). London, England: Routledge.
Woolf, V. (1921). *Monday or Tuesday* [ebook 29220]. Retrieved from http://www.gutenberg.org/files/29220/29220-h/29220-h.htm.

Chapter 5

Bad dad – negative father complex

'Omar answers'
The wisdom of the wisest of the wise
Is but the pinch of powder in the eyes
Thrown by the fingers of the fiend, that we
True things from false may fail to recognise.

Hafiz, *Hafiz in London* (McCarthy, 1886, p. 90)

André Green's concept of the dead father effect leads to the negative father complex in Jungian analytical psychology. Together they illustrate, although in different ways, the absent father compromising a daughter's development in the world, her career, her relationships and her own self. Early contacts with the father are significant in shaping character, emotional habits and attachment patterns. Both André Green and Carl Jung noted this all depends on the nurturance or toxicity of the father–daughter relationship. They both recognized a father influences how a daughter's personality opens, or contracts, to life.

The construction of the negative father complex derives from absence and abandonment in many ways. It depends on the type of absence, the position of the mother figure and the personality of the daughter if she remains apologetic, guilty and without the impetus even sometimes for life (Kast, 1997, p. 161). Self-knowledge comes from recognizing the hurt places, events and feelings within this complex. Both Green and Jung, with the concept of the collective unconscious, note that trauma does not have a locale solely in the self as it is beyond the person yet, at the same time, being the person created (Bollas, 1999, p. 100). In other words, wounding personal experiences link to the collective through the conscious and unconscious realms.

In Jungian analytical psychology the father complex involves a range of thoughts, feelings, behaviour patterns and somatic forms of expression, both healthy and unhealthy. Classically, complexes occur where the energy is dammed in an area of unconsciousness. The further from conscious awareness, the more autonomous the complex and its tendency to repeat and attract attention. When negative, the father complex is marked by a daughter's destructive impulses, separating her from the instincts and natural reactions in her psyche and body. Negative father complexes appear in the dream series presented here calling forth the psyche for self-regulation and equilibrium.

To know our self is to know our complexes individually and distinctively and to become aware of how they change and morph through life.

> As we live, we grow and our beliefs change. They must change. So I think we should live with this constant discovery. We should be open to this adventure in heightened awareness of living. We should stake our whole existence on our willingness to explore and experience.
>
> (Buber, quoted in Kramer, 2019, p. 5)

Complexes are dynamic and powerful, the lens through which we view the world, a coloration granting experiences their distinctive hue. The complex modifies the present in response to the intercession of prior memories, not as pathology but as an informative part of the personality. The complex is not ever really expelled but becomes apparent, so the energy can shift and be consciously used. Complexes inform our trajectory, and although we cannot escape them, the challenge is how to be aware of and use them.

The absence of father provokes and sustains a negative father complex, making the world bleak, oftentimes hopeless, until understood. The negative father complex can adversely affect a daughter's confidence, promote the idealization of others and crumple assertion and initiative. The negativity of this complex arises from a trapped, disquieting place the ego avoids. It can empty the daughter of self-definition, whereas becoming conscious separates her from being under its spell.

> A traumatic complex brings about dissociation of the psyche. The complex is not under the control of the will and for this reason it possesses the quality of psychic autonomy … Abreaction then is an attempt to reintegrate the autonomous complex, to incorporate it gradually into the conscious mind as an accepted content, by living the traumatic situation over again, once or repeatedly.
>
> (Jung, 1954b, pp. 131–132)

The complex is a network of pathways with various characteristics, a web seemingly inaccessible to change. The complex with its many roots in childhood wounds and relational failures can seem insidious, leaving a daughter with little choice but to accede and go unconscious. The negative father complex wraps around a daughter like the wind and often goes unnoticed as she is so used to its presence. It is familiar but compels her to remain hostage, unconscious and unaware of herself or how she feels.

The origin of the complex is 'frequently a so-called trauma, an emotional shock or some such thing, that splits off a bit of the psyche' (Jung, 1960, p. 204). A complex turns negative and hardens due to tendencies that interfere with natural desires and impulses. The psychological fallout from the negative father complex appears through various symptoms of depression, depersonalization, dissociation, despair, anxiety, all representing the disturbed connection to self and others. A father figure negatively inhabiting a daughter's psyche can prevent her from living in an autonomous and creative way, which is possible only when there is separation from the father (Carotenuto, 2015, p. 26). The complex can act through internalized persecutory male figures, creating a hostile inner world, rage or numbness. Until comprehended, the daughter might remain in violent protest against the father and all he represents, locked in a self-perpetuating negative cycle. Progressively more and more out of touch with her own thoughts, needs and feelings, she develops a pattern of negative male figures submerging her self.

The negative father complex leads to denial, confusion, self-sabotage, numbing and an inability to find adequate voice or expression. This scenario can despoil a daughter's sense of what it is to be a woman, and she feels incapable, as her inner compass is off. The more severe the wounds from the father absence, the more autonomous and ego-dystonic or unconscious are the complexes. Exploring this leads to self-knowledge.

In addition to personal experiences, the complexes are influenced by the era and place in which a person lives, including the impact of various religious, social and cultural structures. What seeps in from the unconscious is played out through the complexes.

> To have complexes only means that something discordant, unassimilated and antagonistic exits, perhaps as an obstacle, but also as an incentive to greater effort, and so, perhaps, to new possibilities of achievement. Indeed complexes are focal points of psychic life and they should not be missing, for otherwise psychic activity would come to a fatal standstill.
>
> (Jung, 1971, para. 925)

As denoted in Merriam-Webster's, the word *complex* contains multiple parts of speech and senses. It refers to a whole made up of complicated or interrelated parts. As a verb, its original meaning is 'to join or unite'. *Complex* comes from the Latin *complecti*, which means 'to entwine around, to embrace', a word that is based, in part, on *plectere*, 'to braid' and 'an intricately interwoven combination of elements in a cohering structure'. A negative complex splits off from the central personality and begins to function autonomously, ranging in effect from being hardly disturbing to being so strong a daughter disappears into it. This is what has happened to many of the daughters in this book, propelling them to seek inner knowledge and growth through Jungian analysis.

Learned dismissiveness

Without images and experiences of loving fathers, daughters can likewise become dismissive and defensive to themselves and others. Kaleigh is a composite example, a woman raised with a father she labelled a thug. Her parents divorced when she was four, and subsequently she saw him on rare occasions. He did not protect her, especially when he married a woman who rejected and acted punitively towards Kaleigh. When he remarried, although the children went to live with him, they did not receive good care and were simply ignored. Kaleigh, in effect, raised herself, travelling many pathways through drugs, alcohol and various sexual partners from a young age. She was angry with her father for abandoning them, marrying an evil woman and then being cruel. Most of all, now that he was dead, which she had wished for so many times, she was confused about why she missed him.

Although she hardly saw him for years, when he died, she was still arguing with him in her mind while also fearing him. She wanted him to be kinder and better and did not understand his compelling dark power in her psyche. She decided she would just not think of him anymore, but his absent presence still dragged at her. On the other side of this, her adopted attitude of fierce independence covered the helplessness and over-dependency she felt for her father, keeping her in an infantile state (Seligman, 1985, p. 82). This conflict revealed itself in the form of destructive and oppressive energy turned against herself, enacted in periodically smashing her artwork, finding no consistent partner and being frustrated professionally. At the beginning of a relationship Kaleigh would assume the role of a femme fatale, malleable, without definition and living to please the man as she evaporated into his image of her.

Kaleigh had a brief but impactful dream. *In it, much as she tried, she could not step beyond her boss. She was frozen and unable to move.* In person, Kaleigh, in her late thirties, appeared tightly coiled, often wearing sexy outfits. In the dream, the boss was her father's age, an imposing leader in his field, wielding force and threats to keep people in line. The dream illustrated the paralysis Kaleigh experienced with males and the masculine, impacting her apprehension about achieving success. Anticipating failure, she would stop any forward progress. Kaleigh was at an emotional impasse and in a quandary about how to move beyond the negative and feared father/male image. This scenario happens to many daughters who are without the possibility of internalizing good-enough fathers. And in Judith Butler's words, 'Possibility is not a luxury; it is as crucial as bread' (2004, p. 29). They had no one to ask and no one to show them. They express loneliness, holding sorrow and hiding their perceived flaws with outer bravado.

Kaleigh seemed confident, energetic and had many creative ideas and talents. She could maintain this façade for a time and then she would suddenly collapse into self-denigrating, unsatisfied, destructive behaviours and thoughts. She was apprehensive about intimacy, even though she yearned for it. Meanwhile, her aloof veneer confused people, holding them at bay.

Negative father complex dreams

Dreams can help liberate and clarify the psyche by exposing the psychological complexes in the natural quest for accessing life. They reveal the unconscious realms of the psyche in symbolic language unfolding into more than the literal or obvious. The symbols in dreams help decipher thoughts and emotions, personal and collective, historical and present. Jung wrote: 'The dream is a spontaneous self-portrayal, in symbolic form, of the actual situation in the unconscious' (1960, p. 505).

The perspective of Jungian analytical psychology affirms the reality of the psyche, the unconscious holder of symbols, images and messages of blockages, compensations and hopes. Dreams are like crystals to be turned to the many facets of the personality. They are natural ways of dealing with problems and help restore balance to one-sided attitudes from the negative father complex. Dreams are both subjective and objective, reflecting inner and outer figures and situations. Jung stated: 'Only they are always a little bit ahead of the dreamer's consciousness' (1976, p. 244).

The psyche is a self-regulating system, and the theory of compensation is a basic law of psychological behaviour. This perspective lies at the heart of the Jungian approach to dream interpretation. One of the key questions raised when confronted by a dream is what conscious attitude it compensates, as the dream is not isolated from daily life. It portrays what has been lost and needs to be re-found and how this can happen. Dreams illustrate the rhythms of the inner life. When the daughter is held in a negative father complex, when he has her energy and she is passionless, depleted of her life force, this manifests in her dreams. These disconnections and dissociations foster the seeking of self, taking her inward to the answers and guideposts held in the dream world.

In returning to Kaleigh, we find a daughter who raged at her father but was insecure. Her rage went nowhere and was diminished rather than directed. She internalized a father who was absent and terribly cruel. *Kaleigh dreamt of throwing things at her father, yelling at him; she was exhausted, and he was impervious.* She didn't know what prompted the altercation in the dream or how she got there. Would she continue the anger and remain unconsciously attached to this negative father complex? From the deprivation and/or absence, the possibility of a good father is withheld, and the investment remains with the absent, elusive and cruel father. She wondered whether it was all too entrenched.

Kaleigh had low self-worth and felt incompetent and unsure she could survive. In despair she often felt emasculated and hopeless. Hating her father and, at the same time, desiring love from him kept her intertwined with, yet disconnected from, her father. A father should provide enough ego-functioning to help a daughter evolve a solid self. Yet her father absolutely did not, and she now needed constant confirmation from others since the toxic osmosis with him had a soul-squashing effect. She could not break into or out of his orbit. A wedge developed between a loving and reparative self and a hating and persecutory self, and the latter took over in the form of the negative father complex.

Rather than experiencing the full range of her senses and movements, Kaleigh, like many in similar circumstances, learned constraint and to encase herself in a suit of armour. She became desensitized and aware of herself only in situations of intensity, crisis or excitement; otherwise, her emotional life was muted. Kaleigh's efforts to perceive and define her self were frustrated by the overshadowing father, who in his threatening absence, was forbidding and foreboding. He became an exaggerated and angry inner presence with constant accusations about what was wrong with her. Kaleigh took care of her body, but it is like an object for others to see rather than her to feel. Her natural impulses to express her individuality were stifled and she was without personal ease. Even though serious about meditation and yoga practice, her mental vigilance and compulsive thoughts continued. Anxious, she often could not hear in therapy and was suffocated by feelings of shame she was not better.

Kaleigh wondered why therapy had never worked. Over the years she had attended numerous workshops and various modes of therapy, but only for so long. Something eluded her. She remained nervous and uneasy in her skin. She had to exercise for hours to relax and write page and pages in her journal or draw to centre herself. The absent father lived restlessly in her. The anticipation of rejection would take over like a poison, and she could abruptly cut off, stomp out and disappear. Early on, she learned her emotionality was shameful and devalued by her father. However, she needed these emotions for differentiating from the impact of the oppressive father.

The script of the daughter/feminine/female as inferior creates self-isolation. Kaleigh could not experience good relationships and lacked sufficient love. Again, due to non-attachment with her father, anxiety, vulnerability and loss kept her solidly defended and on the defensive. Relationally, she withdrew from the terror of dependency, from the apprehension that she could be destroyed by the power of the other person (Knox, 2010, p. 154).

Everyone has a father complex, but when negative he appears overly impressive, out of proportion and the daughter diminished. This projection becomes a life-long pattern metastasizing into a belief the daughter's reality is wrong, invalid. As Jung commented: 'Children are so deeply involved in the psychological attitude of their parents that it is no wonder that most of the nervous disturbances in childhood can be traced back to a disturbed psychic atmosphere in the home' (1954a, para. 80). When the childhood paradise is destroyed too early with a father's absence prior to the time of natural separation, the emotional disturbance can feel like a crime against the daughter's personality, often resulting in self-persecutory actions and internal vengeance. Jung spoke about the 'inertia of the libido, which will relinquish no object of the past, but would like to hold it fast forever … [an] original passive state where the libido is arrested in the objects of childhood' (Jung, 1967, p. 253). Tumultuous feelings over time increase in velocity and power, fragmenting the mind and body and scattering the personality through self-disavowal. Busy compensating the loss, independence of self is seemingly not there. The daughter may try to compensate with achievements or getting lost in others or maybe she will just give up. In any case, the lack remains, and she is harassed and closes in on herself.

Father gaze

As an infant, the daughter looks around and sees her reflection in the face and eyes of her father. A daughter is concerned with such things as 'Are you there? I am here. Are you here for me?' The mirroring of father to daughter is made up of his empathic responses to her needs, wishes, experiences, behaviours and gives legitimacy, validation and a sense of worth.

Many daughters, however, do not have good experiences because they do not see or feel anything related to them. She might see doubt, insecurity or absence, a father's lack of love and care, and this becomes how she views herself, with lack and absence. The daughter attempts to incorporate the attributes associated with the paternal image, but she cannot find the safety to get close. The feeling of containment establishes peace of mind, but when the father is not present, it is not possible to access peace. She must relinquish coherence for incoherence as the world is not as she expected (Britton, 1998, p. 79).

The negative father complex can alienate her from her body, and various physical reactions point to anxieties about unmet needs and desires. Because self-realization is embedded in all psychological processes, and the psyche like the body strives to keep balance, what happens with the absence of the father figure (Samuels, 1985, p. 15)? A daughter learns to compensate with persona formation, as if there is no problem. But this persona is like a carapace or shell and not always internally connected to the real inside. It becomes a deceptive pseudo-covering to compensate for the discontinuous emotions, identified with filling a role and acting (Mizen, 2014, p. 316).

She internalizes nostalgia, regret, resentment, attempting to sever his hold while always hoping to find love. The psychological process of cancelling his claim on her spirit requires a dance between the forces that are threatening. This means getting close enough to understand but staying far enough away to not get caught in him. Jung commented: 'The images of the unconscious place a great responsibility upon us. Failure to understand them brings fragmentariness to life' (1963, p. 192).

Meanwhile, the symptoms of distress course through her and circle back to the wounds originating from not being with a solid and caring father figure. The traumatization, loss and melancholic identification with the father contributes to the negative father complex. There is emotional shattering, premature separation and psychological deprivation. Insufficient father nurturance creates guilt and sorrow, and his betrayal makes the daughter desolate. Missing out on his validation for her strength and independence, she has to search various pathways to find her authority and voice.

'[T]he things which have the most powerful effect upon children do not come from the conscious state of the parents but from their unconscious background' (Jung, 1954a, para. 84). Too often the daughter within the negative father complex is unable to sort her thoughts or organize her life so it feels like a tangle of confusion and confabulation of directions. She is susceptible to living out the father's shadow, enacting *his* perceptions of father and daughter, feminine and masculine, separation and differentiation. The daughters without a father are left with an exaggerated image of the father in their psychological life and they end up defining themselves in father terms (Shorter, 1985, p. 177). In these instances, by default and at the same time overpowered, a daughter could enter a psychological paralysis, become ineffective, a rote follower – of him. Jung referred to the father-ideal as a potentially dangerous object of a daughter's fantasy.

> The fateful power of the father-complex comes from the archetype, and is the real reason why the *consensus gentium* puts a divine or daemonic figure in place of the father. The personal father inevitably embodies the archetype, which is what endows his figure with its fascinating power.
>
> (Jung, 1961, para. 744)

Rather than imagine otherwise or explore options within her personality, the daughter remains young, unreflective and in imitation of the father. This has also been described as a 'fixation of delusion' (Shorter, 1985, p. 179). Fusion with the negative father complex defends against reality, and the necessary separation becomes more difficult. In other words, when in the throes of the negative father complex, the daughter could become what she does not like in the father.

'The binding of the daughter to the father ... that to which she falls defensively has a lethal aspect ... where the masculine appears not graciously and paternally but aggressively' (Shorter, 1985, p. 180). She might avoid, delay or circumvent her natural bent towards the creative and edgy, towards rebelliousness and the bending of rules because it is not in the father tradition. She cannot find her way, attain womanhood or value her particular qualities when wrapped up in support-ing the absent father's ways and living within the negative father complex.

Complexes contain conflicting emotions difficult to reconcile with the con-scious mind and appearances. The negative father complex often blocks access to a variety of effective and helpful masculine images and figures. The daughter lacks inner support to realize her potential or use her energy with passion or spirit. As Jung said:

> The children are infected indirectly through the attitude they instinctively adopt towards their parents' state of mind: either they fight against it with unspoken protest (though occasionally the protest is vociferous) or else they succumb to a paralysing and compulsive imitation.
>
> (1954a, para. 154)

Demonic complex

From the absence of a father, a woman can fall into developing a father complex that acts like a demon holding her in its clutches (Leonard, 1983, p. 88). Internally, she forms attachment to the abyss of the father. She is unable to differentiate herself: 'The process by which the human soul comes to be is a lifetime activity … I come to be by differentiating myself from the world into which I was born, but success at that project requires that I become a differentiated unity' (Lear, 1990, p. 177).

Cassey dreamt there were scorpions in her father's house. He was not present there. She worried the toads, in addition to the mushrooms and scorpions in his house, would poison her dogs. Some male professors were present and told her to go into a dark room and stay there. She complied but became afraid. She couldn't stay, panicked and frantically got out. In the dream she realized there was no one to help her.

Upon awakening she commented that getting out would displease the professors. She said nothing about how this felt or her emotional reactions. In discussing the dream Cassey did not associate the fact her father was a professor. Nor did she put together the professors in the dream acting like she described him – cold, unrelated, unsupportive and dismissive. Her flat affect also indicated she was unconscious of the hurt from this absent father, who she described as a forbidding and formidable man, distant, unemotional and strict. Life with him had been too much to manage. Bullied by other children as a child, she never told because he would ridicule her as weak. He focused on himself, often absent, quite suddenly taking unexplained long trips for his work. No one knew when he would return, and he provided no communication when gone, sometimes for months at a time. She walked on eggshells around him and was uncertain if and when he would cruelly disapprove. He gave no expressions of love, care, guidance, protection or emotion, only trepidation. She still wanted his approval, but he hardly took any interest in her.

He did not play with her when she was a child, and any activity was determined by him, not according to her wants or needs. About this she again registered no anger or disappointment, no sorrow or loss. Emotions were disallowed in the home, and by the time we met, she was reduced to a flat line. Yet, the dream told her she had to get out of her father's house as it was filled with poisonous insects and plants. The other professors as iterations of her father were certainly not helpful. If she followed their advice, she would remain in the father's house, unaware of her life, repressed and trapped, unconscious, her psyche in the dark.

Cassey received no encouragement from her professor father to get an advanced degree and certainly not to be a professor, although she was intelligent. In her early forties now she could neither find a career she liked nor decide whether to be a mother. Instead, she floundered, working in jobs for doctors like her father, her mind focused on worrying about being correct and getting approval. She had medical problems, quite serious ones, but did nothing about them.

This form of the negative father complex denotes a pull to depression, defeat and resignation, like Cassey taking no time for self-care or attention, forgetting herself and her mind wandering away. Cassey did not know why she did not matter and searched online for the meaning of self-care. She was unable to decide or be definitive about almost anything, as she remained unsure whether others would agree. She had been depressed and fatigued for years since college. She was tied to the negative father dilemma and unable to move or amass energy. She wondered whether there was a repressed memory, fearing she would discover something awful, yet she had no idea what. Could it be self-knowledge she avoided?

A father's absence can fuel a daughter's compensatory drive towards heroism and fame, or equally it can ignite the flames of despair and gripping self-doubt. An absence of emotional containment or reverie by the father leaves this daughter with neither containment nor the ability to reflect creatively on herself.

> It is of course not possible for parents to have no complexes at all. That would be superhuman. But they should at least come to terms with them consciously; they should make it a duty to work out their inner difficulties for the sake of the children.
>
> (Jung, 1954a, para. 219)

Cassey's father seems to have worked out nothing and she has taken on the negative and repressing effects.

Jung commented: 'The dark sun of the feminine psyche is connected to the father-imago … Unfortunately, this source is often sullied just where we would expect clean water' (1970, para. 232). Without a father, a daughter grows up in a twilight state, non-differentiated, unformed. This can become an internal tug of war between wanting to come alive and pulling back. Tension exists between her independent and dependent self. In not knowing where to go, she does nothing. Anxiety, fear of fragmentation and lacking a creative existence are the result of attachment to the absent father and the unmet yearning, keeping women like Cassey unborn to themselves. Cassey continued in Jungian therapy for a while and then abruptly stopped. She seemed wistful about this, reluctant, unsure. Not much had changed outwardly, but perhaps the recognition of a self to be valued had some impact. Maybe she will decide to pursue her development later or in other ways.

The absence of father energy creates problems, longing, unfulfilled desires, intense needs and the rage turned inward (Hillman, 1989, p. 208). The daughter's life comes to mean nothing and she regards it as futile. James Hillman, archetypal psychologist, addressed the idea that what actually individuates is not us, but our passions, talents and places of wounding. As complexes shake off their infantile associations and find maturity, reality and connection between psyche and body, the personality becomes a rich, multidimensional canvas (Slater, 2012, p. 30). With knowledge, complexes can become conscious and their negative and restrictive impact reduced. The father complex brings out the possibility to restore a better inner father. Analyzing dreams, keeping track of feelings consciously, spending time in self-reverie helps restore and bring a daughter's psyche out from the negative father complex. Being herself requires the withdrawal of projections, differentiating parts that are hers from those that are not. From this painstaking interior and relational work, the integration of complexes then leads to self-understanding and enhances the personality.

> Individual self-reflection, return of the individual to the ground of human nature, to his [or her] own deepest being with its individual and social destiny – here is the beginning of a cure for that blindness which reigns at the present hour.
>
> (Jung, 1966, p. 5)

References

Bollas, C. (1999). Dead mother, dead child. In: G. Kohon (Ed.), *The Dead Mother: The Work of André Green* (pp. 87–108). London, England: Routledge.

Britton, R. (1998). *Belief and Imagination*. London, England: Routledge.

Butler, J. (2004). *Undoing Gender*. London, England: Routledge.

Carotenuto, A. (2015). *To Love, to Betray*. Asheville, NC: Chiron Publications.

Hafiz (1886). *Hafiz in London*. J.H. McCarthy (Trans.) [eBook 51392]. http://www.gutenberg.org/files/51392/51392-h/51392-h.htm.

Hillman, J. (1989). *Puer Papers*. Dallas, TX: Spring Publications.

Jung, C.G. (1954a). *The Development of Personality*, Vol. 17. Princeton, NJ: Princeton University Press.

Jung, C.G. (1954b). *The Practice of Psychotherapy*, Vol. 16. Princeton, NJ: Princeton University Press.

Jung, C.G. (1960). *The Spirit in Man, Art, and Literature*, Vol. 15. Princeton, NJ: Princeton University Press.

Jung, C.G. (1961). *Freud and Psychoanalysis*, Vol. 4. Princeton, NJ: Princeton University Press.

Jung, C.G. (1963). *Memories, Dreams, Reflections*. New York, NY: Vintage.

Jung, C.G. (1966). *Two Essays on Analytical Psychology*, Vol. 7. New York, NY: Pantheon Books.

Jung, C.G. (1967). *Alchemical Studies*, Vol. 13. Princeton, NJ: Princeton University Press.

Jung, C.G. (1967). *Symbols of Transformation*. Princeton, NJ: Princeton University Press.

Jung, C.G. (1970). *Mysterium Coniunctionis*, Vol. 14. New York, NY: Pantheon Books.

Jung, C.G. (1971). *Psychological Types*, Vol. 6. Princeton, NJ: Princeton University Press.

Jung, C.G. (1976). *The Symbolic Life*, Vol. 18. New York, NY: Pantheon Books.

Kast, V. (1997). *Father, Daughter, Mother, Son*. Zurich, Switzerland: Element Books.

Knox, J. (2010). *Self-Agency in Psychotherapy*. New York, NY: W.W. Norton & Co.

Kramer, K.P. (2019). *Martin Buber's Dialog: Discovering Who We Really Are*. Eugene, OR: Cascade Books.

Lear, J. (1990). *Love and Its Place in Nature*. New York, NY: Farrar, Straus & Giroux.

Leonard, L.S. (1983). *The Wounded Woman: Healing the Father/Daughter Relationship*. Boston, MA: Shambhala.

Mizen, R. (2014). On the capacity to suffer one's self. *Journal of Analytical Psychology*, *59*(3), 314–32.

Samuels, A. (Ed.) (1985). *The Father*. New York, NY: New York University Press.

Seligman, E. (1985). The half-alive ones. In: A. Samuels (Ed.), *The Father* (pp. 69–94). New York, NY: New York University Press.

Shorter, B. (1985). The concealed body language of anorexia nervosa. In: A. Samuels (Ed.), *The Father* (pp. 171–86). New York, NY: New York University Press.

Slater, G. (2012). Between Jung and Hillman. *Quadrant, XXXXII, 2*, 15–37.

Chapter 6

Father archetypal dynamics, symbols and images

When Judah saw his daughter-in-law, he thought she was a prostitute, for she had covered her face. Not realizing who she was he said, 'Come now, let me sleep with you' ... About three months later Judah was told, 'Your daughter-in-law Tamar is guilty of prostitution, and as a result she is now pregnant'. Judah said, 'Bring her out and have her burned to death'.

(Genesis 38:13–18, 24)

This archetypal story from the Old Testament conveys the unconscious side of the father absent to his daughter. With the father projected onto her, she is punished and killed for his sins. It illustrates another old and archetypal story, replicated through the time and space of history with personal and collective conscious and unconscious effects. Here, the linking of archetypal patterns to contemporary relationships reveals the father as selfish, absent in his awareness of the daughter and his cause of her demise. Too often this story is the current reality.

Classically the archetypes function as a template or set of expectations against which life is experienced. Inner and outer images arise from the interactions of the archetypes, real-world experiences, cultural and interpersonal relations. Jung said: 'It [the archetype] persists throughout the ages and requires interpreting anew. The archetypes are imperishable elements of the unconscious, but they change their shape continually' (1959, para. 179). The word *archetype* derives from the Greek *arche* meaning 'primordial', and *typos* meaning 'typical elements of the human experience'. The *archetype* expresses the perennial dilemmas enacted in the psyche of the individual. The archetype is, so to speak, an 'eternal' presence, and it is only a question of whether it is perceived by the conscious mind or not. (Jung, 1968, para. 329). These images present themselves in dreams, relationships and life, reflecting their symbolic and historical roots. Part of the Jungian approach to the psyche is to recognize, not label or rigidly categorize these patterns, to discover their meanings and functions in a particular life.

Jung said: 'The father archetype corresponds to the *yang*. It determines our relations to man, to the law and the state, to reason and the spirit and the dynamism of nature. "Fatherland" implies boundaries, a definite localization in space' (1970, para. 65). The archetype of the father has a history of being portrayed as huge, authoritarian and powerful; his rule is law. Further descriptors of the father archetype appear in mythology, art, religion, tales, videos and so on, and relate to his qualities as a ruler, king, as sky imagery, a mental or spiritual principle, a wise old man or the God of the Old Testament (Greenfield, 1985, p. 202). As defender of the dominant position, father is known as the guardian of the status quo. 'The father … represents authority … He is the creative wind-breath' (Jung, 1970, para. 65). As father he is a protector, law-giver, owner, a figure whose power can overwhelm with roles of order, intelligence and authority. Father is also depicted in stories, tales and legends in the guise of a ghost, fiend and wizard. He has been aligned with the birth of ego consciousness, or awareness of oneself, movement out to the world and the separation from home and mother.

'The tremendous energy of the archetype lends a numinous, spiritual feeling to experiences of father in the young child, especially when it is not appropriately mediated by the personal father' (Jacobi, 1959, p. 9). In other words, when he is weak, unable to protect and guide or just absent and offering nothing personal to go on, the archetypal images take over. The absent father can mean the daughter inhabits stereotypical and male-defined roles and images, but not her own. She defines herself in father terms, reflecting the lowered expectations and limiting possibilities many daughters are still raised on. Because we are in a patriarchal structure, a daughter tends to determine her life by such attitudes and behaviours, until she begins to examine her psyche. Self-development depends on 'her deconstructing the dead self that is a male opus and discovering a living self. She must replace the copy with her individual nature' (Gilbert & Gubar, 1984, p. 19).

Current Jungian analysts have been expanding the concept of the archetype, emphasizing its active and changeable qualities. The archetypes and their imagery are not to lead to ossification but can be interpreted as contentless general forms. For instance, Jean Knox, British Jungian analyst remarked: 'Archetypes play a key role in psychic functioning and are a crucial source of symbolic imagery, but at the same time are emergent structures resulting from a developmental interaction between genes and the environment that is unique for each person' (Knox, 2003, p. 8). She described these as image schemas providing 'the initial scaffolding for archetypal imagery and the implicit and explicit mental models that organize and give a pattern to our experience' (p. 9). Rather than static, the archetype holds a range of possibilities expressed personally, culturally, consciously and unconsciously. The archetype is not hardwired in us but rather 'it appears, is made actual and emerges from self-organizing systems forming through life. The possibility is that new archetypes are born out of constantly evolving experiences' (Saunders & Skar, 2001).

Example of archetypal dreams

> Ona! pale and weak!
> To thy father speak:
> O the trembling fear!
> O the dismal care!

William Blake, 'A Little Girl Lost'
Songs of Innocence and Experience (1901, p. 65)

Because there are many influences on the archetype and its image, even if the father is absent, the daughter's imaginative experience of father and her attachments to other men may suffice (Samuels, 1985, p. 30). Aidy, unfortunately, had no such substitutes. Her father was a solitary man who became more solitary after her mother died when she was 12. Aidy, as the only girl with two brothers, learned to take care of the house, cook, do her school work, be a model pupil and was so busy she had little time to mourn the loss of her mother. Meanwhile, her father became increasingly withdrawn and pecuniary and left Aidy and her brothers alone. He did not know how to nurture; he did not try; and he hardly noticed how they were coping. They were just to be obedient.

The archetypes are known through dreams. Here we can feel their influence on the personality. Jung described dreams as the psyche's attempt to communicate to the dreamer what is really going on. They are symbolic representations of elements within the dreamer's psyche. The personal associations to the dream, as well as amplifying the images with archetypal, collective and cultural themes, compensate the conscious attitude. 'In the dream, ... there are numberless interconnections to ... associations of ideas (or perhaps in certain poetic creations which are often characterized by a borrowing, not always conscious, from myths)' (1959, para. 259). They expose the influences shaping conscious life and have a role in individuation. As Jung said: 'This struggle has something to do with creation, with the unending battle between affirmation and negation' (1969, para. 72). The disconnections and dissociations from self are also a seeking of self ultimately taking her inward to the dream world.

Aidy had several dreams that seemed to embody the archetype of the all-powerful father, repeating the themes appearing in many myths and tales where the father lets the life of his daughter go or he kills her himself. Aidy dreamt: '*I am with a man I label the sadistic father. He is after the children and me. I am trying to get away or am the one trying to help the others. The man is very crafty, and it seems there is no escape. He can jump over fences or merge through them*'. In the dream, he can get to her no matter what fences or defences she erects.

Aidy's reaction to the dream was surprising. She did not realize it was this dire. She wondered what she should do. The dream offered no help to fend off this powerful male inside her, the sadistic father with malevolent intent towards her and the children. The appearance of the dream indicated she had not dealt sufficiently with him, and he had become more insistent and threatening. 'A demonic father figure takes possession turning the creative into images of self death' (Kavaler-Adler, 1993, p. 78).

Cultures and their stories repeat the archetypal patterns of the absent father, depicting various situations of personal and mythical deadness, absence, neglect and danger. In such scenarios he is cold, unrelated, corrosive or even violent. This is the death-dealing archetypal father, like the Greek myths of Uranos and his son after him, Zeus, devouring his children and killing their essence. He will not allow the natural generational advance. This old king refuses to die. In another version of this scenario, the female is raped by this energy as a punishment for trying to escape his dominance (Greenfield, 1985, p. 205). These archetypal stories illustrate how a father can dominate through neglect, emotional derision or abuse, and they occur in many real situations. Too often,

> The power of the fathers: a familial-social, ideological, political system in which men – by force, direct pressure, or through ritual, tradition, law, and language, customs, etiquette, education, and the division of labor – determine what part women shall or shall not play, and in which the female is everywhere subsumed under the male.
>
> (Rich, 1976, p. 57)

If there were no sons, daughters were allowed to inherit their father's land (Numbers 27:7,8).

In response to her childhood, Aidy had become invisible in order to survive. Her father was thoughtless, had no reflective awareness, dominated through the omnipotence of his absence. She seemed imprinted with apprehension and bewilderment, immersed in fearful circumstances robbing her of vitality. She knew no love or trust and certainly had no time to be creative or carefree as she was busy caring for others while her needs were unattended. As described so poignantly by Adam Philips, 'Life is punctuated by spells of boredom: that state of suspended anticipation in which things are started and nothing begins, the mood of diffuse restlessness which contains that most absurd and paradoxical wish, the wish for a desire' (2001, p. 68). The dream showed she also had the ability to grab the gun and defend herself by running away.

Following an interlude of many other dreams, Aidy dreamt, '*I see a man who looks like a gremlin. He asks me to stay with him and not go out with others. He is seductive and attractive, but small in size. I am attracted to him, but suspect it is a trick. Although he keeps me from my art, I also know by his size he has unusual powers. The question I want answered is how I can acquire his special forces without losing myself?*'

The gremlin, mischievous, causing malfunctions, could represent an archetypal trickster figure with his special powers. This time they could work for her betterment, but the dream warned her to not get seduced by him. She had to stay alert. Her experience with an absent father set up Aidy to be lured by the gremlin, or perhaps he was similar to a demon lover. Although this figure did not sound especially demonic, he might represent enchantment, but he was not there for the stability of relationship or evolving the foundation for love. That he seemed all right was similar to the deception encountered with an absent father who appeared fine, talented and even majestic to the outside world but who was never there for his children. To Aidy the feedback from those who felt sorry for her father, lauding him as burdened, having to cope with three children, made no sense. What could she say? For years she could not recount to anyone how lonely it was at home and how quiet. No one was to disturb her father, who often just stared into space, and she could not do anything.

All this came out in therapy as Aidy began to explore the depths of her psyche. Denied attention until she was in her thirties, only then did she begin to wonder why relationships did not work. Why was she always lonely and feeling out of it, out of sync with what others seemed like? Her self could not attach to life, creating an absence, a vacuum at the centre, overwhelmed with feelings of loneliness and solitude (Modell, 1996, p. 164). Aidy began to have a series of confusing dreams. This brought her to Jungian analysis as the dreams kept nagging at her. She knew she had to do something because she felt so bereft.

In discussing the previous dream Aidy was confused by the gremlin character. She had wished someone would save her for so long. Could that be him? Yet, the absent father is part of what propels the daughter to be susceptible to what is called the demon lover. She has little related experience with the male. The demon lover acts with little reliance or trust, but he is convincing and seductive. He is like the absent father, not really there and with a dark side, always aloof and untouchable. She might agree to sell her soul or diminish her life to acquire what she missed with the father – love, care and attention. The problem is that, just like the absent father, the demon lover deceives, even ignores, yet keeps her enthralled. Both the absent father and demon lover figures only offer unrequited love, yet she still falls for their promise, hoping for love.

Later Aidy dreamt, '*A family goes to a good wizard for help. I seem to know the plot. The wizard goes to the door and speaking in another language is saying "The Arrangement". At the door is evil. The wizard screams, "Go away". But whose name should he use, in which power should he give the order?*'

Here Aidy faced evil forces beyond herself. All three of these dreams seemed related. In each, she had to cope with immense danger. Their occurrence also brought up many unanswered questions. Had things become so bad and so unconscious that evil was needed to bring awareness? The dreams also displayed the strength she did not realize. The end of the last dream implied a spiritual energy, something of the unknown, unusual, set apart from daily life. Although she had little father support growing up, in the dream, she now had the assistance of the good wizard. Yet upon awaking, she worried whether the evil was in her. The self-referencing of this problem was her automatic initial response, indicating the underlying insecurity and anxiety of her life. The dream reassured her, as it seemed the wizard was a knowledgeable figure who could help. Perhaps she could now learn the arrangement referenced in another language in the dream. Jung commented: 'The mind ... consists of the sum of the inheritance from the ancestors, the "unseen fathers" whose authority is born anew with the child' (1969, p. 54). It is this authority Aidy missed, and the dreams revealed what was lacking, the qualities and strengths she now had and how she could use them. 'To be human is necessarily to be a vulnerable risk-taker; to be a courageous human is to be good at it' (Lear, 2006, p. 123).

The daughter–father issues reach to the psychological depths – to issues of self, culture and the complexes a daughter acquires leading to the stunted and then subsequently acquired growth. Aidy continued in Jungian work for a long time as layer after layer of grief, loss and acknowledgement of her aspirations emerged. Her aloneness when young and all the nurturing from books previously sustained her personality to a point. Now she could access the potentials she was unable to acquire with such an emotionally absent father.

Jungian analyst Jean Knox interpreted the archetype-as-such or what she called 'image schemas'. She commented: 'Archetypes play a key role in psychic functioning and are a crucial source of symbolic imagery, but at the same time [are] emergent structures resulting from a developmental interaction between genes and the environment that is unique for each person' (Knox, 2003, p. 8). She described these providing 'the initial scaffolding for archetypal imagery and the implicit and explicit mental models that organize and give a pattern to our experience' (p. 9).

Aidy felt the impact of the archetype with a visceral and psychological reaction. Similar reactions can be aroused relationally and socially and when accessed consciously can shake up the personality system necessary for expansion. Aidy's dreams apply to many daughters as the archetypes contain the seeds of past, present and future. They are concerned with the problems affecting this daughter and many daughters with an absent father. Jung commented: 'The personal father inevitably embodies the archetype, which is what endows his figure with its fascinating power' (1961, para. 744). This means the personal father is connected with transpersonal images and is why the father carries so much power and potential, if he can convey it to his daughter.

During childhood and continuing through life, we are confronted with various representations of the father. The father image is a composite from the personal and symbolic father, reflecting cultural attitudes and expectations. We are exposed to a singular father who also is plural through these images. These, along with the expectations at a biological and psychological level of what a father is or should be, shape the internal father/male/masculine images. The power of archetypes comes from a momentary unity of outer and inner, material reality and perception, culture and body, history and experience (Jensen, 2009, p. 3).

British Jungian analyst Andrew Samuels took a twist on understanding the archetypal construction in the psyche when he said:

> The view is gaining ground that what is archetypal is not to be found in any particular image or list of images … What stirs you at an archetypal level depends on you and where you sit and how you look at things and on your personal history. The archetypal therefore can be *relative, contextual, and personal*. This reframing of archetypal theory as a theory of affects is something that has not yet reached conservative academic Jungians.
>
> (Baumlin, Baumlin, & Jensen, 2004, p. xiv,
> original emphasis)

Mediating the archetypal images occurs through the personal father as he impacts the development of self-agency. The daughter forms a self and personality through knowing his attitudes and values (Samuels, 1985, pp. 24–25). In classical

Jungian interpretation, these archetypal images and symbols form the structural core of the father complex. He might represent positive archetypal qualities to one daughter, whereas to another he might represent negative meanings, depending on the quality or lack of their interactions and relationship. The following quote gives another idea about the father archetype and the impact of its psychological workings.

> Because our culture is a patriarchy the very air she breathes, the boundaries of her consciousness, the contents of her personal unconscious psyche, and the complete cast of the collective psyche, are full of The Man: his image, his history, his definitions, his requirements, his expectations, his needs, his desires, his threats, his power, his laws, his religions, his gods, his money, and his ambivalent, unrealistic image of her.
>
> (Cowan, 2013, p. 12)

The father is responsible for participating in developing emotional ties and exhibiting correct erotic energy without overpowering. Eros and the erotic can be interpreted in many ways, but more broadly we could say it means life energy and relatedness with interconnection and interaction based on respect for a daughter's individual self. Yet, many fathers have difficulty as a daughter grows in establishing Eros correctly. The absence of his appropriate use of Eros in their connection leaves her puzzled, as if she has done something wrong or is wrong, and she becomes confused about her libidinal energy for life, sex and relationships to self and other (Samuels, 1985, p. 31). Due to his position and how he uses it, the father with incorrect Eros sends confusing messages.

In life and as revealed in dreams, the absent space of the personal father means the archetype and its symbols can become too prominent and develop into pathology. A lack of fit between the innate sense of wanting and needing a good father and the negative and dangerous residue from the absent father set up internal dissonance. If father is not there, the daughter cannot see how he relates to a partner, how he interacts with himself, nor can he be a good mirror for her. A daughter needs the personal father figure to mediate these archetypal energies (Samuels, 1985, p. 27).

The qualities imbued with the archetype of the father are traditionally those of authority, ideals and values, social and cultural roles, and power – politically and religiously – in the family and culture. As patriarch the father was considered invulnerable. He is portrayed through the qualities of will, intellect, leadership and generativity. When he has been well related and present to his daughter, he passes on these qualities and she learns to modify them to fit her life. Jung commented: '[If] the connection between the personal problem and the larger contemporary events is discerned and understood, it brings a release from the loneliness of the purely personal, and the subjective problem is magnified into a general question of our society' (1971, p. 119). 'In this way the personal problem acquires a dignity it lacked hitherto' (p. 119).

References

Baumlin, J.S., Baumlin, T.F. & Jensen, G.H. (Eds.) (2004). *Post-Jungian Criticism: Theory and Practice*. Albany: State University of New York Press.
Blake, W. (1901). A little girl lost. In: *Songs of Innocence and Songs of Experience* [Etext 1934]. Retrieved from https://www.gutenberg.org/files/1934/1934-h/1934-h.htm#page65.
Cowan, L. (2013). Dismantling the animus. *The Jung Page*. Retrieved from http://www.cgjungpage.org/learn/articles/analytical-psychology/105-dismantling-the-animus.
Gilbert, S. & Gubar, S. (1984). *The Madwoman in the Attic: The Woman Writer and the Nineteenth Century Literary Imagination*. New Haven, CT: Yale University Press.
Greenfield, B. (1985). The archetypal masculine: Its manifestation in myth and its significance for women. In: A. Samuels (Ed.), *The Father* (pp. 187–210). New York, NY: New York University Press.
Jacobi, J. (1959). *Complex, Archetype and Symbol in the Psychology of C.G. Jung*. R. Mannheim (Trans.). New York, NY: Princeton University Press.
Jensen, G.H. (2009). Introduction to the puer/puella archetype. In: S. Porterfield, K. Polette & T.F. Baumlin (Eds.), *Perpetual Adolescence* (pp. 1–12). Albany: State University of New York Press.
Jung, C.G. (1959). *The Archetypes and the Collective Unconscious*. New York, NY: Pantheon Books.
Jung, C.G. (1961). *Freud and Psychoanalysis*, Vol. 4. Princeton, NJ: Princeton University Press.
Jung, C.G. (1966). *Two Essays on Analytical Psychology*, Vol. 7. New York, NY: Pantheon Books.
Jung, C.G. (1968). *Psychology and Alchemy*, Princeton, NJ: Princeton University Press.
Jung, C.G. (1969). *The Structure and Dynamics of the Psyche*, Vol. 8. Princeton, NJ: Princeton University Press.
Jung, C.G. (1970). *Civilization in Transition*, Vol. 10. Princeton, NJ: Princeton University Press.
Jung, C.G. (1971). *Psychological Types*, Vol. 6. Princeton, NJ: Princeton University Press.
Kavaler-Adler, S. (1993). *The Compulsion to Create*. New York, NY: Other Press Professional
Knox, J. (2003). *Archetype, Attachment, Analysis*. London, England: Routledge.
Lear, J. (2006). *Radical Hope*. Cambridge, MA: Harvard University Press.
Modell, A. (1996). *The Private Self*. Cambridge, MA: Harvard University Press.
Phillips, A. (2001). *Promises, Promises*. New York, NY: Basic Books.
Rich, A. (1976). *Of Woman Born*. New York, NY: W.W. Norton & Co.
Samuels, A. (Ed.) (1985). *The Father*. New York, NY: New York University Press.
Saunders, P. & Skar, P. (2001). Archetypes, complexes and self-organization. *Journal of Analytical Psychology*, 46(2), 305–23.

Chapter 7

Who is she really? The 'as-if' personality

In therapy sessions Tiffany explained that she related to people based on a need to please and have them like her. She could not tolerate mistakes or disapproval. Having little guidance as a child, an absent father who, when home, she feared, she learned how to be a person from books. She observed the parents down the street as well as others. She learned not to ask for anything, not to expect or want help, and she put on a front that she needed nothing. And her father hit her many more times than he said he loved her. Such a father, with no capacity to relate to the child's mind and emotions, has a direct behavioural and emotional impact (Knox, 2010, p. 132).

Tiffany remained dimly aware of a space inside herself that no one saw, a place where she hid in corners for safety. She constantly looked outward, checking to make sure it was safe, but her fear lived inside herself, masked from the view of others. She experienced a form of isolation from herself, from her body sensations and from the immediacy of her experiences, leaving her devoid of spontaneity or aliveness. She determined from a very young age that no one was going to know about this place. Tiffany still held tightly on to it. Now she was with a partner and had a small child, but the façade was cracking with the pressure of getting older, seeing her body change and wondering about resuming her career. These burdens and stresses were her ostensible reasons for making a foray into Jungian psychotherapy.

She dreamt her father put his hand on her thigh so forcefully it burned her flesh to the bone. Branded, she could not rise against the resistance of his hand. Later, she thought about filling the wound with concrete. How could this wound heal? Concrete would make her flesh inflexible, heavy and non-human. His branding gave her a father wound, imprinted on her for life. Although emotionally absent, his influence was heavy-handed and her skin could not breath in concrete. Yet, this dreamer registered no horror at the dream's ghoulish image, neither rage nor defiance at the father, but passively accepted this as her fate.

Tiffany's dream was personal, a statement of oppression, related without any display of emotion. It could be taken as an impersonal portrayal relevant to collective and cultural situations. The dream father was forbidding, larger than life, unrelated, forcing his mark on her, and she had no way to resist. 'It seems to me more and more that heredity is seduction by the father' (Masson, 1990, p.

212). Nonetheless, the imaginal world, the dream world, also carried guideposts to access potential through opening the wounds, mirroring messages from the unconscious, pushing the envelope for self-discovery. The dream gave Tiffany a strong message about what was unconscious and suppressed. And the dream recurred on and off for 15 years.

Tiffany said she was numb from too much stress. Was she referring to current or old stressors? She didn't know, as they blurred together. She often went silent in therapy, not understanding how to express or formulate what she felt. Blocked inside, she side-stepped conflict, avoided what she called burdening others, not asking for or getting what she needed; she was passive. She did not make many decisions and found it safer to give up. Tiffany worried she would offend, worried someone would accuse her, get mad or put her down, and she would crumble. At all costs she masked any emotional and personal responses.

Tiffany represents what is referred to in the Chinese Book of Wisdom, the I Ching, as Hexagram 18, called 'Corruption' or 'Work on what has been spoiled, decay'. Throughout the hexagram is a call for 'setting right what has been spoiled by the father'. It entails facing the reality of problems, mucking in the decay, comprehending the deleterious effects of the not-there father. The hexagram demands consciousness to engage with the negative, limiting and self-effacing patterns learned without the good presence of a father. In Jungian psychotherapy she was embarking on the painstaking yet rewarding process of fashioning a related, helpful and kindly father image.

History of the 'as-if' personality

Tiffany typifies those described by the 'as-if' personality, which originated with the Freudian psychoanalyst Helene Deutsch in the 1940s. She diagnosed this person as an impostor type without genuineness, acting in mimicry of others (Solomon, 2004, p. 637). Deutsch herself described 'a spasmodic, if skilled, repetition of a prototype without the slightest trace of originality' (Deutsch, 1942, p. 303). She noted 'another characteristic of the "as-if" personality was that aggressive tendencies were almost completely masked by passivity, lending an air of negative goodness, of mild amiability with an absence of feeling connection' (pp. 304–05).

This personality type was typified as inauthentic, although social and able to assume expected appearances, seemingly capable of warmth, but with stunted emotional depth. At that time, this personality was associated with someone who could neither engage nor adequately utilize inner work. According to Helene Deutsch, as well as the analytical methodology and thought of that era, this person was considered psychologically unreachable.

Hester Solomon, British Jungian analyst, has written about this personality type more recently. Now this person is no longer assessed as hopeless and is accessible for psychological treatment, understanding and growth. In an interesting parallel and similar to the daughter/father dynamic, however, the concept and description of the 'as-if' personality have remained a somewhat neglected part of the psychological literature. Bringing it to the fore here also links it with the puella archetype in Jungian analytical psychology and the personality of narcissism, both described in later chapters. The focus here is on aspects illustrating how the absent father affects and even taints a daughter's personality.

The 'as-if' personality is marked by an internalization of the presence of an absent other – here the father – and is associated with the feeling of a void. The lack of maternal devotion or the experience of an alpha father affects the development of this personality type (Riesenberg-Malcolm, 1992, p. 115). Although not consciously recognized, the father figure is internalized as negative and domineering through thoughts and actions. The daughter is disturbed in self-agency, perhaps developing eating disorders, methods of self-harm, addictions and psychosomatic and borderline phenomena (Knox, 2010, p. 132). The possibility of relating to the good object of a father has been denied and the only option is investment with the absent object of the father. Often these daughters are burdened with carrying his shadow, the unresolved feminine and masculine aspects and fulfilling the roles he prescribes. Her freedom to separate becomes more intricate when she cannot connect.

The phrase 'as-if' can be characterized by a person seemingly confident while just under the surface resides fragility and feelings of fraudulence bounded by a wall of impenetrability. The daughter has impoverished or absent emotional relations to both inner and outer events and people. Moreover, she is insecure and inundated with a harsh internal scrutiny set up against impossible standards for perfection. She appears well functioning, but under it all believes she is not and feels helpless and scared.

The 'as-if' adaptation is an aspect of the psyche, one with splits and dissociations formed in defence of the self to the point of the daughter being described as emotionally stricken (Solomon, 2004, p. 637). The internal dissociation develops as a survival attempt but reflects there is a void where the feelings and emotions should be. Unnerving is the yet-to-be-discovered layers behind the veils, mirrors and empty cheer. There is a lack of passion, the kind that comes from sidestepping the depths rather than going to them. At some point, life events cause her to halt abruptly and take a step back into accessing her core self. This often means stripping away the very mechanisms through which she has seemed to survive.

A benevolent inner structure remains unavailable, elusive and often felt to just not be there. The 'as-if' woman attempts to hide the hurt, the sorrows held within, and presents outwardly with a coherent and polished personality. However, all the internalizations and identifications that she has adapted from the outside – and there are many – do not obviate the absence and void at her centre that is felt to be primary (Solomon, 2004, p. 642). The 'as-if' daughter is unreal with herself and also with others. British psychoanalyst D.W. Winnicott said:

> The world may observe academic success of a high degree, and may find it hard to believe in the very real distress of the individual concerned, who feels

'phoney' the more he or she is successful. When such individuals destroy themselves in one way or another, instead of fulfilling promise, this invariably produces a sense of shock in those who have developed high hopes of the individual.

(1965, p. 144)

Such a daughter learns to put on a sparkling appeal, a cover usually fostering positive projections but ones she neither sees nor accepts. The consistency of self is porous, and the sense of self-value not within her purview. She lives behind the façades, feeling small and needing insulation from others who seem threatening and able to hurt her. So tremulous within, she cannot risk showing herself due to the apprehension of negative judgements of being incorrect, insufficient and lacking. While the façade makes it appear she is there when she is not, it also keeps her from knowing herself. Closeness is threatening. She is too hurt, cut off, afraid, damaged and lonely.

Not uncommonly, many women remark on the inner forces interfering, the limitations based on sexual stereotypes, social and family pressures, leaving their selves distorted, disguised and in shards. These daughters present one-dimensional personas and are not really living. This death-in-life existence is registered 'as if'. Yet they hold themselves together by following the rules according to father and his conventions. These are the very things that undermine the spirit.

A dream reveals

Later in therapy Tiffany dreamt, '*I am with new people. A man begins looking at me. I start to avert my gaze because I am uncomfortable and wonder how to look at him. Then I see he has a blue light coming from his forehead in the place of the third eye. Like watching a play, a scene opens and I see my father. I realize this is the time as a child when I began to make him better than he was in order to deny my fear of him and to ignore such feelings. Then the scene closes and I wake up*'.

From the dream she gained the previously denied knowledge her father was not the person she wished him to be, a truth she did not want to admit. There was ambivalence as he looked to be special with the blue light on his forehead, but his look was discomforting. Why is that? Like so many daughters here, her questioning of the relationship originated years later, as only then could she acknowledge he was not the father she made up. The dream brought forward her underlying wishes for him to give safety, comfort, guidance, understanding, support and protection, but it showed he did not. The dream demonstrated the impoverishment of the self, attributed to the early traumatizing experiences with the longed for and idealized other (Solomon, 2004, p. 639). Turning inward, Tiffany was gradually discovering the material previously forced away, submerged and ignored.

Yet the risk to encounter her real self seemed daunting. Her system was not experienced as stabilized or harmoniously ordered (Dieckmann, 1985, p. 223). She felt anxious and easily overwhelmed. Seeking the protection and security she did not feel within, she was precariously held together by repetitive behaviours and routines. Life had been marked by mistrust of others and feeling unsure of acceptance. As this peeled off in therapy, Tiffany faced the task of unravelling the complex father issues thus far negated.

Tiffany engaged in flights from the present, escaping into dreams of the future. This preserved her from the anticipated disappointments close to the surface and kept her from being reality-centred. And then, quite suddenly, she was flung into the moment, the bottom dropped off, and she descended into the dust (Hillman, 1989, p. 26). This descent surprised and upset her but was needed for grounding and becoming what she is from the inside. Yet she lived 'as if' in Neverland, a place of infinite postponement and half-identity (Solomon, 2004, p. 639), slumbering in the land of the almost-living. To avoid anxiety, insecurity and conflict, her mind shut off. Women like Tiffany only partially engage, remain emotionally unavailable, mostly to themselves, unable to commit or to find their depth, meaning or fulfilment. Their talents are there but the follow-through often remains elusive.

Distress occurs when the outer methods that formerly worked to contain the personality are exhausted and the inner reserves collapse, no longer sustainable. Something stops. The bravado ends. These are the defences failing as she reaches a limit and can no longer sustain the emotional deception or false fronts. For many, this brings about physical and/or psychological changes, usually accompanied by alarm.

Without a father figure to trust or who gave her security, Tiffany had to grow up too fast and deny her childhood emotional needs only to have them emerge as an adult. A false maturity covered an infantile state of mind. The immaturity derived from insufficient nurturance. The father's lack of attention and caring attitudes towards her intellectual and creative interests planted the seeds for feeling insufficient and unable. Developing a sense of worth depends on having a father who smiles, recognizes and listens with patience, encouragement and support. These are the places desired, feared, so vulnerable, anticipated to vanish or just not ever appear. An internal conflict ensues between wanting and not getting. Tiffany could only become more and more veiled in the persona adaptation to what she thought was wanted rather than what she wanted. This 'as-if' woman seems hollow, mostly to herself, anticipating that the falsity will be discovered and that she will be found out as insufficient and an imposter. Tiffany felt and would acknowledge the artifice, tensions and her fragile emotional framework. No one was to see her real self but she actually did not know who that was. If she remained on the surface, she might get by without encountering these issues.

Doing so meant waging tireless struggle against her body. Looking at her, you see a put-together woman, but over time you become aware she seems to be superimposed and the finished personality a sort of double exposure. Layer upon layer of obfuscations prevent knowing her, for she is continually and unconsciously dodging. The carefully designed façade conceals the losses, fuels the feverish activity and makes it seem as if she does not need anything or anyone. The experience without a good father leaves her compulsively chasing ideals, perhaps through drugs or alcohol, body alterations, achievements and other external manifestations – as if these will help mask what is real. Behind it all, the actions are also driven by negative and demeaning thoughts and behaviours, signifying interior restlessness and unease. Tiffany retained the nagging belief she did not achieve enough, as the aching loneliness propelled more achievement but did not allow her intimacy with self or others. Sadly, she doubted anyone could know or want to know her. And she was tired of it all.

By putting on a performance and acting 'as-if', the needs for love and attention get obfuscated in a deception to self and others (Solomon, 2004, p. 639). Such is the mask that many wear, often unconsciously. No wonder such a daughter feels inauthentic and at a remove from life. What seems like self-absorption is actually a defence against intimacy and interior reflection. She exudes an emptiness and lack of warmth because the genuineness of the inner experience is missing, including the capacity to love (Sheehan, 2004, p. 413). To love is to be vulnerable and open, to trust, face the risks and possible rejections and also to be seen, but these were all excruciating for Tiffany. Feeling unlovable, she experienced shame based on the conviction that she was not good enough. Assuming she did not deserve love was painful, and she avoided the possibility of that pain (von Franz, 2000, p. 8). The avoidance of love and loving resulted in lack of engagement and depersonalization. These daughters dwell 'as if' in twilight, non-differentiated, usually anxious and fearful of falling apart yet they cannot admit the depth of the apprehension, nor find its causes (Seligman, 1985, p. 70).

Yet Tiffany began to hear and respect the rumblings within. She continued in therapy and persisted, uncovering the life of her personality. In the words of Rumi, 'Move outside the tangle of fear-thinking. Live in silence. Flow down and down in always widening rings of being' (quoted in Collopy, 2002, p. 109).

The poseur

> To know harmony is to endure.
> To endure is to be enlightened.
>
> *Tao Te Ching* by Lao Tzu: Verse 55

At the first therapy session a woman named Sydney exhibited a flair for the dramatic seemingly intended to ward off others. She presented an impeccable appearance, speaking in a modulated tone with composure and confidence. There was an indication the transference, probably similar to what occurred in other relationships, could remain stillborn and the personal connection not fully taken. She exuded an unlinked quality and guardedness, distant and off-putting. Sydney seemed preoccupied, as if inhabiting a place barricaded against anyone else entering.

Indeed, much later in therapy Sydney revealed she called her presentation 'the poseur' and often felt like a fraud and worried about being found inauthentic. Her word *poseur* simulates the Jungian term *persona*. The persona is our outer presentation to the world and can be heavily influenced by social expectations. The persona as an accurate self-expression reveals personal integrity and expresses authenticity. Although it can reflect the truth, for Sydney the perfect and appealing persona was a necessary guise relied upon for enclosing her in a semblance of safety. Her defence was to withdraw further and compartmentalize, segregating one part of the mind from another but leaving little energy for real fulfilment.

Sydney hid the severe periodic depressions, self-attacks and times of cutting off from the world. Her partners were abusive; she could not escape being taken advantage of. This happens when transformation has been impeded by an absent father. Sydney learned to diminish her needs for being understood and appreciated by her father, a man who was absent from her life until she found him in her early adulthood. He left when she was very young, with no explanations forthcoming about why or where he was. She was barricaded from the truth. She felt something must be wrong with her to be without paternal love or presence.

When she found him, he provided no explanation for not acknowledging her all those years. She did not question him. His being gone remained a mystery. During childhood she yearned for him secretly in what she called her 'melancholic mind'. Without a father, she experienced alienation and difference from others, felt doomed to an indescribable loneliness. She could not get rid of the pall of depression. If her father did not want her, who would? Here she enacted the sad and lonely displacement put onto her from the unreachable yet looming father figure.

During the course of therapy Sydney had few dreams about her father. He was both so present in her conscious mind as well as so repressed there was little from the dream commentary. Here was one dream she remembered. *'I am finishing a wonderful visit with my father. He lives in a beautiful home with every kind of animal, including tamed falcons. I am preparing to leave, frantically putting all my presents in a paper bag to save them from disappearing. I've had a dream foretelling at the end of my visit his wife will show up and stop all the joy. My father is jovial and happy – like Old King Cole. He's dressed up for a party in robes and asks me to help him find his crown. The party is in his honour, an annual event at a neighbour's house where they crown him. It's a joke. He's very happy. His wife has not fulfilled my prophetic dream, but I expect it to begin any minute'.*

In the dream Sydney was asked to find the crown for her father, referring to her position as the one who secured his position of king. This father masquerading as a king induced strong loyalties in his daughter. According to the dream, Sydney envisioned leaving him, but she also wanted his gifts and did not realize there was a huge cost. None of his gifts were ever without strings, but she ignored this fact. She would have to sacrifice something to free herself from his spell. The dream contained another dream within it, accentuating she had knowledge, but it was enfolded in layers of unconscious material. The dream impressed upon Sydney the reality that her father had a wife and she must break his wrongly composed connection to her.

In being true to a father emotionally, physically and creatively, a daughter can become over-identified with the male world and ignore her own. Sydney was insecure in attending to the quality of her mind, keeping herself small and her father large. She assumed he knew more and could guide her, although he never had and there was nothing to substantiate her assumptions except her longing and need to make him stay and be wonderful.

Sydney's therapeutic tasks included uncovering the denials that guarded against her knowing, the fantasies that protected and the bonds that inhibited roles. She expressed wariness about what she called the abyss, worried she might fall in. As she put it:

> I am finding I can no longer garner the energy to keep cycling through the fruitless changes. The anticipation of more years of emptiness and lethargy is intolerable. The exhaustion with this routine is translating into a deep, abiding urge to simply no longer be.

Her apprehension was if anyone got close, then what she considered the ugly truths would be noticed. This is a hallmark of the 'as-if' personality, and in reaction the personality forms what can be called a *pocket* or *psychosomatic space* (Solomon, 2004, p. 649). This place resides within the larger personality, segregated in the 'as-if' area. The personality is affected and over time eaten slowly away, eroding from within. Much psychic energy is spent avoiding this area until a psychological and physical shattering occurs and breaks apart the façade.

Sydney exhibited similar somatic aspects as noted with the 'as-if' personality, such as weight gain or loss, autoimmune disease, allergies and general body unease (Solomon, 2004, p. 649). She described times of only eating, doing drugs and sleeping with no impetus for life, encased in darkness. Constantly defeated by thinking nothing would make any difference meant she just got by. She admitted to not really knowing how to care for herself, what it looked like, nor did she have memories of getting personal care beyond the essentials. Certainly she received nothing from the father.

The absence of a father placed Sydney in a dilemma. Lacking the basics, she admitted needing what she called a 'how to be a person manual'. Jean Knox explained this as follows:

> In order to be loveable and loved, she must cease to exist and so must destroy all her aliveness in a constant struggle against being who she is. This conflict and resistance becomes a kind of self-torture. On the other hand, to experience oneself as a real person, with a sense of self and a capacity to make her own choices brings the risk of violent retaliation … It is an irresolvable impasse, which eventually leads the daughter to a state of despair. To love means to exist and to want to have one's independent existence recognized and responded to by the loved other.
>
> (2007, p. 544)

In therapy Sydney brought favourite passages from the books she read to share them, with the idea of being understood – having her life witnessed.

Sydney described being an understudy, especially in relation to her mother who was purported to be the loveliest of all and enticing to men. She felt she could not equal this marvellous mother in getting men and, of course, in having the man she wanted – her father. She wrote about the disintegration of self and silencing of her voice, describing this in her journal as follows:

> This is a woman who would live inside herself, making her hair a long shading roof, her eyes the basement door, the space between her legs a half-opened window where only the most tenacious of thieves may enter. This woman would be stone. She would grow her own food in a damp place. Oh, look at this, pressing at her face, wondering if she can be opened. Decides she cannot. Picture this woman plucking at herself like cardboard.

Sydney's subjective experience reflected a psychic deadness from the father's relational lack. It seemed 'as-if' she was only the image taking prominence over the real. Sydney described herself as a performer. She knew it was a performance but one she relied on and could let go, acutely aware of a hole at the centre of herself. She wondered if she would ever regain the spark she thought she once knew. She clung to her boyfriend, desperately wanting him to know her. She wished he would ask her questions, be emotional and open to her many frustrations. She worried about what would happen in the future with him. She felt more like a doll who must make him happy, doing almost anything to escape her anticipation of abandonment and falling apart.

Yet Sydney was ambivalent about accepting love and tried to lessen her hunger for love. She could not process her affects or handle their intensity. There was a gap of self-understanding made more difficult because she did not know how to verbalize or meet her needs. Sydney's efforts were oriented towards pleasing others with a performance and if she stopped, what would she do? Therefore, she had to act 'as-if' real when she felt a fiction of herself (Sheehan, 2004, p. 420).

Sydney questioned the meaning of her life. She said its structure was wrong. Although accomplished in many areas, she felt cut off at the knees and proceeded to recount a recent experience of falling and skinning her knees. Taken by surprise, she realized she had been out of balance. She reported feeling unprepared, needing to learn more, read more books and take more courses. But once completed she did not use the information she had learned, unable to accept competency, leaving it all on the shelf. She kept her special possessions hidden in case something happened, anticipating being robbed. These material goods were like her psychological goods, precious but unused. With no early guidance or protection from a father, what was hers felt fragile, subject to dispossession and being taken away by others.

Over the years Sydney went in and out of Jungian therapeutic work, each time stimulated by emotional and physical problems and malaise. The losses and despair impacting her body and soul seemed unending, and it was as if her system might collapse under the weight of psychological burdens. Many women without fathers are 'in a state between what they fear in their own minds and what they fear in the outside world' (Solomon, 2004, p. 639). There is a need for the illusionary and the wished-for world to compensate for the weight of the pervasive anxiety.

A partial life

The 'as-if' personality concerns 'the defensive dissociation from early experiences of internalizing the presence of an absent object, creating the sense of an internal void at the core of the self' (Solomon, 2004, p. 635). These people are emotionally unavailable, mostly to themselves. This psychological constellation manifests in various forms of narcissism and hatred towards self. Paternal neglect, abandonment and emotional lack make it difficult to consistently love or care for themselves. In effect, there is a paralysis of spontaneity, and the 'as-if' personality is devoid of sustained enthusiasm, fearing any surprises.

The daughter has become the lack of her father, an absence so ponderous that it leaves her without access to her true self (Solomon, 2004, p. 641). To compensate and hide the loss, acts of self-creation occur through a series of identifications and internalizations with other sources of environmental nourishment, like a need for achievement, the perfect look and the pressure of hyper-functionality. These are attempts to substitute for what the daughter feels has to be constructed around the sense of internal emptiness (p. 641).

Without a secure attachment to a father figure, self-identity is compensated with mimicry and falsity. These indicate that connections to the core are adrift. Life is reduced to illusion and cover to hide what feels like confusion, a dull ache and lack of animation. This daughter feels a forgery, reacting from pseudo affectivity and living a sham existence. She needs excellence and to be liked and even adulated, impossible goals that will not make up for the void and emptiness when a father is not there.

The fast-paced and surface mentality in Western culture is replicated in the 'as-if' personality who learns to bypass the underpinnings. The more measured and methodical approach is unsatisfying. It feels too tedious, like sorting peas. She lacks the patience and feels incapable of delving into the issues. Rapidly glancing from one topic to another, she avoids the deeper spaces foundational to comprehending disturbing emotions.

In addition, because life seems ethereal, she postpones. Life feels precarious and she has trouble finding her stance. There is a pressure to have complete success, every day, even in the smallest details; no slips are allowed. She plummets if she makes a mistake; her life is like riding on narrow rails. To compensate she is vigilant in trying to carefully and accurately discern the needs of others. To her, to respond for real, or be real, shows a dependency that early on she learned to check as unsafe and disallowed. There was no place to curl up into, no protective father to teach her, nothing solid to rely upon. The apprehension and insecurity keeps her on the surface, in a dream-like existence, acting a memorized part in a play.

To obfuscate her internal distress, she needs a shell that glitters, as her insides and outsides are disparate. This is evidenced in some of her comments:

> I cannot accept the fact that I am who I am. My work is not good enough. I do not remember what I did, felt or thought yesterday. I do not want others to be angry at me as I cannot take it.

She grows more and more emotionally disconnected. The negative self-images occur day after day, affirming the message that life is a disaster, not a celebration. Without an accurate inner mirroring, she assesses herself to be either inferior or superior to others.

In therapy this daughter needs care to reach beyond the veneer of the tight persona and grandiose attitudes. This type of daughter often has a fragile ego, feels diminished and caught in the grip of what was missing with the father. Resisting change, she has trouble managing the space between what was known and predictable and what will be and remains a mystery.

Eventually the call from the unconscious begins, emerging from the unaddressed places. Life can no longer be avoided or hidden with perfectionism and ego goals for outer approval. This involves recognizing the missed connection to the body and inattention to the mechanics of daily living. To recover herself is a process requiring a dive into the unconscious. To come closer to the self brings about a feeling of being real, giving personal existence its meaning with beneficial effects upon the psyche and body.

The blown-apart place

When a father is too distant, a daughter can become inhibited, frightened and unable to access healthy aggression and assertion. When the father figure has no limits and is either all-giving or a rigid disciplinarian encased in a distant and foreboding authority structure, the daughter has not been personally touched by the masculine. This becomes a life-long pattern, easily metastasizing into the script of inferiority with aggression turned inward.

Years ago a woman named Sophia, a composite of many, in her mid-forties and divorced, entered Jungian analysis. Over many sessions we roamed the landscape of her psyche – delving into the disturbed relation to her natural physical and emotional instincts. Sophia described therapy as lancing an abscess in the painful uncovering of disappointments, obscurities, mysteries and tears. Session after session addressed the reactions, perceptions, thoughts, ideas and emotions she had not acknowledged with anyone. We listened carefully and followed her rhythm.

There was little love between her parents, who put up a façade for years until it came out her father was homosexual, which was disallowed by their religion.

The mother's emotional distance and the father's deceptiveness in his sexuality and his illicit work ethic created a foundation of distrust and insecurity, affecting Sophia's body and psyche.

Sophia assiduously followed the religious teachings of her father and family until she left the church in her late twenties. Looking back, she felt her soul was disconnected, and the strict father and church rules disregarded her essence. Internalizing this form of the paternal, what remained was an inner division arising from the psyche's defences early in life protecting the self from dissolution (Solomon, 1998, p. 229). These took the form of obsessive drives and self-persecutory compulsive thoughts, spending too much money, worry about calories, pressure to perform at her work as a radiologist.

Sophia longed to be in a relationship, but she regarded herself as flawed and the fear and distrust of her physical-sensual nature instead resulted in isolation and alienation. In order to survive, Sophia outwardly hardened emotionally while her interior landscape receded. 'What to the rational mind seems a flaw is often a profoundly mysterious key to the secret of individual life … When we pathologize human foibles in our relentless way, trying to subdue and "purify" life, we kill the soul' (Hinton, 1993, p. 58).

A father is absent through being unconscious of himself and also of his daughter. The father chiefly interested in himself squashes her initiatives, refuses her challenges. Sophia's childhood did not support her instinctual, emotional, intellectual or physical foundations. Her father's distance and disconnection can be seen in a story Sophia told about when as a teenager she got a knife stuck in her foot at dinner. No one noticed as she carefully walked out of the room with the knife sticking out of her bleeding foot. She remembered trying to walk normally to avoid the shaming and blaming attention expected from her father.

In one of the first dreams Sophia brought to therapy, *she was being transported from the city, signifying the roots of her religion. She was carried in a large procession because her legs were frozen beer bottles. The people were taking her south where she actually lived and where her legs would thaw.* In therapy she periodically returned to this dream, as it seemed basic to her problems and solutions. The city in the dream she associated with the law of the patriarchal church, the empty origins of her life with her father's emotional attachment and focus on the church, not on her. Beer was forbidden in this religion, but she drank it now, and the beer legs represented a spiritual, phallic and sexual standpoint. This all became frozen by the religion, aligned in her mind with her cold and unempathetic father. As the dream showed, Sophia's adaptation of psychic numbing was a form of desensitization or dulling of experience. Trying to be normal or fit according to a father whose rules and religion he deceived and violated sent confusing messages to Sophia.

Sophia unconsciously picked up her father's sexual secrets and desires disallowed by their religious scripture. The father's deception produced unease in Sophia, and she buried part of her ego in his paternal necropolis. For her, it translated into the perception she must be flawed and unacceptable, like him. She thought she was unlovable and should reduce the longing for love to nothing. She was ashamed if she got close, as it would expose her lack of worth, neediness and insecurity about accepting or giving love. She learned self-denial from the lack of care and insufficient father love. These are the psychological holes that create the inability to love or make the most of one's talents (Green, 2001, p. 176).

So she could survive, Sophia based her interactions on rules she made up about how she should be. One of the purposes of therapeutic inquiry is to heal the splits characterizing the personal and collective conscious and unconscious with a spiritual imperative. Living as part of the whole starts from the reality we are participants, part of the cosmos and interconnected. For Sophia, her journeys into nature became something like this cosmic participation, as she had none with her father. Sophia gained a sense of self while hiking alone, sometimes in dangerous territory, facing the elements and physical discomfort. She became restored in barren nature, yet at the same time she longed to be with someone she loved.

A recurrent dream

Jungian analytical psychology recognizes the psyche as a self-regulating system, maintaining its own equilibrium just as the body does. Similarly an adaptation too extreme inevitably calls forth compensation by bringing the unconscious into relation with consciousness. Sophia reported *a recurring dream in which a man was chasing her over, around and through buildings. The dream took place in a cityscape – crowded, impersonal, chaotic and concrete and amorphous. Throughout the dream she hid and dodged and knew that although remaining uncaught, the man could eventually get her.* This city might represent the distance, the concrete structures and coldness and lack of empathic response from her father. We discussed the dream man as an aspect of her father and the shadow parts she could not face.

What else can we understand of this dream? The barrenness might be how she felt internally. The unknown man chasing her might represent the others, both within and without, chasing her – like the patriarchal culture, society, family and religion, devoid of spirit and life, cold; she was the pursuer and the pursued, dodging and on the run.

The dream image also revealed much that was present in Sophia's psyche – how she avoided seeking help; she was alone and steeled herself to get through, each time barely escaping the threat. This replicated what can happen when there is lack of experience with a well-involved father. Sophia did not expect help, assuming no one would understand, much less care. In this dream image, we have a sense of what is both absent and present, the psyche struggling to be heard and seen, yet scared. For Sophia it was a risk to be exposed, human and vulnerable as she learned with a deceptive, secretive and absent father.

Emotional and physical lack and the subsequent grief suffered affect the imaginary realm and symbolic entry so early that the child can neither name what she has lost nor what she mourns. For Sophia, the paternal presence and experience of being seen or having resonance was almost completely barren and she subsequently experienced the world as offering her little.

The defence of 'as-if'

A defensive structure locked Sophia in internal combat and her attacks on herself were vicious, leaving her lacerated and torn apart. By negating and rejecting parts of herself she remained unseen, with a sense of strangeness even to herself. Sophia's emotional numbness was juxtaposed with vulnerability, illustrated by the tears shed in therapy even though they embarrassed her. Her sadness represented an expression of the depth of the wounding, the profound loss and mourning of a father not there. Sadness became her emotional object for attachment. The optimal beginnings in a warm, loving environment with a father never happened for Sophia. These were the feelings of aloneness and 'offness' she experienced with others.

When instinct turns self-destructive early in life, the ego lacks cohesion and falls into bits. The anxiety and feeling of being destroyed from within is what remains, and Sophia often could not think, feel or find orientation. At times she was terrified, describing the loneliness punctuated by uncontrollable crying or wildly eating ice cream and cookies. Her psyche and body wept for the lack of resonance, the unrequited longing for love and the emotional neglect and lack. Others, she assumed, did not know this psychological place like an abyss separating her from them. Sophia was often internally bombarded by what she should or should not do, be it exercise, a coffee, work or reading. She never knew what she wanted. Sophia called this the blown-apart place where rules had to substitute for the spontaneous self she did not trust. The self was not emergent but fragmented, dissipated, eclipsed.

Sophia lived 'in a solitary confinement of the self … There was fear of opening to another at the risk of psychological annihilation' (Solomon, 1998, p. 228). The lack of paternal devotion meant that the unfolding of the self met a blank, hostile or inappropriate environ so she felt unseen and/or noxiously related to. Her self sought a benevolent and creative inner structure but could access neither.

For a long time Sophia seemed unable or resistant to getting in touch with these interior places. French psychoanalyst André Green interpreted this situation as a person needing the container of the analyst for the content to be presented. According to Green, both analyst and analysand witness how the bad object keeps being resurrected and both face the emptiness that returns as layer after layer of the emotional neglect becomes unwrapped (1986, p. 42). The transformation of the self needs this interactive space so the analysand can safely begin to open.

Sophia's apparent need to be disengaged and alone to find herself was paradoxically mixed with an inability to engage with herself. This came from a failure in the father holding environment, as there was little constancy established in her world. As Arnold Modell, American psychoanalyst, opined: 'the traumatic inter-actions without an early paternal caretaker was replicated in an equally traumatic internalized object relationship, leaving in its wake the true self waiting to be found' (1996, p. 86). Rather, a grandiose self affords magical protection and an independent or omnipotent self needs no others as compensation for the absence of safety (p. 88). The loss of contact with an authentic self can result in closing off from others. Estranged from an affective core, life seems meaningless, empty and futile.

Sophia not only felt like a stranger with her father but also was the recipient of his emotional deficiencies and inaccessible love. Her psyche and body wept, quite possibly from the lack of resonance and unrequited longing. Sophia described an eerie sense of absence in the presence of the other. She felt like a shell, covering what she described as a gap, a persistent and agonizing hollowness at the core. The far-reaching effect of his neglect meant Sophia disdained and denied her physical instincts that became ridden with negative body feelings; she was also dismayed and ashamed about her sexuality (Modell, 1996, p. 76). This splitting or parcelling of the self had been happening for as long as Sophia could remember. It was like an experience of fragmentation, a feeling of being trapped, a sense of nameless dread, a sense of disintegration, the inability to bear absence. Connecting to others was threatenening, anticipating cruelty, bombarded with too many sensations and not having time to compose thoughts or reactions. She searched for what she called 'needing someone to make her whole'.

Anxiety and feeling destroyed within is what remains when there has been no father. Self-doubt and despair can become excruciating and life feels brutalizing. André Green named this emotional situation *blank mourning* and aligned it with emptiness (1986, p. 146). It can also be associated with the negative father complex. A daughter survives the emotional neglect and grief but may not be able to waylay the progressive life numbness. Amid the mourning and loss, the longing for the father does not diminish.

Absence indicates a blank place to be filled. This happens through the recollection of what was lost and damaged, a process of individual and collective healing. The repressions, misalignments and lack of development from the past appear in and influence the present. The unconscious becomes activated by intent, fear, hope or any strong emotion. Through this process we attempt to master loss and emotional wounds of all kinds: internal and external, acute and cumulative, personal and collective. The search requires being exposed and also distraught, feeling flayed and sometimes exhaustive. The world opens as we do and likewise narrows if we refuse or turn away.

Consciousness is not linear but loops back to reincorporate the sentient and foster the imaginative in newly emergent ways. This is an effort at broadening and deepening, a going towards inner reflection. It is by descending into the effects from the absent father that the complexity and wealth in the psyche emerges.

> If you contemplate your lack of fantasy, of inspiration and inner aliveness, which you feel as sheer stagnation and a barren wilderness, and impregnate it with the interest born of alarm at your inner death, then something can take shape in you, for your inner emptiness conceals just as great a fulness if only you will allow it to penetrate into you.
>
> (Jung, 1970, para. 189)

'Nor can we ever be carefree when we think that whenever we are observed we are appraised ... yet the life of those who always live behind a mast is not pleasant nor free from care' (Seneca, 1997, p. 5).

References

Collopy, M. (2002). *Architects of Peace: Visions of Hope in Words and Images*. Novato, CA: New World Library.

Deutsch, H. (1942). Some forms of emotional disturbance and their relationship to schizophrenia. *Psychoanalytic Quarterly*, *11*(2), 301–21.

Dieckmann, H. (1985). Some aspects of the development of authority. In: A. Samuels (Ed.), *The Father* (pp. 211–28). New York, NY: New York University Press.

Green, A. (1986). *On Private Madness*. London, England: The Hogarth Press.

Green, A. (2001). *Life Narcissism, Death Narcissism*. London, England: Free Association Books.

Hillman, J. (1989). *Puer Papers*. Dallas, TX: Spring Publications.

Hinton, L. (1993). A return to the animal soul. *Psychological Perspectives*, *28*(1), 47–60.

Jung, C.G. (1970). *Mysterium Coniunctionis*, Vol. 14. New York, NY: Pantheon Books.

Knox, J. (2007). The fear of love: The denial of self in relationship. *Journal of Analytical Psychology*, *52*(5), 543–63.

Knox, J. (2010). *Self-Agency in Psychotherapy*. New York, NY: W.W. Norton & Co.

Masson, J.M. (1990). *Final Analysis: The Making and Unmaking of a Psychoanalyst*. New York, NY: Basic Books.

Modell, A. (1996). *The Private Self*. Cambridge, MA: Harvard University Press.

Riesenberg-Malcolm, R. (1992). As-if: The experience of not learning. In: R. Anderson (Ed.), *Clinical Lectures on Klein and Bion*. London: Routledge.

Seligman, E. (1985). The half-alive ones. In: A. Samuels (Ed.), *The Father* (pp. 69–94). New York, NY: New York University Press.

Seneca (1997). *Dialogues and Letters*. Oxford, England: Oxford University Press. Retrieved from https://archive.org/stream/Seneca/Seneca_djvu.txt.

Sheehan, M. (2004). The hours: The 'as-if' personality and problems of loving. *Journal of Analytical Psychology*, *49*(3), 413–20.

Solomon, H. (1998). The self in transformation: The passage from a two to a three dimensional internal world. *Journal of Analytical Psychology*, *43*(2), 225–38.

Solomon, H. (2004). Self creation and the limitless void of dissociation: The 'as if' personality. *Journal of Analytical Psychology*, *49*(5), 635–56.

von Franz, M.-L. (2000). *The Problem of the Puer Aeternus*. Toronto. Canada: Inner City Books.

Winnicott, D.W. (1965). *The Maturational Process and the Facilitating Environment*. London, England: Karnac Books.

Chapter 8

The dialogue of therapy

Willow came to therapy at a loss about what to do, what to feel, what to think. What was her purpose?

> In many cases in psychiatry, the patient who comes to us has a story that is not told, and which as a rule no one knows of. To my mind, therapy only really begins after the investigation of that wholly personal story. It is the patient's secret, the rock against which he is shattered. If I know his secret story, I have a key to the treatment. The doctor's task is to find out how to gain that knowledge. In most cases exploration of the conscious material is insufficient … In therapy the problem is always the whole person, never the symptom alone. We must ask questions which challenge the whole personality.
>
> (Jung, 1963, p. 118)

The Jungian therapeutic approach consists of neither releasing nor repressing, but of holding and working with the psyche to uncover the internal and external challenges. Through Jungian analytical therapy, Willow made conscious the absent father appearing in her dreams, thoughts and feelings, affecting her relationships with self and others. The aim was also to elicit meaning from the unconscious that related to her future attitudes (Jung, 1971, para. 702).

This chapter discusses experiences in therapy, focusing on concepts in Jungian analytical psychology such as the transcendent and reflective and symbolic functions leading to the transformation of self. The transcendent function and its appearance through symbol formation regulate and balance the psyche, and with this emerge new attitudes. Put another way, the self is supported in its development through the symbolic nature of the transcendent function so the creative resources residing in the unconscious become accessible (Solomon, 2007, p. 244).

Daughters with absent fathers express having lost a sense of basic belonging. They represent the predicaments of many twenty-first-century women, their dislocation, alienation and internal divisions. These are some of the personal, cultural and historical processes explored in therapeutic endeavours (Kimbles, 2004, p. 201). Therapy is a process of reconstructing and reassembling the personality fragments formerly dissociated in order to take the steps for reintegration.

Discontinuities of thoughts and feelings arise from the recesses of the daughter's psyche as she recalls the inner stories too disturbing to touch. Although difficult to articulate, they come into awareness with the therapist. Connection is reframed and reconstructed. Talking about things formerly not spoken of, but without the pressure for immediate solutions, can be comforting, sparking creativity and new ways of perceiving. Self-identity occurs through exploring her subjectivity and imagination. In a broad sense 'modern humanity's great adventure is to … plumb the depths of the human soul … to open completely new dimensions' (Guggenbühl-Craig, 1999, p. 142).

In-depth psychological work constellates self and other, patient and analyst, depicting together the movement of the psyche. The analyst's challenge is to assist the patient in finding her unknown aspects so she can escape the limits she has inhabited. 'In the final analysis, the therapist must always strive to constellate the healing factor in the patient' (Guggenbühl-Craig, 1999, p. 92). The therapist provides a mirror for the daughter to perceive what she could not previously due to the arrested images of her starved psyche. The process is facilitated by dreams, the therapeutic relationship and other life events. All these lead towards her cherishing herself, an attitude not acquired when an absent father did not cherish her.

Re-enacting the father

The daughter's earliest relationships, including those with the father, are re-enacted in psychological treatment. The attachment to the absent father may be preserved in a melancholic and/or invisible interior space. The father, even if absent, always walks through the therapy door. Often shadowy and undefined, the father is like a ghost pervading the therapeutic process (Modell, 1999, p. 80). He makes appearances in a daughter's projections onto the therapist's office, gestures and voice and in her reactions to those. The longing to which the father is connected comes forth in the therapeutic process of recovering what has been thus far unmourned (Perelberg, 2018, p. 44). This emerges in what lies between the therapeutic participants. The real analytic object is neither the daughter's nor the analyst's side, but in the meeting of these two and how they communicate in the space between them. Both carry effects from the absent father, whether culturally or personally, consciously or unconsciously. Together they open what has been the closed but internalized space of the unconscious, abandoning, deadened father.

The absent father, just because he was absent, controlled the daughter's freedom of expression, confidence and ease in being. Unconsciously he took up psychological energy so a daughter might have no room for other thoughts or space for interpretation. These can make the therapist's comments seem intrusive or overbearing, like the father. Rather than this being an impediment, it exposes the memories, adaptations and also the unconscious situation. Here are the origins of the gaps between herself and others, the idealizations, her need for defence, her feeling less than. Margaret Wilkinson, British Jungian analyst, commented that therapeutic work includes relational as well as interpretive agents of change.

These bring about the integration and increased connectivity between and within the hemispheres of the mind–brain, leading to a change in the nature of attachment that will then permit the self to emerge more fully through the process of individuation (Wilkinson, 2004).

The female therapist inevitably carries the father projections. The question is: How does the therapist manage them? This is a difficult area, as the father figure is elusive, undefined yet too dominating at the same time. He affects both participants but often in diverse ways. The patient might, for example, experience the female therapist as an idealized or overly critical and harsh paternal figure. In other instances she might expect the therapist to meet or be unable to meet the absence of the paternal. Understanding the origins of these disappointments is crucial. It is equally important for therapists to understand and be aware of issues with their own fathers and how these emerge differently with each patient. The therapist representing the father has the responsibility to remain conscious of the unconscious images and symbols on which both participants, differently as well as similarly, were no doubt raised. Their communications oscillate verbally and nonverbally, encountering the father's lack and exposing its relational wounds, emotional traps and distortions. This daughter often cannot feel the therapist as a container and mediator as she experiences only the negative transference and its destructive effects and affects (Meredith-Owens, 2008, p. 468). Psychological life is complex and not easy to grasp, as even in therapy this daughter often fights her desires and represses dependency needs.

Long ago she drew a magic circle around herself, knowing she had to be self-sufficient. She may have withdrawn intra-psychically and interpersonally acts raw, prickly and sensitive to others. The therapist, rather than backing off from the negative projections, sensitively holds them. Jung commented:

> Individuation involves the transformation of the analyst as well as the patient, stirring up in his or her personality the layers that correspond to the patient's conflicts and insights ... Archetypal dynamics will affect any analyst, but particularly one whose life is not fully lived and needs to be.
>
> (Jung, 1954, p. 172)

The illusions

Illusions create a precarious hold for a fragile self. The process of stripping off the veils of the illusionary is painful. It takes much patience in therapeutic work because the unmasking of reality can be tricky due to the patient's vulnerability and repression.

> When we analyse the persona we strip off the mask, and discover that what seemed to be individual is at bottom collective; in other words, that the

persona was only a mask of the collective psyche ... In a certain sense all this is real, yet in relation to the essential individuality of the person concerned it is only a secondary reality, a compromise formation.

(Jung, 1966, para. 245f)

Being unmasked and feeling nakedly exposed in therapy is threatening. In psychological treatment these daughters face difficult tasks. Therapy is a gradual unpeeling of layer after layer, unwrapping her needs in a tender process. What felt like the bad parts are revived, and the emptiness along with the shame and internal discomfort becomes overt to both in the analytic relationship. The patient hesitates to move beyond the wishes substituting for the truth and finding out who she is and who her father is. A daughter expresses: 'Inside me is silence. Who and what am I? I feel only inner pain and panic'.

Therapy provides a place where she can safely evolve with a therapist who is emotionally involved in this joint endeavour. Both are engaged in a search for the silenced self and the lost desires within the relational bond. She enters therapy because 'there is something [she] cannot forget, something [she] cannot stop telling [herself], often by [her] actions, about [her] life. And these dismaying repetitions ... create the illusion of time having stopped' (Phillips, 1994, p. 15).

Comfort with self and others is not easily learned without a father. The creation of self was inundated by the 'environmental failures, a profound and lifeless void and what the psyche does to survive this bleak and often life threatening experience' (Solomon, 2004, p. 642). These dynamics affect body and psyche, patient and analyst, conscious and unconscious. André Green interpreted this situation as a person needing the container of the therapist for the content to be presented in a self-to-self mutual steeping in the issues (Kohon, 1999, p. 42).

The unconscious becomes activated by intent, fear, hope or any strong emotion. Dreams are impartial, spontaneous products of the unconscious psyche, outside the control of the will. They are

pure nature; they show us the unvarnished, natural truth, and are therefore fitted, as nothing else is, to give us back an attitude that accords with our basic human nature when our consciousness has strayed too far from its foundations and run into an impasse.

(Jung, 1970, para. 317)

They poignantly express the emotional, developmental and psychological needs unaddressed yet now clamouring for attention. Answering these unmet needs is part of developing security of personality and solidity in the self.

Much as we may want them, new attitudes are not easy to manage or accept. Each psychological phenomenon, like that of the absent father, contains within itself the means for interpretation and understanding. The varied positions in the unconscious bring the psyche forward, out of polarization and the oppositional states, enabling the process of individuation (Solomon, 1998, p. 232). Therapy explores loss and wounding of all kinds, internal and external, acute and cumulative, transgenerational, personal and collective. The therapeutic process promotes the kind of psychic activity requiring tolerance for contradiction and holding the energy that pulls in many directions. The paradoxes and the back and forth, the psyche with its principle of synthesis and balance, bring forth aspects of the submerged personality 'From the activity of the unconscious there now emerges a new content, constellated by thesis and antithesis in equal measure and standing in a *compensatory* relation to both' (Jung, 1971, para. 825, original emphasis). Breaking away from the old brings pain and resistance, even as we want to move towards movement and renewal.

Reflective function

Jean Knox addresses the reflective function in the analytic process, describing it as the capacity to be aware of oneself and others. It is an attitude of independent psychological and emotional reflection on one's life. Being an analyst requires constant focus on the subjective, intuitive, poetic, symbolic narrative that emerges in an analytic session. This requires the therapist's capacity to resonate with the multiple and sometimes contradictory threads of the patient's narrative in the co-construction of a symbolic space (Knox, 2003, p. xx).

Because numerous obstacles can obstruct the therapeutic process, patience is required for exploring this relational journey. The daughter's particular language, including her sorrows and mourning, become known and witnessed. Although emotionally charged, the analyst and analysand uncover their nature and become authentically real through the crucible of relationship. 'The vicissitudes of experience within the analytic dyad facilitate the development of the self-regulatory capacity and the emergence of the reflective function' (Wilkinson, 2004, p. 98). Reflection is activated through the imagination and fantasies integral for psychic movement. New contents become articulated, understood, clarified. Analysis reinforces apprehending the material (Shorter, 1987, p. 104). Through reflection and its repetition, perceptions change and release former constrictions.

Therapy can provide an experience of ego-self relatedness becoming gradually internalized as the reflective function begins to work. This means the conscious ego deepens as it accesses more layers of the basic and foundational self. Therapy concerns itself with reflection, so the unconscious and its images rise to attention, connecting to conscious life. Reflections on the absent father bring forth the wishes, resentments and desires activating old patterns, scripts and expectations. The father is crucial here, as the reflective function develops from childhood where it begins to be nourished and supported. This occurs when a father figure can hold the daughter in his mind and care for her emotionally. In this way she learns to relate to herself.

The reflective function is located at the root of our experiences, forming mind and personality. The daughter needs presence combined with early experiences of appropriate absence to form thoughts and make creative use of the symbolic and the imaginal (Colman, 2007, p. 566). In other words, the right amount of presence and notice, respect and love, foster the self and other connections for bringing about a coherent self. Coherence is necessary for resilience and the emergence of other attitudes and feelings. When this function has not been developed or has been damaged, the therapeutic relationship becomes the vessel where the walls of defence and control can slowly be taken down. It supports a natural reflection on self and life. The reflective function is compromised when the distress and anxiety provoked by the absent father predominates, leaving little room for the daughter. From his absence or absent presence, she became invalidated, internalizing unease and self-doubt.

The shields that these daughters develop for protection can obstruct the in-depth examination that fosters self-reflection. They have been so shaken by father neglect and absence that the amount of hurt they've experienced can be resistant to therapeutic intervention. The 'often perilously obtained clinical experience and information along the hazardous journey is difficult and requires much patience on the parts of both participants' (Solomon, 2004, p. 635). Therapy involves waiting and surrendering, making it hard for the scared person clinging to the superficial, to what's easy and fast. The ego worries and is impatient for the suffering to stop. Although the daughter wants clarity and guidance, the sure path she desires does not happen on the ego's time frame.

Therapy includes naked and tender moments of being seen, acknowledged and accepted so she can develop an ability to observe herself yet still retain the mask until she feels safe taking it off (Bromberg, 1983, p. 379). The process evolves slowly as it is discordant with the controlled and watchful self. Her personality, even if seemingly alive to others, is internally deadened and in despair, inhibited, lacking confidence or assertion, when the father was absent for love.

Transcendent function

The transcendent function bridges the border between self and other, psyche and body, guiding the psyche towards individuation. The word *function* derives from the Latin verb *fungere*, to perform. *Transcend* is a compound of two Latin words: the prefix *trans*, 'beyond, across', and the verb *scandere*, 'to climb'. When something *transcends* it goes above, beyond or below. This process is an active confrontation between conscious and unconscious, resulting in the emergence of new symbolic forms. Dreams and the complexities and dissociations of the psyche reveal the transcendent function in therapeutic work. These transcend internal conflicts and, by doing so, lead to increased psychic wholeness.

The transcendent function describes the psychic functioning necessary for meaning to emerge from suffering and loss. This derives from the process of the various psychological elements, pushing and pulling at her personality, transcending into a third, or different, perspective of another order while embodying properties made from the disparate parts. The transcendent function operates between patient and therapist; from this space between, symbols emerge as communicative gestures from the unconscious to conscious. The active confrontation between conscious and unconscious results in new symbolic forms moving beyond, yet composed of, the pair's internal conflicts. The flow between the therapeutic pair leads to greater psychic wholeness within. The energy released from these conflicts, the discontents and stress are re-experienced so new emotions, reactions and thoughts can come forward.

Bridging the gap between conscious and unconscious, the transcendent function depends on the ego's ability to hold the clash of what seem like opposing forces while keeping them in dynamic interplay. This occurs both within each person and within the therapeutic couple. About this Jung said:

> The shuttling to and fro of arguments and affects between conscious and unconscious represents the transcendent function of opposites. The confrontation of the two positions generates a tension charged with energy and creates a living, third thing ... a living birth that leads to a new level of being, a new situation. So long as these are kept apart – naturally for the purpose of avoiding conflict – they do not function and remain inert.
>
> (1960, para. 189)

Therapy allows the expression of desires formerly lost, frustrated or abandoned (Toril, 1986, p. 84). A woman noticed a tree in the yard outside my therapy office and described one branch reaching out and leaning on the other. She perceived it was without burden as this connection provided support. She previously could not imagine that relying on anyone else was other than burdensome. The image helped release her from the accentuated self-reliance imposed by a distant father who overlooked her. She was the competent child in the family and, therefore, received little attention – her needs unseen, unmet and unacknowledged. This happened so often she learned to ignore them herself. The tree in the yard symbolized the emotional leaning she now could feel and receive.

The transcendent function is valuable in the clinical setting. mediating unconscious contents with the conscious attitudes. 'The tendencies of the conscious and the unconscious are the two factors that together make up the transcendent function. It is called 'transcendent; because it makes the transition from one attitude to another organically possible' (Jung, 1966, para. 145). The transcendent function can be difficult to access, however, if there is a deficit in symbolic functioning. The inability to easily symbolize comes from absence, and this daughter only feels difference, otherness and gaps negated, not present, not enough. She can be quite literal, holding on to the concrete, needing evidence and to know what is right and needing to be directed. She clings on to what's solid, as life has been too insecure and its foundation unsupported so early in her life. 'Absence can only be tolerated by means of early representations that eventually lead on to symbol formation ... An intolerance of absence and an incapacity to symbolize tend to go hand in hand' (Colman, 2007, pp. 565–66). Both options seem intolerable to a person when it has been impossible to think, feel or encounter psychological space. Such a daughter's discomfort in the symbolic arena can be surprising when her intellectual and verbal facility is evident, but the analyst must remember there is often fear of the unconscious.

Accessing the transcendent function in therapy changes a person, opening the personality. The union of therapist and client, the conscious and unconscious, bring forward the third element, aspects different from either but composed of both. As Jung said: '[It is a] new content that governs the whole attitude, putting an end to the division and forcing the energy of the opposites into a common channel. The standstill is overcome and life can flow on with renewed power towards new goals' (1960, para. 827).

The transcendent function breaks the impasse obstructing personality differentiation and potential. The opposing elements are bridged, and the new or third contains another level of complexity. This third is comprised of the representational space necessary for emergent meaning. In this sense, the transcendent function is an attempt to depict the creation of the psyche's meaning-making function (Colman, 2007, p. 566). Here, suffering and emotional distress is given meaning, and the energy released from sorrow and loss can now be utilized.

Transference/countertransference

We become ourselves through interactions with others, and in this experience, we find the face of others within ourselves. The containing relationship of therapy creates experience anew, not just from the past, but evolving from the present. 'Dreams dreamt as an integral part of an analysis have an integral part to play in the process of transforming the effects of poor early relational experiences ... particularly in the development of the patient's own internal analyst' (Wilkinson, 2006, p. 44). Therapy can provide safety for the self to unfold by accepting the confusion of sifting through what seems like the ashes or chaos of the personality. For these daughters, the self found no security or confidence from the father figure, so the authenticity and safety of the therapeutic relationship is even more essential (Solomon, 2007, p. 240).

For example, Willow worried that as her therapist I would say her father did his best. She thought my job was to defend him and confirm she had the problem, like she and everyone else had done her whole life. But her father did not show care or affection. When he disapproved of her life choices, he cruelly threw her out of the house when she was 17 years old with no money and no place to go.

In a recent dream *her father did not pick her up when she fell. She was bleeding, and the blood spread in tattoos up her arms. Her hands were shaking like they used to as a child with him. As she looked up in the dream, she saw his shoes and they were now abhorrent to her. Then in a scoffing tone, he said her fantasies and books would lead nowhere.* She was upset the day following the dream and very uneasy. Now she remembered why. Quite alone in her family and her own imaginal world as a child, her unemotional, detached father said children were to be broken so they would obey. This cruel father kept to himself, his emotions icy and his distance only broken with harshness and disapproval. She assumed with others she should put herself aside and did not communicate her emotional needs.

'Relationship treats relationship . . . For it is the relationship as the space in which our wound was inflicted, it must also be the space in which we are healed' (Carotenuto, 2015, p. 51). When the father is absent, the blank space around him can adversely affect security, the ability to relax and share feelings and reactions, spontaneity and enthusiasm. This also replicates itself in the therapeutic relationship. Willow assumed she must please everyone, including myself as her therapist. She looked for approval with each of my gestures, forgetting or fearful to focus on herself and worried she might cry or be too much to handle. So busy looking outward, she was unseen and unheard, abandoned and alone. She was masterful at her own self-deception and afraid of incurring my derision, just like from her father. In her mind he remained too present with his emotional absence and harshness, leaving her emotionally bleeding.

With this background, many experiences are made difficult, as evidenced in finding similar reactions to the therapist (Knox, 2010, p. 126). Immersion in the uncomfortable, searing and painful material in therapy brought Willow into view to reconcile these unaddressed components. Because she experienced father absence and unavailability, therapy evoked many feelings, including repressed expectations, yearnings, longing and desire, love and hate. She was brought up against the formerly negated and avoided. The dependencies denied and refused by the father were the very ones precipitated in the context of the therapeutic transference.

The lack she experienced with her father influenced several factors in her psychological treatment: the emotional core of myself as her therapist had to be available enough as a container; the extent of her need to preserve sameness; and the unresolved negative transference with its potentially destructive affects (Meredith-Owen, 2008, p. 468). The process of self-awareness required becoming conscious of and grieving losses, developing an independent self and reigniting lost desires and passions.

Willow dreamt *she was working for the therapist. There was a problem at the therapist's office, and she solved it. When the therapist entered the room, there was no notice of her, no appreciation of her solving the problem, no attention at all. The therapist was self-absorbed and dismissive. Although she tried, there was nothing, and then she gave up and left, feeling awful, defeated and in despair. In response to the felt badness, she withdrew, reflecting the emotional and relational withholding and inhibition of personality that resulted* (Knox, 2003, p.130).

The dream reminded Willow of the awful emptiness in her home, the not-there father; only his authoritarian demands to comply existed. Her father was a distant tyrant, frustrated and angry; he criticized her brains and offered no emotional understanding or holding. This situation was replicated in the therapy in her dream. In it, I embodied the position of the father in which my comments were interpreted as accusatory and critical. Meanwhile, she searched for exact attunement, but when this was not possible she took on the fault as her own (Knox,

2003, p. 130). Receptivity to the contents of the unconscious, like in the dream, requires an acceptance of disappointments. If the disappointments are small and manageable enough, the daughter can grow by dealing with them. But when the disappointments, like those Willow experienced with her absent father, are more than the daughter can handle, she resorts to the aloneness she has always known.

Willow retreated from sessions; driving home she cried, disappointed and frustrated. She displayed none of this in the therapeutic session, only reported it later as if it was not safe to express or feel in the presence of another person. Willow was insecure in therapy, vigilant but also fearful of the magnitude of her unmet needs. This is not uncommon as the absence of the father means the daughter is most familiar with an emotionally absent object: the father (Knox, 2003, p. 141). Unable to access her voice, she maintains a defensive attitude to remain hidden, self-deceptive to her raw feelings, cut off from her body's reactions. For this daughter, new relational experiences are initially resisted, as they are not easily recognized. The emotional confusion lands between self and other as she is so used to watching out for problems that her interior life loses focus.

Willow had many dreams about our therapy relationship – being in bed with me or resting at my house, taking a shower and even staying over in a room. But then she became anxious revealing these dreams, anticipating refusal, as perhaps she wanted too much. The dream's sexual components and their expression of emotional needs like being in bed were also indicative of pre-sexual needs. As we discussed these symbolic meanings, she was allowed to address these needs, finding emotional containment and the safety sorely needed and missed long ago without the right father figure. In these situations, my reactions and emotions were relied on to remain aware of the effect of the father's absence and to feel her mental processes emotionally, reacting in an intuitive response to symbolic communications (Knox, 2001, p. 614).

In therapy, when emotional contact is risked, the apprehension is that it may, in fact, prove disappointing, thus reconfirming the former spiral of disillusionment and withdrawal (Meredith-Owens, 2008, p. 438). Anticipating rejection and being dismissed, the daughter perceives the therapist as neglectful, like the absent father. Within the therapeutic relationship she might interpret my tone, expression and movement as disturbing, making her uneasy sharing her tender vulnerability.

In therapy Willow verbalized a terror of non-attachment, like floating in the universe without a thread to connect to the earth. This was a frightening image but more so as it was accompanied by her sense of being shell-like and susceptible to the inevitable looming disaster. Willow expected disappointment so she must be watchful. Although she might be intuitively knowledgeable about her psychological needs, she was unconsciously defensive. Willow's foundation was weakened early on from being erased and ignored by her unavailable and unrelated father. The needy place within her shut down and she had to frequently test the therapeutic relationship.

Inevitably as I carried reminders of the father, Willow felt the old apprehension; she could neither relax nor let down her guard. This reaction reflected the depth and extent of the emotional lack and how much it took for her to keep the therapeutic connection alive. As layer after layer of the emotional neglect became unwrapped, the analytical relationship offered a corrective experience. Willow commented: 'Since the last session I came away with a heavier feeling but greater understanding. I want change more than anything. I don't know how to begin to unravel this. Way more layered than I ever realized'. Her words referred to a kind of repair for re-membering the wrenching and broken connections of self to self and self to other. Jung contended both parties in analytic work are changed as self and other unite in this manifold process (1933, p. 49).

Analysis exposes the innermost ravages and co-constructs the patterns of self and other, psyche and soma. Jung commented that analysis is a mutual and dialogical process. There is no understanding of the story without the one who understands. This understanding is negotiated between author and listener, patient and analyst (Jung, 1959, para. 314). The therapist is a witness to the former chaos of emotions, needs and lack. The patient transfers something to the analyst and the analyst transfers something in return. Through this exchange a kind of truth formerly missed evolves through the verbal and nonverbal interactions. 'Effective analytic work arises out of the transference and countertransference which is the unconscious interchange between analyst and patient, taking many forms, so we are always learning' (Knox, 1998, p. 83).

The therapist must be attuned to the gaps, silences and reversals in each session, listening to how the absent father might be an invisible presence. The unmasking of reality threatens the hidden, tender vulnerabilities in the patient's heartbroken world. There she lived insulated, concealing the fragile core where she was falsely safe but numb. In therapy, Willow was confronted with the opportunity to express and repair the wounds and disappointments from the lack of father love. From our therapeutic interactions, new perceptions and more ease in relating emerged, expanding her personality as she was getting closer to herself.

The therapeutic relationship tries to bring the nascent self back through establishing bonds of authenticity. The therapist provides a place to explore the wounds in the unfolding narrative, even though the retrieval of the personality means re-experiencing the original and traumatic losses. This process brings with it fear of disintegration or annihilation as experienced with the father. It can feel threatening and her defensive attitudes become even stronger. In the search for understanding, emotions erupt, as the therapeutic relationship is a 'haunting repetition … of those traumatizing situations that created the original dissociative responses' (Solomon, 2004, p. 642).

> Change occurs only perilously … there are positive forces that seek to move the psyche into the future, there are powerful retrograde forces that seek to prevent such movement. These … often create the experience of a shared area of tumult and turmoil that requires engagement from both parties in the analytic consulting room.
>
> (Solomon, 2007, p. 142)

Such a therapeutic attitude is important, as the deficient experiences in emotional meeting and attachment with the father occurred early. These occurred before the daughter could process the onslaughts that were both too high and too low in physical and psychological arousal (Solomon, 2004, p. 646).

Through the ups and downs of therapy, the inevitable misunderstandings elicit defences. The daughter finds fault, problems; the therapist is wrong, does not care; she is not special, and she reacts with distrust as it repeats the story with the father. She feels humiliation, loss, worried about connection and locked in internal combat. It is difficult to get through her feelings of being marred and unacceptable. These are the feelings of the father's absence still holding her in their grip. They do not let other stories in and preserve her position of helplessness and lack experienced with the absent father.

Willow reported the hours away from therapy were, at times, painful, shame-filled, panicky with feeling disconnected and falling apart. In addition, her need for the veneer of sophistication and confidence complicated the transference. Uneasy about her connection or her not mattering to me, she wondered if she could depend on me. This came up as her unmet former dependency needs emerged. She thought maybe she did not count. Maybe she would not be met. Maybe she would not get what she wanted. Could she ask? A form of distancing and anxiety came out in the hurried, detailed but psychologically unreflective report of her daily comings and goings, surprises and disasters, persons and places. She said this was her defence and what she had to do before she could get into the difficult material. Willow hesitated.

She projected power and control onto me as the therapist, like with the absent father. She could not help wanting what she thought I had, needing to hide this because it also signalled the dependency she feared would be unmet yet again. She might have a reaction, not to what was said, but to what was not said or to a possible implication of what hadn't been said but was expected. Paradoxically, she had to be right, even prepared before sessions to reaffirm she was intact. She perseverated on what she considered mistakes and avoided not knowing. As time went on she realized something had been wrong, particularly as the good periods became more infrequent and the bad periods more intense and terrifying.

She might have taken flight into a precocious intellect as a defence against feelings and emotion, appearing to live in a twilight state, non-differentiated and trapped (Seligman, 1985, p. 71). She might have felt she was not really living or have the sensation of sleepwalking. She now faced the previously avoided material. In therapy, recognition and empathy was given to the deadness acquired as an adaptation to the deadened father and his absence rather than leaving it unaddressed. If disregarded, it would continue in the unconscious and damage the therapeutic work. The deadness was signalled by responses in both participants, like sleepiness or lack of interest, confusion and sometimes anger, or seemingly impossible demands. Once noticed and explored, the deadness could be afforded its vital place in the work (Goss, 2006, p. 688).

Willow dreamt, *There was a tower on my right that looked like the tall forest watchtowers. My therapist was in the tower counselling someone. I was very jealous and wanted time with her. A young kid started rocking the tower. I tried to warn the people inside. It is going to fall over. I feel lost. Then I am standing in a dark hall with heavy dark wood panelling and knock on the door to her office. There is no answer. I open the door and she is with someone talking and ignores me. A small animal starts to run out, fur? feathers? Not sure what it is. I catch it and try to push it back in as I close the door. I try to hide my face and don't want to let her know I want to talk to her. I close the door and leave. I am feeling self-destructive. No one has time for me.*

In discussing the dream Willow associated the therapist to her father in his tower locked away from everyone, as she was forgotten and hidden in shame. The dream made her realize how much was projected onto our therapeutic relationship, how much she needed trust and acceptance and how she worried it would not happen. The small animal might be the uncontrolled tender and young feelings running out. From experiences with the absent, nonresponsive father and resulting distressing internal restrictions, she anticipated the therapist would prefer another person. Willow assumed she would be the rejected one, as in the dream, alone and self-destructive. The dream was a message to her and to me about what was happening between us and the early childhood issues aroused and needing attention. This helped the symbolic function and addressed the damage from traumatic failures of attachment, which might be re-established through the analyst's behaviour in the present (Colman, 2010a, p. 298).

The dream showed I was also in service for building the paternal presence from within (Seligman, 1985, p. 69). Through the therapeutic transference, this daughter came in touch with the old yearnings, replicating those of the present day. When anticipating there was no way to be seen, investment in the absent father scenario remained, confirming the old cycles of disillusionment and withdrawal. She tried to hide the envy but also assumed I had everything and she did not. Due to her vulnerability, she might resort to the old methods of protection and cut off, become secretly depressed, give up in despair and distance, desires for connection denied. It was wrenching for her to get into the sadness. She did not easily communicate sensitive feelings or reactions, anticipating the misunderstandings she knew from her father. She could too easily submerge the discomfort in being exposed, abandoned and re-traumatized, the very feelings that needed to be acknowledged.

To relax and feel safe enough to emote is precarious. Self-reflection brings recognition of the collapsed psychic space. The act of turning inward for psychological development is difficult when the daughter's inner world is populated by what she calls monsters. She is embarrassed and unwilling to admit what she considers these deficits. As the father gave no praise or caring attention, she became nervous, fearing mistakes and making wrong choices, lamenting how many of the basics she was never told.

Partially because she could express so little with her father, the internal strife comes out in therapy. A daughter expressing herself with the therapist reflects that the therapeutic setting makes her actually talk in a different way (Perelberg &

Kohon, 2017, p. 130). Therapy helps re-negotiate the wounded places, dismantle the defensive strategies and, in the process, also reveals the psychic panic. The therapist must be willing to manage the 'real existential anguish, doubt, not knowing and the risk it takes for them to reveal emotions and real feelings' (Solomon, 2004, p. 643). The therapist might be perceived as a persecutor or intruder, not understanding and even harmful. The therapeutic support was only a dimly imagined wish. She is sensitive to any nuance or change in the therapeutic routine, translating it as loss and being left out.

The therapeutic process of questioning and self-exploration dredges up elements of desire, passion and suffering – all ingredients for renewal to the psyche. It is a time of heightened feelings when the old defences are ready to be abandoned and a precarious time in the therapeutic process (Solomon, 2004, p. 647). This work disrupts memory, disturbs the ego's status quo and pierces the psychological complexes. It requires becoming conscious of and grieving the losses for finding her voice, developing an independent self and reigniting desires and passions.

Mourning

The capacity to mourn is consonant with the process of individuation, as becoming oneself is connected with the capacity of the mind to process separation and mourn what was lost (Cavalli, 2017, p. 187). The lack of father affects the daughter's intra-psychic world and returns her to the grief. Although she cries and suffers and feels sad, doing so might not address the complex and more intricate mourning for the father. Without a capacity to bear pain and mourn losses, the self defensively tries to stay identified with the lost object and becomes attached to the absence. Grief involves recognizing the investment of energy in the wishes for the father who was not there. It means walking the line between the pain of the absence and the unaddressed need for presence. The task feels great.

Mourning also refers to the alchemical phase called the *nigredo*, a time of darkness accompanied by difficulty, melancholy and unease. It is a stage for descending into the psyche indicating mourning and despair as part of psychological development. And mourning is an aspect of therapy propelling individuation.

However, an absent father often goes unmourned. How does a daughter mourn a father who did not exist for her, with her, around her, caring for her? He was like a shell of a person without history or personality. Absence has become part of her life in an unconscious allegiance and replication of the absent father. A lump of grief remains at the core of the daughter creating melancholic reactions. The rupture happened so early on she often cannot name what was lost. Mourning the father becomes especially difficult when he is not linked to memory, representation or perception. One of the results of experiencing grief and mourning is feeling de-centred. Staying in the sadness and waiting is hard, as she wants to escape the distress. Grief eventually expands the boundaries of the self and, at the same time, brings the reality of what cannot be replaced but also never was.

Mourning is linked with the capacity to open up, live through, separate and integrate experiences. Therapeutic work brings the capacity to represent the loss and re-create the lost object. Over the course of mourning, powerful emotions are not only worked through but also a capacity to represent the lost object, the father, in the mind; this can function as a reparative act (Fordham, 1974, p. 21). As mourning is recognized, the daughter begins to connect with the disowned or split-off parts of her personality. Any sign of the emergence of the self into consciousness in its symbolic form is highly valuable. But these experiences are other than what she has heretofore known. The symbols tend to act as focal points for integration, fostering a sense of pattern and meaning. They are, as Jung called them, 'uniting symbols' (Colman, 2010b, p. 291). By being with, and even immersed in, the sorrows, she no longer needs to keep defensive positions or protective barriers or seal off the pain. She begins to share in therapy.

Yet when unable to access her foundations, the changes required can seem daunting and filled with obstacles. The repetitive and self-deprecating behaviours and thoughts create distance from herself like with the absent father. The emotional unfilled space forms a vacuum. She feels unlovable, alienated from the physical, resulting in various forms of self-attacks and numbing behaviours. Without desire or libido, a non-nourishing self-absorption arises as a defence against intimacy, be it to self and/or to others. '[She] started out in the world with averted face ... and all the while the world and life pass by her like a dream – an annoying source of illusions, disappointments, and irritations' (Jung, 1959, para. 185).

She needs an opening of the doors for psychological understanding. The 'act of self-recollection or the gathering together of what is scattered indicates the integration and humanization of the self' (Jung, 1969, para. 400). The psyche is fluid, multidimensional, alive and capable of creative development. Over time, the daughter becomes less armoured, more open. It takes courage to keep looking and searching in the uncovering of self.

Jung paradoxically said: 'The secret is that only that which can destroy itself is truly alive' (1968, p. 93). This requires the daughter to recognize the lost object of desire – the father – and retrieve her life. Transformation, not the erasure of the memories, brings the submerged energy into conscious awareness. She learns to live, not denying the feelings about the father who was absent, but by developing her own cannon of being. It also means realizing the history that haunts and shapes her, influencing the therapeutic experience. As André Green paradoxically noted, the representation of an absence of representation also suggests it contained what could not yet be represented (Green, 1999). Herein lies the possibility of symbolic creation and imagery within the personality to repair the painful absence and come alive through the relational space of therapy. The re-creation of representation evolves in the dialogue of therapy, verbal and nonverbal, conscious and unconscious.

The psychological journey involves finding what is called in Jungian analytical psychology the 'treasure hard to attain' or the knowledge residing in the unconscious and brought to conscious life. The therapeutic relationship and dreamwork are processes of honouring the body, mind and soul. The therapeutic discourse gives additional meaning to past, present and future events, enabling her to take possession of her abandoned or undeveloped potentials. She discovers the meaning in her personal drama as a step towards separating from restrictive paternal attitudes. This comes through the use of the reflective function, the symbols arising from the union of the opposing tendencies and new perspectives emerging with the transcendent function. The discovery of her self occurs through this minutely reflective and relational process integrating both the chaos and order of the psyche.

> The therapeutic situation is the only place explicitly provided for in the social contract in which we are allowed to talk about the wounds we have suffered and to search for possible new identities and new ways of talking about ourselves.
>
> (Kristeva, 1988, p. 6)

References

Bromberg, P. (1983). The mirror and the mask: On narcissism and psychoanalytic growth. *Contemporary Psychoanalysis, 19*(2), 359–87. doi:10.1080/00107530.1983.10746614.

Carotenuto, A. (2015). *To Love, to Betray*. Asheville, NC: Chiron Publications.

Cavalli, A. (2017). Identification – Obstacle to individuation, or: On how to become 'me'. *Journal of Analytical Psychology, 62*(2), 187–204. doi:10.1111/1468-5922.12303.

Colman, W. (2007). Symbolic conceptions: The idea of the third. *Journal of Analytical Psychology, 52*(5), 565–83.

Colman, W. (2010a). The analyst in action. *International Journal of Psycho-Analysis, 91*(2), 287–303.

Colman, W. (2010b). Mourning and the symbolic process. *Journal of Analytical Psychology, 55*(2), 275–97.

Fordham, M. (1974). Jung's conception of the transference. *Journal of Analytical Psychology, 19*(1), 1–21.

Goss, P. (2006). Discontinuities in the male psyche: Waiting, deadness and disembodiment. Archetypal and clinical approaches. *Journal of Analytical Psychology, 51*(5), 681–99.

Green, A. (1999). The intuition of the negative in *Playing and Reality*. In: G. Kohon (Ed.), *The Dead Mother: The Work of André Green* (pp. 205–21). London, England: Routledge.

Guggenbühl-Craig, A. (1999). *Power in the Helping Professions*. Thompson, CT: Spring Publications.

Jung, C.G. (1933). *Modern Man in Search of a Soul*. New York, NY: Harvest.

Jung, C.G. (1954). *The Practice of Psychotherapy*, Vol. 16. Princeton, NJ: Princeton University Press.

Jung, C.G. (1959). *The Archetypes and the Collective Unconscious*. New York, NY: Pantheon Books.

Jung, C.G. (1960). *The Spirit in Man, Art, and Literature*, Vol. 15. Princeton, NJ: Princeton University Press.

Jung, C.G. (1963). *Memories, Dreams, Reflections*. New York, NY: Vintage.

Jung, C.G. (1966). *On Psychic Energy*, Vol. 8. New York, NY: Pantheon Books.

Jung, C.G. (1966). *Two Essays on Analytical Psychology*, Vol. 7. New York, NY: Pantheon Books.

Jung, C.G. (1968). *Psychology and Alchemy*, Vol. 12. New York, NY: Pantheon Books.

Jung, C.G. (1969). *Psychology and Religion*, Vol. 11. New York, NY: Pantheon Books.

Jung, C.G. (1970). *Civilization in Transition*, Vol. 10. Princeton, NJ: Princeton University Press.

Jung, C.G. (1971). *Psychological Types*, Vol. 6. Princeton, NJ: Princeton University Press.

Kimbles, S. (2004). A cultural complex operating in the overlap of clinical and cultural space. In: T. Singer & S. Kimbles (Eds.), *The Cultural Complex* (pp. 199–211). Hove: Routledge.

Knox, J. (1998). Transference and countertransference: Historical and clinical developments in the Society of Analytical Psychology. In: I. Alister & C. Hauke, (Eds.), *Contemporary Jungian Analysis* (pp. 73–84). London, England: Routledge.

Knox, J. (2001). Memories, fantasies, archetypes: An exploration of some connections between cognitive science and analytical psychology. *Journal of Analytical Psychology*, *46*(4), 613–35.

Knox, J. (2003). *Archetype, Attachment, Analysis*. London, England: Routledge.

Knox, J. (2010). *Self-Agency in Psychotherapy*. New York, NY: W.W. Norton & Co.

Kohon, G. (Ed.) (1999). *The Dead Mother: The Work of André Green*. London, England: Routledge.

Kristeva, J. (1988). *In the Beginning Was Love*. New York, NY: Columbia University Press.

Meredith-Owens, W. (2008). 'Go! Sterilise the fertile with thy rage': Envy as embittered desire. *Journal of Analytical Psychology*, *53*(4), 459–80.

Modell, A. (1999). The dead mother syndrome and the reconstruction of trauma. In: G. Kohon (Ed.), *The Dead Mother: The Work of André Green* (pp. 76–86). London, England: Routledge.

Perelberg, R. (Ed.) (2018). *The Psychic Bisexuality: A British-French Dialogue*. London, England: Routledge.

Perelberg, R. & Kohon, G. (Eds.) (2017). *The Greening of Psychoanalysis*. London, England: Routledge.

Phillips, A. (1994). *On Flirtation*. Boston, MA: Harvard University Press.

Seligman, E. (1985). The half-alive ones. In: A. Samuels (Ed.), *The Father* (pp. 69–94). New York, NY: New York University Press.

Shorter, B. (1987). *An Image Darkly Forming*. London, England: Routledge.

Solomon, H. (1998). The self in transformation: The passage from a two- to a three-dimensional internal world. *Journal of Analytical Psychology*, *43*(2), 225–38.

Solomon, H. (2004). Self creation and the limitless void of dissociation: The 'as if' personality. *Journal of Analytical Psychology*, *49*(5), 635–56.

Solomon, H. (2007). *The Self in Transformation*. London, England: Karnac Books.

Toril, M. (Ed.) (1986). *The Kristeva Reader*. New York, NY: Columbia University Press.

Wilkinson, M. (2004). The mind–brain relationship: The emergent self. *Journal of Analytical Psychology*, *49*(1), 83–101.

Wilkinson, M. (2006). The dreaming mind-brain: A Jungian perspective. *Journal of Analytical Psychology*, *51*(1), 43–59.

Chapter 9

If he loves her, where is he?

'How can I cut off my own child's hands'? Then the Evil One threatened him and said: 'If you do not do it you are mine, and I will take you for myself'. The father became alarmed and promised to obey him. So he went to the girl and said: 'My child if I do not cut off both your hands, the Devil will carry me away, and in my terror I have promised to do it. Help me in my need and forgive me the harm I do you'.

Fairy tales trace the natural and archetypal development of the psyche through their cultural and psychological images. In childhood, a time of natural closeness to the world of the unconscious, we wholeheartedly believe in fairy tales. Imagination and fantasy are as real as the so-called real world. Children are wise enough to know the truth in the fairy tale and are touched by and want to hear the story over and over again.

Oftentimes, when grown up, this connection is lost, as what is assumed as rational and reasonable takes over. After all, to whom do we say, 'I spent the day reading and contemplating a fairy tale'? The adult world often labels such behaviour as ridiculous or regressive, and so we miss out on the excitement and enchantment of the fairy tale. The lessons depicted in the stories contain the age-old truths of complex psychological processes. They describe archetypal and basic patterns, larger than the individual arena yet applicable in different ways to each person and culture. Depicting transformation and growth they are vehicles for insight into our human tendencies, replicating patterns of the unconscious naturally occurring in conscious life. They also illustrate the brutal, destructive ego and power-driven aspects of the psyche. And they show us how to get through suffering while illustrating endless variations on the psychological journey.

Fairy tales recognize we are all princesses and princes, queens and kings in different forms. In fact, each of the characters can be interpreted as aspects of the personality. This includes the evil, demonic and servile. The fairy tale charts what is out of balance personally and collectively and parallels the circuitous mode of the therapeutic process. The fathers in the fairy tales selected here reveal their hubris, treachery, betrayals and abandonments. These fathers neither represent trust nor security; they do, however, represent what have been the predominant collective patriarchal attitudes. Fairy tales also show through many trials and efforts daughters who integrate the varieties of masculine and feminine qualities.

In almost all, once the daughter leaves, as she must, she does not return to the father's kingdom.

Only the beginnings of several tales are presented here as this is when the father disappears, leaving the daughter to fend for herself. Although he might be present at the beginning, he is insufficient, not protective and usually unconscious of her and what she needs. Commonly assumed as simple, these stories illustrate the constellations of many current families and the distress from their fractured and disastrous relationships. The fathers in these tales do not take on caring roles and often are poor at providing money or emotion. They are failures in almost every way, and the daughters suffer. The deficient father is a staple of the fairy tale, although he has rarely been as condemned as the stepmother has been. This, in itself, indicates how much father absence and neglect have been ignored and his position has been unchallenged. The tales also reveal that an absent father does not determine a daughter's fate as she takes her own path away from him.

The fairy-tale father is almost predictably portrayed with emotional absence, unconsciousness and lack. Fairy tales illustrate what a daughter has to do to extricate herself from him. On her journey she works in menial jobs, engages in tasks requiring the help of animals or trusting an unknown figure. She is usually isolated in this work. Although separated from all she has known, and stripped of finery, in a barren or desolate place, there she discovers her capabilities. Only at the end, or close to it, is she again in connection with a male figure. He also usually has to perform his own tasks, indicating change in the masculine realm and in his relationship to her.

Understanding these timeless stories is an aspect of Jungian psychological work, connecting the modern person with narratives common to the human condition. They are grounding and sobering, and from them one learns life signals. Even when the outcome is unknown the daughter's attitude of openness indicates respect for the unconscious. All this illustrates the intricate work of finding her individuality. Growing up in the families portrayed in fairy tales is neither happy nor fulfilling.

The unconscious father creates no end of problems for the daughter. In them and in many families the daughter is used as the feeling function for the father. This fact becomes more significant as the tales often occur when the daughter is at puberty. The situation indicates this type of father cannot manage the sexual reactions around his daughter appropriately. And he cannot encourage her growth as he tries to hold her back. In his immaturity and lack of psychological development, he cannot cope with her difference. Something is sorely wrong with the father who neglects the daughter, indicating his feeling side is undeveloped. She is unable to be nourished by his Eros or relatedness (von Franz, 1988, p. 77). Likewise, in today's families there are psychological effects when the daughter has not been encouraged or supported to be herself and separate from the father tradition and to exert other choices.

These fairy tales portray a daughter escaping the negative, narcissistic and unaware father and getting outside the family enclosure. Her refusal of the father exerts a high price, but the cost of staying is her soul. She will discover her own desires as being other than his, rather than existing as a substitute or replication of his ideas. She is charged to access her force and movement, no longer constrained or diminutive. The journey she undertakes is longer and more arduous than she imagined. Along the way she heals from the wounds inflicted by the father by accessing her stamina and abilities. These stories make the point a daughter can break the visible and invisible ties to her father and his world. They demonstrate it takes hard and basic work to claim herself, her authority and place in the world.

In any number of tales evil enters through the father's unconsciousness and lack of emotional attachment, threatening the daughter. The father will do anything to save himself, even at the expense of sacrificing his own daughter. Even when fathers in fairy tales are rulers or kings, they are still often self-serving and negligent. Or, if poor and depleted, they are unable to provide economically or emotionally for the family.

Release from this system only comes through extreme events. Paradoxically, the absence of the father as a good related figure is a precursor to the daughter's embarking on her own journey, finding an identity wider than only being a father's daughter. There are many aspects to the father's betrayals pushing her alone into the world, as she feels the pain and reality of his betrayal, but through her trials she awakens to her independence and strength. In this way his betrayal can be seen as the abandonment needed for development. But basic trust has been broken; a daughter has been let down, failed, love misdirected and refused. She is left exposed and unprotected, yet in these fairy tales she expresses no resentment or vengeance and goes on, although she does not deny what has happened. James Hillman wrote on father betrayal:

> If betrayal is perpetuated mainly for personal advantage (to get out of a tight spot, to hurt or use, to take care of Number One), then one can be sure that love had less the upper hand than did the brute power.
>
> (2005, p. 198)

For example Cinderella's father did not notice or just ignored the overt physical and emotional abuse perpetrated on her by the stepmother and stepsisters. Asking no questions about the disparity, the father brought the requested dresses for her stepsisters and a twig for Cinderella and then he disappeared. Cinderella was left to deal with their mean, selfish envy as the father exposed her to these unsavoury shadow parts. Again, his lack means she will have to manage hard life lessons as well as find her strength.

In 'Rumpelstiltskin', the miller is poor, unable to provide economically or emotionally. To get money he proclaims his daughter can spin straw into gold. Motivated by his own greed the king takes the father up on his boasting and the daughter ends up doing all the work, locked in a room, threatened with death if she does not succeed. The father not only sets her up to do the work but also puts her life in possible peril. She is saved from death when an imp appears to spin the straw into gold. As payment he extracts a promise for her first-born child. He only agrees to give up the child if she guesses his name. He dances in glee, repeating his name – Rumpelstiltskin – thinking he got the best of her, but she overhears him. By knowing his name she gains freedom from him and her father. They both seem similar, colluding in her demise and willing to sacrifice her to get what they want. Both are masculine figures without connection to the feminine or themselves. In this tale the daughter becoming a queen supersedes the father, going beyond what he could ever give her.

Similarly, in 'The Handless Maiden', the poor miller father agrees to give the unknown old man what is behind the mill in exchange for gold. Unconscious of his own daughter's whereabouts, he thinks it is the apple tree. Upon arriving home, his wife asks about the gold they now have, and the miller explains they got it from the man who wanted what was behind the mill. Although he did not know the daughter was behind there, the mother knew. The situation clearly illustrates the daughter subject to the father's unconsciousness.

Poverty represents the loss of energy in the father. For a daughter initial poverty results in not being sufficiently nourished by Eros or the principle of relatedness in the father. In fact, we might ask where are the fairy tales demonstrating the supportive father to the daughter? The absence of the father for relatedness and feeling allows the negative animus in the form of the devil to come in and attempt to take possession of her. The father's unconsciousness, inability and greed are obviously dangerous.

In classical Jungian thought, the anima is the psychological principle of the feminine in a man and is assumed to be the young maiden daughter. Jungian analyst Marie-Louise von Franz believed this situation denotes that the excluded principle, or the feminine, has to be brought into consciousness. In addition, the daughter's task is to liberate herself from this situation as it is revealed in the devil's appearance (von Franz, 1988, p. 31). When the devil comes for the daughter, the father who wants his money and his life apologizes to her for what he must do. He could be the sacrifice, but instead sacrifices her, chopping off her hands as the devil demands.

Again, the father exposes the negative male in the form of the devil and himself. The daughter does not rebel and willingly lets her father take her hands, leaving him to perform the blameful act. She cries so much on the stumps of her arms, the devil cannot get to her. She provides her own protection; the father does not. The outpouring of tears and her sorrows begins her departure from the father and releases her from the devil and the father, as both are destructive. The natural expression of sorrow saves her, whereas the father lack maims her.

The miller father displays a cruel face, cuts off the daughter's participation in life and leaves her unable to go on for a time. So disconnected from the ramifications of what he has done, he now offers that she can stay with him. She refuses. It is too late, and how can she trust him? To stay with him is to remain encircled by the paternal world, in the shelter and trap of the father, unable to grow up. Independence and self-respect emerge when the role of the good obedient girl is no longer extant. Eventually, this daughter becomes a queen, has a male child called Sorrowful and spends seven years alone in nature with her child. During this time her hands heal. The father of the child, the king, also has to take a journey of his own to find her. The masculine must also change for new psychological perspectives to develop.

In fairy tales the figure of the devil is part of the setup for the crisis a daughter encounters with her father. In other words, the devil's attempt to get at the maiden and capture her is part of her fate and she must deal with him. If not for the devil, the girl would have remained within the family, unaware of the world and ignorant of herself as a distinct person. The very fact of the devil appearing shows how negative, disconnected yet powerful the masculine has become, which happens when the father figure is too remote psychologically and takes a compensatory, exaggerated and adversarial role. When the masculine has insufficient connection to the daughter, internal pressure threatens to crush life, creating a situation of distress and upheaval. Yet, the formerly unconscious contents bring awareness, loosening the constricting perception of reality for personality expansion.

In a dream

Emily began analysis with the following dream: *I was going to be killed by my father. I tried to stall for time. He had already killed my sister, and this made me mad and sad. I tried to remain cool on the outside as he pointed a gun at me. I grabbed the gun through a struggle and ran and ran and woke up.*

In this dream her very life was at stake and she ran away, but to where? The dream illustrated the understanding of feminine psychology to include attention to the father as a destructive figure. The father is part of what models the daughter's feeling relationship to man, to men in general, to culture and to the feminine. There are meaningful coincidences between dreams and body processes. For Emily, the dream illustrated the task was to escape this type of father with his murderous actions. Part of the feminine self or the shadow/anima in the form of the sister had already been destroyed. To prevent being overtaken, she grabbed the gun and ran, saving herself from the lethal father's energy. This harsh dream was a psychological step towards consciousness.

Many educated and independently minded women apologize, however, sabotaged and degraded for being forceful, threatening the male way. Bringing this out, as in the dream, means sometimes grabbing the gun and running; fighting is necessary. Otherwise, the daughter would be killed by the paternal way. Realistically, as in Emily's dream, it can become this extreme.

As with the example of Emily, a daughter cannot rely on being merely charming, beautiful and compliant as it will not suffice. Emphasizing such qualities reduces and denies her development. The dream illustrates a break from father and an end to ignorance. It means consciously experiencing life and this reality. There is no protection if she does not realize how bad the father really was. So many daughters keep on giving the father excuses and taking the blame themselves, making him less important than he was in shaping their life trajectories.

The remainder of the father's damaging rule is sustained through her wounds. She has to face the perverted masculine aspect and leave the innocence manifesting in helplessness, dependence and being a victim and assume responsibility for her strength (Leonard, 1983, p. 85). As in the fairy tales described in the previous section, severing from the father psychologically and physically requires finding the necessary inner resources, personal stamina and inspiration. 'It is because I dove into the abyss that I am beginning to love the abyss I am made of' (Lispector, 2012, 39).

The animus

The animus is an irksome concept, out of date, misogynist as traditionally delineated in classical Jungian analytical psychology. If we look with a wider lens, the animus does not function from static definitions, but it can assist in connecting aspects of the psyche. Even so, there are many well-founded disagreements with Jung's interpretations of the animus reflective of his era. It was a different time, yet some aspects are applicable to our own. This concept in its updated form includes the belief that we have both sexes within the unconscious processes, and these are not in themselves gendered (Perelberg, 2018, p. xix).

American Jungian analyst Thomas Moore noted the animus as defined in classical Roman psychology,

> connoting several modes of intellect and spirit; identity; active mind including criticism and judgment; artistic imagination; thought of the heart; character and temperament; will and purpose … is less interiorizing reflection and more the outpouring of mind and heart . … It also appears as genius (including the *genius loci* and the family spirit), conscience, and daimon … It is a source of light in the underworld. And it can also be monstrous, upending our expectations of a genteel *coniunctio*, revealing the power of our own spirit.
>
> (Moore, 1987, p. 131)

Moreover, the word *animus* means breath or spirit and represents potential activity and a quality of discernment. Another definition of the animus includes the following:

> To contemplate some action is to have it in one's animus. To turn one's attention to something, an idea or object in space is to turn the animus towards it … When one loses consciousness, the animus leaves. Moreover, to collect one's faculties and spirits is to collect one's animus.
>
> (Onians, 1973, p. 179)

These words depict the healthy and related animus/male able to accompany the female with conscious awareness and intent.

In the present day, French psychoanalyst Julia Kristeva describes a multiverse of sexuality (2019). Her interpretation of the psyche includes many expansive possibilities when the sexes are recognized as a multiverse of expression. These forms of identity are not fixed but fluid and lead to a more flexible and creative cohabitation of the masculine and feminine. Kristeva contends the feminine is in an endless process of transformation, releasing men as well from narrow paternalistic roles. The postmodern approach to sexuality and gender sits at an intersection. Kristeva calls this a crossroads, a time of pluralization of the psyche and how we relate to each other in this multiverse. She notes an expansion from the singularity of narcissism with its insistence on sameness and fusion. In addition, we are facing the question of how to live with the other in many varieties as part of the recognition of psychological and social pluralization. The multiverse reflects both the force of history and the potency of the unconscious for continual growth and development.

Energy swings between male and female, masculine and feminine, morphing throughout life. Individual possibilities are broad and not merely a simplified union of static and narrowly defined polarities. Rather, there is a range of aspects existing within each person. 'It appears that the real exists as at least three: a real corresponding to the masculine subject, a real corresponding to the feminine subject, and a real corresponding to their relation' (Irigaray, 2002, 111). Current Jungian thought broadens the animus images that are not of men per se but 'a metaphor for the richness, potential and mystery of the other' (Samuels, 1993, p. 143). The animus, like all aspects of the psyche can affirm and solidify development through life. When expanded beyond the narrow confines of gender, the animus allows for understanding otherness based on difference rather than opposites (Samuels, 1999, p. 223).

'To move beyond the discourse of opposites requires something plural, decentered than the simplified sameness-difference' (Benjamin, 1995, p. 50). The integration of masculine and feminine dimensions implies not only the need for but also the incompleteness of both. 'This is not to be confused with man and woman but is an ever active intertwining ... each is linked to the other, defined by their differences and "extraordinary articulations"' (Perelberg, 2018, p. 42).

When these aspects are out of relation to each other, a woman will be frustrated in expressing the range of her individual femaleness and maleness. Especially in our current era of flux and change, it cheapens and is simplistic to prescribe a fixed set of properties to the masculine or feminine. Rather, the concept of the animus leaves in 'suspension' the 'question of "masculine" and "feminine" ... even, and the word is used advisedly, in some confusion' (Samuels, 2016, p. 94). Each person possesses sexual otherness, division and difference, promoting links and opportunities for various formations between self and other. The psyche seeks balance and can be likened to a dance between the partners in many combinations, arousing passion and life energy. These aspects are part of our psychological roots and the natural compass for richness in life.

The animus includes the use of intellect, mind, thought, feelings, emotions and the creative. This gives the daughter the freedom to live as she is rather than being constrained by convention, her father or the traditional patriarchy in which she lives. Here is how a woman in Jungian therapy described these interior aspects of her personality:

> The man and woman looked at each other, searching for signs. Are they willing or not to face the truth of the drama? By this time they knew they were in it together. Each wondered at the courage of the other, the fragility of the other's mind. Each was tempted to stay and suffer the unfolding ... For a moment their eyes met once more. But doubt possessed them, courage and desire deserted. They turned, walked out and said goodbye. Neither ever knew what the drama was really about or what truth could have been theirs.

Her words leave us wondering what they imply about her inner connections working in concert, or not. 'To the degree that [a person] does not admit the validity of the other [she] denies the "other" within [herself] the right to exist – and vice versa. The capacity for inner dialogue is a touchstone for outer objectivity' (Jung, 1954, para. 187).

If dominated by the masculine, the feminine suffers; desires are repressed, as the daughter avoids direction and choice. For example, from the distorted and negative animus, she considers herself ugly and this inhibits her life process so that she is unable to express affection with the body (Carotenuto, 2015, p. 129). Further, in its negative aspect, the animus constellates as the inner critic, judge, sadist, murderer who informs the woman she's worthless, stupid and unlovable. This disrupts love relationships, sabotages possibilities and creates impotence, shakes her confidence or, if she has been successful, deflates her. An inner tyrant holds sway.

It takes a consciously aware father to foster both the femininity and masculinity of the daughter (Samuels, 1985, p. 31). When a father is not present to affirm her, his refusal generates injurious consequences like masochism, an inability to leave the father world. She gives up her identity to become his idea of the feminine. Or she might engage in defiance and vengeance against the masculine. Either attitude fosters the disappointments and internal depletions taking up residence within her. Because the father is the other love object to align with in both sameness and difference, it is not necessary to steal or envy masculinity but to rightfully have it (Benjamin, 1988, p. 129).

The concept of the animus recognizes the bisexual nature of the psyche. Jung opined:

> She should take care that her animus does not escape because if it gets away from her unnoticed and falls into the unconscious, it can be destructive. The animus can be either positive or negative. He can be like a dragon guarding the bridge trying to prevent us from reaching the other bank. If we do not try to evade him, but go on courageously he becomes manageable and we can pass through without harm. If we run away because the dragon seems too powerful we lose vital energy and become soulless.
>
> (Jung, 1967, p. 269)

As illustrated by Jung's quote, the animus can be wonderfully creative or powerfully destructive, depending on the female's relationship to it. Integration means adapting the animus to her personality rather than being subservient to it. With inner connections to the flexible and open animus/male energy, she can access vitality, openness, love, confidence and security.

The animus contains the complex of feelings about males learned from mothers as well as fathers. This includes how the animus functions within her, the interactions between the mother and father figures and between them in the world. When flexible, these aspects model healthy dependency needs and mutual reliance. When the father is unavailable, unsupportive and not present, the daughter can experience disappointment, promises unmet, without models for coupling, working things out, and love is broken (Seligman, 1985, p. 73).

Delayed damage

Darelle found herself angry much of the time, filled with negative judgements. She described herself as having toads falling from her mouth and could not help the nasty, cutting and distancing comments, which reflected inner misery. As a child she had to avoid a forbidding but demanding father for whom nothing was good enough. Always morose he never smiled and shared nothing personal, asking nothing about her. She was unaware she had adopted his attitudes. Every time she tried to enjoy herself or rest, the negative male/animus taunted her with the accusation she should work more and be productive. Without access to inner soothing words or actions, she just proceeded from task to task, keeping busy, performing, being efficient. Hounded by incessant demands for doing more, she could not access her real desires and took refuge in giving to others. Over time, Darelle became defeated, beaten down by weariness, tainted by a sense of nullity.

Darelle avoided her desires and hesitated to find love, assuming she would meet rejection. She took the blame that she did something wrong when relationships were not reciprocated. Questioning how to be female, unable to gain self-esteem, Darelle was unsure of her ability to attract anyone and tended to disregard her natural intuition. She thought she should erase the longing for intimacy, hide from being exposed as needy. But this attitude left her helpless and flattened with few sparks of hope. She was like many daughters who long to come alive yet don't know how.

She did not understand for many years the damage she had suffered from being mirrored inadequately by a distant and overbearing father. He commented on her body, how women should look, always in a sexual and lecherous way. She learned to stay out of sight and definitely out of the limelight. The father who should have supported her authority and strength was not around. Although in distress and lonely herself, her mother said to accept and understand his brutal and crass dominance; after all, he provided for them. Yet Darelle knew her mother was deeply unhappy, and she rarely saw her parents express any love. A quiet desperation and defeat lay in the home atmosphere.

In such a situation she could not access the interactive dynamics of the masculine and feminine. Her adaptation was to go unconscious, erase her father's influence, modify the story and make him not count. She was uncomfortable in her skin, often changing clothes many times a day, as if to gain some ease. She was vigilant, careful, watching others more than herself, trying to fend off any surprises.

Many daughters often remark that they could not ask their fathers to show them much, if anything. They become frustrated in how to use their strength and talents yet hide behind a persona of needing nothing. Rather than experiencing the full range of their senses, these daughters become constrained and act self-consciously. When the father is absent emotionally, the animus can assume negative forms, inappropriately in charge of the daughter's psyche, in conflict with her instincts, expressions of individuality, affecting relationships with self and others. The animus is a natural predisposition intended to function with her feminine intellect (Jung, E. 1978, pp. 12–13). Yet no one attended to Darelle's mind.

After much therapy, Darelle was beginning to acknowledge her father was a man like the Wizard of Oz, a fake and puny character hiding behind his curtain of bluster and bravado. Having no magic abilities, it became clear her father, like the wizard, was also a fraud. This figure became like a demon within that would not allow her to succeed, be human or fail, constantly scolding, calling her stupid and weak, inconsequential. Emma Jung said the following:

> What women have to overcome in relation to the animus is the lack of self-confidence and resistance of inertia. It is as if we have to lift ourselves up … up to spiritual independence. Without this sort of revolt, no matter what she has to suffer as a consequence, she will never be free of the power of the tyrant, never come to find herself.
>
> (1978, p. 23)

A form of the negative animus/male energy manifested in Darelle's self-denigration and general ignoring of herself. She denied her father's inadequacy by turning it into her inadequacy to fix it. Tortuous and powerful male voices took over inside and she disappeared. 'To discriminate between oneself and the animus, to limit its sphere of power is extraordinarily important … to free oneself from the fateful consequences of identifying with the animus and being possessed by it' (Jung, E., 1978, p. 38).

A daughter who learns to be out of touch with her body will be fearful of her heart and cut off from emotions. Darelle found it difficult to be still and was ridden with compulsive internal preoccupations. She stayed so hidden emotionally she unconsciously lived according to the masculine, the animus tyrant; little did she realize she was him, blinded by the masculine, defensive, on the alert (Shorter, 1987, p. 103). There was no inner good animus energy to help, support or balance, to differentiate the healthy from the destructive. Her behaviours ranged from withdrawal to negative thoughts and actions, emotionally harassing and destroying herself through doubt and insecurity, separating her from herself. She had little pleasure or peace. She knew she was too anxious but could not stop. The pressure mounted within; she was wound tighter and tighter. As she was so outwardly focused, she could hardly comprehend what it was to just be.

She might become like many daughters and eventually give up trying, becoming progressively alienated and lost. Idealizing the male/father, she might disown elements of her own psyche. The wounds underneath indicated a missing nourishing connection between the ego and body. Darelle ignored her body's signals, forgetting to breathe; frozen, she had no idea of her uniqueness. She was embedded in a world lacking colour or liveliness. In the meantime, she engaged in an unending war between parts of the self – a war of internalized voices, sadistic, unrelenting, often paternally based, but voices she obeyed, dominated by the negative animus.

In therapy Darelle said she wanted to be like Athena, the Greek goddess she associated with war and being strong. She said Athena did not need anyone, but she forgot Athena was always obedient and loyal to her father, Zeus, the heavy-handed, self-serving king of the Greek pantheon of gods and goddesses. Athena as the dutiful daughter did his bidding no matter what.

The father figure can turn malicious and malignant as the daughter internalizes his sadomasochistic enactments (Kavaler-Adler, 2000, p. 85). A daughter with this type of unconscious attachment to her father too easily falls into the arms of what is called a *ghostly lover*. This figure is actually a form of the negative animus, disconnected from the feminine. He seems like an ideal love but presents a romanticized version of a relationship shrouded in unreality. He is the unrelated, selfish male weaving stories about her need for him and her inadequacies. Unable to give or be present while being internally demeaning, he repeats what she thinks of herself. The ghostly lover is a man/child relying on her while she cannot rely on him. She is taken in by his occasional gestures of sweetness, but that is all he has to offer. Everything else remains distant, on hold, with no commitment, as he is not strong enough to meet her.

Dreams with the negative animus/father

The dream unfolds the hidden realms of the psyche, the not-yet-visible but valuable holder of personal issues as well as those of the collective. Dreams carry fundamental images to open the soul. They affect and guide, illustrating the steps for developing consciousness. The dream reveals the drama and experiences of the unconscious side of life, often especially impactful during times of transition. They warn us if we are going astray, encourage and provide insight. Dreams are one of the best and most natural ways for dealing with inner disconnections as they balance one-sidedness. In interpreting dreams we become not only disciplined and logical but also emotional, feeling, imaginative and sensate. Jung commented: '[T]ransformation processes announce themselves mainly in dreams' (1959, para. 235). Dreams are both subjective and objective in their symbolic language, unfolding into many more meanings than the literal ones. The dream and its symbols can be a challenge to decipher as they include thoughts and emotions, both personal and collective, historical and present day, known and unknown. This might explain why dreamwork is difficult yet stimulating and intensely gripping.

The following dream is an example of the dangers of the negative animus as it appeared at the beginning of Darelle's analysis. *A man wanted to marry me. He was Spanish and dark looking with matador clothes. He was attractive to me, but I did not want him to know that as I felt a very strong pull toward him and away from him. He attended my wedding and knew I was married but still persisted. He was rich and his family owned this huge Western town that they kept adding to so that it got larger and larger. Each time I saw him he looked more Spanish and less attractive. At one point he even got into bed with me and I was glad I had a nightgown and shirt on. I said, 'See how ugly I am with my hair a mess?' He did not seem to care.*

In the dream she feared this man, his invasiveness and advances indicating his potency. Under his influence she was drawn to a dark, compelling quality. Because Western culture is a patriarchy, a woman's experience of the masculine will not be simply the reverse of a man's experience of the feminine. For her,

> the very air she breathes, the boundaries of her consciousness, the contents of her personal unconscious psyche, and the complete cast of the collective psyche, are full of The Man: his image, his history, his definitions, his requirements, his expectations, his needs, his desires, his threats, his power, his laws, his religions, his gods, his money, and his ambivalent, unrealistic image of her.
>
> (Cowan, 2013, p. 2)

The negative animus/male/father appeared in a later dream. *I dreamt yet again and have periodically through my life about the man that has always had this strange energy – part erotic, part fear, part draw, part destruction. In this dream I am having him as a patient in therapy. I know he has killed people – like the therapist in the television series,* The Sopranos. *I am not to tell as then he will kill me. I decide to call the police and get him. I am at a seminar with my husband. The man is there but is a shape shifter, a trickster and has put on a disguise. He is now a woman, but I see in his eyes he knows I know who he is, and he knows I am going to tell. I am afraid. He sits behind me and begins to put on meat and bones to change shape. Then I am on a walkway with people. He will elude them. They are innocents. He is like the man in the movie,* Silence of the Lambs. *I wake up fearful and then think I must call 911, the police, and even if he knows, I have to turn him in and get away from this guy or else it will never end.*

The dream made clear in no uncertain terms she had to go public and get protection. She could not continue to treat him therapeutically because there would be no change. He was the bad male/animus/Mafia character who killed without compunction and in cold blood. And she now recognized he had hounded her for as long as she could remember. In a symbolic reinstatement of the absent father, the dream brought attention to her internalized destructive male forces.

The dreams, in various scenarios, expose the demons inside, preventing a daughter from succeeding, speaking in murderous self-defeating voices that she tries again and again to both face and crush. In dreams, other selves are unleashed, often different than those in our daytime awareness. This dream revealed the deadly internal figure set against Darelle. The images illustrated her self as scared, the dream male as dangerous with a consuming and death-dealing quality. The self was under threat because he was absolute evil. And he reminded her of her father. She was shocked. She deluded herself that this man, familiar in his denigrating comments, was perhaps benign or not so dangerous. He had taken up a residence of darkness in her psyche and his dire motivations were now evident.

Upon awakening from the dream, Darelle knew she could not assume she had dealt with this force inside, even though she thought keeping the daily hatred to herself made it benign. She did not previously question her hateful responses but now she recognized the man in the dream was part of her self-loathing and internal rejection. He was like red nails clawing at her from within. The father's destructiveness became the nihilistic trend aimed at her self, and she was fused with his hostility. Darelle recognized her father was the instigator ruling her life, sapping her originality, diminishing her confidence and undermining her potency. He was behind the defeat arising with each new possibility, and the answer was always no, she would not succeed. About this Emma Jung advised: 'When women succeed in maintaining themselves against the animus, instead of allowing themselves to be devoured by it, then it ceases to be only a danger and becomes a creative power' (Jung, E., 1978, p. 42).

Darelle continued to pursue therapy. Each of the dreams, although horrifying, only made her more determined. She became curious, intrigued and stronger. Her pursuit of relationship, self-esteem and self-care was not easy, but her fortitude and career bolstered her with the energy for the process.

Another example

Chanita so wanted a relationship with her father in her late twenties she went along with his proposal they have a drinking and smoking night together. She listened to him as he pontificated about everything, because she wanted to be considered special. It was only now when she was in her early fifties that the childhood of psychological, emotional, physical and sexual abuse became evident. The shock sent her reeling. Chanita had spent her life denying the severity of the childhood damage imposed by her father.

She dreamt *she went to a male hairdresser asking for a trim for her long much-loved hair. He said, 'Why not cut it short? Older women should have short hair'* – she was in her forties, *'and women who are fat'* – she was of average size – *'should also have short hair'. He kept pushing it. She stood her ground but kept arguing with him.* In discussing the dream, it came out she avoided everything, expected to be put down, even destroyed, lessened and shamed by everyone. Chanita had gradually withdrawn from the world, stepping backward into her own home, on the same street, keeping it safe. The dream strongly revealed how this internalized male figure was not listening to her. Surprisingly he spoke the same words as her mother, who predictably took the father's side. These were some of the convoluted processes halting her movement into life.

Gradually in therapy Chanita began to realize why she unquestioningly went along with awful former boyfriends, her need for their approval and how she later dropped her own career. The images of her father in a series of dreams were consistently threatening, as he grabbed at her, pulling her into his too-tight hugs. Images abounded, unrelenting in their repetition. Something was very, very wrong. Her father was not only brutal, unable to give correct love or security, but now he was psychologically internalized, preventing her movement into the world. She dreamt *she was in bed between her father and mother and then realized this was wrong and tried to get out. He began hitting her with hangers and told her to stay. She bolted upright as if to leave but could not, stuck between mother and father.* The sexual and psychological messages of the dream did not escape her but her affect when reporting the dream was dispassionate, even accepting. As the dream ended, she wondered if she had the energy to do anything else.

Eventually, this intelligent and capable woman physically collapsed. Her adaptation to decline from the world indicated a memory severed, but the wounds were in the body where the psyche also spoke. She developed severe allergies and could not go out much, could not eat much and was anxious. She trusted few people. She feared driving, anything assertive, any experiences separate from her partner or that took out of the house alone. Chanita became trapped by what she did not know yet was working in therapy to discover. The unconscious was fearful to her, as this was where she hid her father's brutality and hurt to her psyche and soul.

Slowly unfolding through many dreams, all of which showed her father as the physical and emotional abuser and her mother as colluding, what she did not want to recognize insisted on being addressed. She was molested in so many ways, harmed in living, without any shred of a decent father. He was dangerous. Period. Her father was unrestrained, uncontained, destroyed her childhood safety, and now she was unravelling the pieces to extricate herself from his stranglehold. Her apprehension of him mixed with longing for his love revealed in dream after dream illustrated how trapped she was – both by his emotional absence and by his brutalizing presence. The sweet and loving father she wanted was definitely not those things. This was a hard reality to accept and shook her to the core, yet her dreams corroborated the information. She needed to be released from the identification with the absent father to make room for the language of her real self (Shorter, 1987, p. 105).

The example of Chanita illustrates the problem when the father influence is distorted and anything good and respectful is inaccessible. Blocked identification with father and the lack of appropriate relationship creates horror and defeat. The daughter comes to see herself with shame and humiliation, and this translates into her sense of worthlessness. Symbolically, without the father figure, there is a blank space where she makes herself invisible, compliant and controlled.

The absent father and the negative animus both castrate and rob her of her strength. An anxious and narrowed self-concern keeps her absorbed with negative assessments. She is under his spell, unable to comprehend the reality of these interior places filled with chaos and confusion. She struggles to define herself personally and professionally. In the grip of the negative animus as modelled by both father and mother, this daughter has been cut away from the sweetness of life. If a daughter's identity stays caught in the blank or destructive father image, she assumes similar attitudes towards herself and others.

Awareness of even the most difficult situations helps dissolve the old psychological structures and reform them with a renewed psychological stance (Stein, 1983, p. 108). Chanita bravely faced each dream, although they shook her to the core. She kept on developing, uncovering layer after layer of what often felt like horror. Slowly new attitudes began to modernize and expand the old patterns for renewal.

The use of her psyche became more fluid and less fearful. Choices opened up gradually; we recognized each small victory as significant movement of her psyche. The many variations and connections within the personal psyche and the culture are available to use in conscious, fluid and innovative ways. Eros and psyche, masculine and feminine in their various manifestations, can then be individually lived out. Their interactions bring transformation in a changing dynamic that is not rigid or gender-based but personally shaped with a consciousness freed from restrictive paternal norms. 'Gender is not something that one is, it is something one does, an act ... a "doing" rather than a "being"' (Butler, 1990, p. 62).

References

Benjamin, J. (1988). *Bonds of Love*. New York, NY: Pantheon.
Benjamin, J. (1995). *Like Subjects, Love Objects: Essays on Recognition and Sexual Difference*. New Haven, CT: Yale University Press.
Butler, J. (1990). *Gender Trouble*. London, England: Routledge.
Carotenuto, A. (2015). *To Love, to Betray*. Asheville, NC: Chiron Publications.
Cowan, L. (2013). Dismantling the animus. *The Jung Page*. Retrieved from http://www.cgjungpage.org/learn/articles/analytical-psychology/105-dismantling-the-animus.
Hillman, J. (2005). *Senex and Puer*. Dallas, TX: Spring Publications.
Irigaray, L. (2002). *The Way of Love*. London, England: Continuum.
Jung, C.G. (1954). *The Practice of Psychotherapy*, Vol. 16. Princeton, NJ: Princeton University Press.
Jung, C.G. (1959). *The Archetypes and the Collective Unconscious*. New York, NY: Pantheon Books.
Jung, C.G. (1967). *Alchemical Studies*, Vol. 13. Princeton, NJ: Princeton University Press.
Jung, E. (1978). *Animus and Anima*. Zurich, Switzerland: Spring Publications.

Kavaler-Adler, S. (2000). *The Compulsion to Create*. New York, NY: Other Press Professional.

Kristeva, J. (2019, October 27). Towards an ethics of the feminine. [Webinar]. International Psychoanalytic Association. Retrieved from https://www.ipa.world/IPA/en/IPA1/Webinars/KRISTEVA_WEBINAR.aspx.

Leonard, L.S. (1983). *The Wounded Woman: Healing the Father/Daughter Relationship*. Boston, MA: Shambhala.

Lispector, C. (2012). *The Passion According to G.H.* New York, NY: New Directions.

Moore, T. (1987). Animus mundi, or the bull at the center of the world. *Spring Journal*, Vol. 17. 116–32.

Onians, R.B. (1973). *The Origins of European Thought: About the Mind, the Body, the Soul, Time and Fate*. Cambridge, England: University Press.

Perelberg, R. (Ed.) (2018). *The Psychic Bisexuality: A British-French Dialogue*. London, England: Routledge.

Samuels, A. (Ed.) (1985). *The Father*. New York, NY: New York University Press.

Samuels, A. (1993). *The Political Psyche*. London, England: Routledge.

Samuels, A. (1999). *Jung and the Post Jungians*. London, England: Routledge.

Samuels, A. (2016). Beyond the feminine principle: Personality, morality and the father. In: *The Plural Psyche* (pp. 92–106). London, England: Routledge.

Seligman, E. (1985). The half-alive ones. In: A. Samuels (Ed.), *The Father* (pp. 69–94). New York, NY: New York University Press.

Shorter, B. (1987). *An Image Darkly Forming*. London, England: Routledge.

Stein, M. (1983). *In Midlife: A Jungian Perspective*. Woodstock, CT: Spring Publications.

von Franz, M.-L. (1988). *The Feminine in Fairytales*. Dallas: Spring Publications.

Chapter 10

Idealization of father – a tomb of illusion

> My dreams were all my own; I accounted for them to nobody; they were my
> refuge when annoyed – my dearest pleasure when free.
>
> Mary Shelley, *Frankenstein* (1831, p. 78)

All daughters go through a stage of idealizing the father figure. This idealization
is magnified proportionally and becomes more unconscious when the father has
been absent. His absence exacerbates the idealization so much so that a daughter cannot get a sense of either of their realities. In a review of *To Dance in the
Wake*, the biography of Lucia Joyce, Hermione Lee writes, about Lucia Joyce,
the daughter of James Joyce, that 'she was analyzed by Jung, who thought her
so bound up with her father's psychic system that analysis could not be successful' (2003). By default, this daughter is shaped by the father's definition of the
female, which overrides her own ways. Stuck in an idealization, the masculine/
father remains in place and her sense of self-agency rests on shaky foundations.
Behind the idealization and dependence on males and the masculine lurk anger
and hurt, sorrow and grief from the father's desertion.

This chapter gives an example of idealization through the examination of several dreams of a woman who lacked a father for the right physical and emotional
attention. Identifying with a father who became ideal because both absent and
inappropriately close shaped her psychological situation. Her devotion to him
became the fallout from his psychological manipulation. Such difficult and trying situations paradoxically create even more idealization until understood. The
daughter's inner feelings were largely ones of absence and void, with her perceiving only the fragmentation and disintegration of the self (Kristeva, 1988, pp.
18–19). Sadness and depression provided her with a fragile defence against falling
apart whereas the heavy feelings paradoxically and tenuously held her together.

This type of father uses his position to promote the daughter's idealization
and allegiance. Her development seems a threat, as is her vitality and youth. She
cannot challenge his authority and cannot have a voice other than in deference
to him. She buys the myth of being his object of docility and allure. Her unconscious adoration and idealization make her seem innocent, younger than her years,

unwilling to challenge or rebel against the father and therefore subject to his rule. She recognizes his depression, how his face falls; she feels for him. He needs her, and she will be there, a passive daughter helplessly absorbed. The compelling power and attraction to her father as ideal leaves this daughter submissive, masochistic and flattened under his psychological constraints. Father and daughter are emotionally attached because she serves his needs. The father, by denying his daughter's essence, restricts her to a half-dead life, as she acquires self-depleting patterns and behaviours.

The idealization mixes with and produces depression, passive-aggressiveness and an attitude of waiting for life to happen. This daughter's experiences are increasingly emptied as she stands in the father's shadow. Her solution is to identify with her father, not challenge him, so he retains his desired image of grand master and she merely an extension. Encouraging her idealization, he is her teacher and mentor, the captain of the ship, a master of the currents and she must rely on his genius.

By assuming a role and fitting in, she becomes invisible to others as no one knows her real self. Despair closes in. A sense of isolation prevails, as if she stands outside herself. She is so unhappy and lonely that she cannot envision anyone wanting her. She lives a blank life, flat, without any depth, protecting her autonomy, resisting others. Although she may engage in feverish activity, she does so only to mask the ponderous depression.

When a daughter's identity is tied to idealizing her father, she may look functional but she lives below her potential. Passion is curtailed, individual thought unformed, and her life has no value. She takes refuge in aloneness to preserve the shreds of her identity. This obstructs intimacy and relationships are aborted. Even in the therapeutic situation she not only assumes she is unknown but she also does not really want or expect anything different.

The setup from childhood

Tilisha's adaptations to life began in her childhood. Her mother died when she was very young, but her father had left prior to this, never to be seen until her adulthood. Her mother's parents submerged reality by revising it. The secrets fostered in Tilisha an unconscious, seductive pull towards more secrets and duplicity. It was how she learned to exist. Secrets have profound psychological and physical effects, especially when mixed with unrequited longing. As a teenager she discovered the truth about her early life and what felt like unbelievable betrayals but told no one. At that time, she resolved to find her father.

Even as a child, the bond with him was in her mind, composed of loving images and secret yearning, all the stronger as she was told not to think of him. The wound from the absent father festered. This was fueled by the fact that he had never been present and was surrounded by a pall of silence and disapproval. His inaccessibility opened the sadness and loss in which she began to vanish. She felt a victim, a daughter without a father, and had no peace of mind. She wanted him even though the longing tied her to the emotional wounds and heartbreak.

When she became a young adult, Tilisha located him but never questioned his reasons for not contacting her through the years. She had only learned to find the father, having given up on the natural process of him finding her. This fact expresses the malignant power of the denial of love and relationship underlying the inhibited development of self-agency (Knox, 2010, p. 132). Tilisha believed his excuses for not trying to find her, believing that she would find him, interpreting this to mean he had confidence in her. For Tilisha, the years of imagining a fantasy father did not prepare her for the reality. The dreams of childhood, wrapping her in an embrace with a fairy-tale good father, led to her assumption that all she needed was his return. She never thought he would use the need against her or that the man she envisaged as god-like would instead be demon-like. Her boundaries with him were porous because of his painful absence and her longing. This left her vulnerable to his suggestions and intrusions into her personal space.

A psychological shift occurred between Tilisha and her father as he pressed a misguided, insensitive and boundaryless union onto her. This father invested his daughter with an unsuitable affective burden as though she were his love (Carotenuto, 2015, p. 45). The emotional setup that he initiated put her into a kind of perverse contract to do as he said to keep his love. She felt a destructive energy drawing her to him, but she could not resist. His absence created this concession, as she gave herself over to him so they would remain together always. She had projected her desire onto him for so very long that he became her universe and she existed only in his eyes.

The bond with him meant she had to assume his stains, however, and the shadow of the father fell on Tilisha. She did not yet realize their twisted attachment meant she could not leave him to love another. She agreed to his stories and became what he called his 'spiritual bride', a position reflecting his ideal image of himself while erasing her separate identity. She took on his issues as hers and by receiving his projections mimicked how he wanted her to be. She preserved the image he had of himself through idealizing him. This idealization was also coloured by the fact that Tilisha felt inadequate, adding to her self-doubt. He tried to control her mind, took over her body and made her keep secrets – all the while convincing her they were a special couple, invoking parallels with the ancient kings and their consorts.

For Tilisha, the enclosure with her father was better than the only alternative she knew – no father at all. She could not resist him – even though her development depended on escaping his engulfment. She felt shame for what she was doing with him mixed with how much she wanted him. She could tell no one and became more isolated. Her self became less and less defined as she melded into pleasing him. Tilisha's libido, so linked to the absent paternal image, exerted tremendous pressure. His initial abandonment led to the tight fixation, entrapment and emotional longing.

Her father combined adoring and monstrous attributes that were impossible for her to negotiate, especially because she ignored the monstrous side of the whole situation. His compelling power and profound attraction became glaring assaults on her individuality. Like a puppet, deprived of independent action, she was vulnerable and then owned, unable to separate. The more she idealized her father, the more her vitality was diminished. Yet Tilisha identified so strongly with anything positive about him that even a year into therapy she could not comprehend the ways in which her father had manipulated her.

Along these lines Andrew Samuels stated: 'The father's failure to participate in the mutual attraction and mutual, painful renunciation of erotic fulfilment with his daughter deprives her of psychological development (Samuels, 1985, p. 31). The word *erotic* here connotes attraction and energy used appropriately to ignite her passion for life and for developing her special qualities. But the absence of the father in her early development resulted in Tilisha's personality being deficient of her own authority or foundation.

After she left her father and went to live on her own in another city, Tilisha had a long-term affair with Jeff, described by her as tyrannical, at times denigrating. She could not let go of him even though he hurt her with his crass words and actions. Jeff was dictatorial, telling her how to be and what to do, and she was locked into him, much like she was with her father. During the several years that their relationship lasted, Jeff had affairs with other women. Trained to come second, Tilisha, although hurt, waited for him. She desperately needed male validation and was willing to do anything to keep it, going so far as to augment her own breasts when she discovered one of the women Jeff was dating had large breasts.

Tilisha represented a portrayal of a psychic state lonely to the bone, sensitive to rejection, often stuck in a pit of boredom, anxiety and emptiness. An ongoing sense of involvement was missing, often without her conscious awareness. She wondered whether her accomplishments were mere manipulations and whether she was fake, fooling others. Because the present was experienced as imperfect and insufficient, she would rather go home and shut the blinds. She was confronted with feelings of resignation, loss of hope and self-disinterest. The despair was simply inescapable, pervading her psychic and physical space. She felt an unsettling disjuncture between herself and others. When speaking of her life, she sounded uninvolved and her narration underscored the emptiness of her existence.

Tilisha needed Jeff's acceptance so much that within the space of a therapy session she argued with herself to justify his disgust for her, much like her childhood belief that she was not good enough for her father to call or visit. When in this mood Tilisha was convinced both her father and Jeff were blameless and kind, whereas her friendship and loyalty were merely pathetic and empty. She described feelings of self-hate appearing in the guise of an inner voice calling her a malignant and foul-smelling cancer. With the cruelty aimed inwards, Tilisha accused herself of being what she called a 'creature harming innocent people through her powers to deceive'. She assumed she must be a phony who made people love her and think she was special.

Dreams

Tilisha had difficulty recalling her dreams at first, as she felt too tired to write them down. Then, gradually catching one fragment after another, she began to access the dream world. She brought in a recurring childhood dream. *In the dream I see a figure coming towards me with a dagger on a pillow. The figure goes to the closet and then leaves.* She was frightened after the dream and hid under the covers. She said this dream was scary due to the figure's threatening intentions. It was ghost-like, as if from the underworld, and represented the dark energy surrounding her as a child but still present. Moreover, the unconscious frightened her, as demonstrated by her initial difficulty in remembering dreams and the anxiety permeating this one. She feared something awful was there, something despicable about her hiding in the shadows. The dream brought her attention to the complex personified by the unknown inner figure.

Dreams mirror psyche to reality and reality to psyche (Shorter, 1987, p. 105). They note the wounds and where they can provide passage into new psychic contents. Darkness is where we hide the things we fear, and it is also the place where things are born. The perspective of Jungian analytical psychology affirms this mode of accessing the unconscious and its symbols for union with conscious life. Dreams help liberate and clarify by exposing the complexes viewed from the perspective of the unconscious. Although dreams do not often make a direct statement, they portray information for the quest. As Jung commented: 'They do not deceive, they do not lie, they do not distort or disguise ... They are invariably seeking to express something that the ego does not know and does not understand' (1954, para. 189).

Amplifying the dream is one way to learn how the psyche works. Dreams are natural tools for expanding the personality from their unconscious underpinnings. Associations range from the personal to the impersonal, allowing the dreamer to gain the kind of understanding to include yet transcend time and place.

After a while Tilisha dreamt: *A beautiful blond is trying to steal my man. We have a friendly confrontation where I say I'm onto her tricks. Her efforts are worthless because I will either beat or unmask her.* The blond woman, according to Tilisha, represented the wish to have the same irresistible attraction to men as her mother did, especially since she was told, repeatedly, they were so very different, although they were both blond. She was told not to be like her mother who died young, was beautiful beyond compare and who had married her father. Tilisha learned early on how to be manipulative to get what she wanted and use tricks with men. The relationships she had throughout her life were not really intimate as each was governed by some deception as to who she really was. She felt both distantly inferior and superior and an object set for the image, not the reality. With each partner she felt tossed by fate, like in her early life, riddled with getting less than needed, immersed in secrets and betrayals. As the dream portrayed, it would require conscious effort for Tilisha to step into her real self.

Tilisha's psychological situation and dream paralleled the Grimm's fairy tale 'Alleruiah', noted to be the most incestuous with its overt sexual overtures of the all-powerful king/father who intends to marry his daughter. She must escape his decision. Although the kingdom disagreed, the father/king was obdurate, and it took the entire populace to assist in her escape. Only then did she begin the journey to recompose herself.

While discussing Tilisha's dream in therapy, it became clear the blond woman was an unacknowledged part of Tilisha. The dream illustrated that she wanted to be irresistible to men, yet she aligned women like this with prostitutes. Was this the image she held of her mother? Was it one of the secrets from her childhood? Tilisha actually perceived herself as a prostitute, but again rated second-best – never as good as the adulated mother/woman/feminine she wanted yet lost when she was so very young.

Tilisha's task was set out in the dream – to unmask and understand the unknown feminine/mother. Her jealousy towards the dream woman representing her mother reflected Tilisha's complex psychological bind. How could she develop connection to a mother who was dead and shrouded in secrets? If she was like her, would she also die young? If she got her father, would he leave as before? Being with him would outdo her mother but destroy her life.

Several sessions later, Tilisha brought this dream to analysis about an inner male figure named Dave. *I slept with Dave. Afterward, I look up to see Jeff lurking around the corner. Dave leaps up to defend me. Jeff stabs him quickly, efficiently. Dave and I leave. I go to the grocery store. I'm furious that Jeff found me out. Perhaps he mortally wounded my new love, listened in on my lovemaking and planned the confrontation to ruin my life. I must call the police because there are bloody messes back at my house and I will have to explain it. I will be mortified and ruined by the disclosure and devastated. He planned it so perfectly and to destroy me because I betrayed him.*

The dream was upsetting, referencing secrets, confrontations and betrayals. Several times during the dream Tilisha realized it was a dream and fought to wake up but was weighted down by the rock-heavy bedclothes. She remembered breathing hard and being scared, unsafe because Jeff seemed ubiquitous. The dream occurred during a time when she and Jeff were fighting, and as in the dream scene, she wondered what would happen if she confronted her bloodied feelings. She was afraid the dark unconscious would overpower and pull her into the underworld, imaged as an abyss so deep any insight was flimsy like a piece of tissue paper.

During the course of therapy Tilisha had few dreams about her father. He was so present in her conscious mind as well as so repressed, there was little commentary from the dream world. She gradually came to realize she could no longer maintain the attachment with Jeff or her father as she had previously. She had to give up seeking their approval, making them better than herself, taking the passive role or accepting second place. This meant developing an independent self and accessing her desires, passions and creativity rather than allowing them to go by the wayside in favour of a man.

Tilisha returned to therapy many times over the years when the old pull to death became too much. She remained in sporadic contact with Jeff who helped advance her career and gave her some financial support. She made a form of peace with her father but did not find an appropriate love relationship with him, as he could never keep boundaries. Outside of a few long-term friends, she remained sequestered within herself, and although she began to do her art, when it came to displaying it, she backed off from the old fear of being seen. She said:

> I feel the presence of my father's shadow and the recognition is a small, cold comfort, but comfort, nonetheless, because I can name it. When years ago he was unrecognized, that was the greater horror. To name it is to have some relief. In my mind I see a shrivelled and unrealized cocoon, surrounded by darkness.

We learn about ourselves by examining the damaging roles, unconscious assumptions and perceptions. We each have the personal and generational task of demystifying the father based on idealized, illusionary and wishful fantasies. Jung referred to this when he contended that nothing exerts a stronger effect on children than the unlived life of the parent. The unconscious repetition of the family pattern can be disastrous – likened to psychological 'original sin' (Jung, 1963, p. 232).

> The fact is, I was a trifle beside myself; or rather out of myself ... I was conscious that a moment's mutiny had already rendered me liable to strange penalties, and, like any other rebel slave, I felt resolved, in my desperation, to go all lengths.
>
> Charlotte Bronte, *Jane Eyre*, 1987, Chapter II

References

Bronte, C. (1897). Jane Eyre [Etext 1260]. Retrieved from https://www.gutenberg.org/file s/1260/1260-h/1260-h.htm.

Carotenuto, A. (2015). *To Love, to Betray*. Asheville, NC: Chiron Publications.

Jung, C.G. (1954). *The Development of Personality*, Vol 17. Princeton, NJ: Princeton University Press.

Jung, C.G. (1963). *Memories, Dreams, Reflections*. New York, NY: Vintage.

Jung, C.G. (1967). *Alchemical Studies*, Vol. 13. Princeton, NJ: Princeton University Press.

Knox, J. (2010). *Self-Agency in Psychotherapy*. New York, NY: W.W. Norton & Co.

Kristeva, J. (1988). *In the Beginning Was Love*. New York, NY: Columbia University Press.

Lee, H. (2003, December 28). No she said no [Review of the book *To Dance in the Wake*, by Carol Leob Shloss]. *The New York Times*. Retrieved from https://www.nytimes.com/2003/12/28/books/no-she-said-no.html.

Samuels, A. (Ed.) (1985). *The Father*. New York, NY: New York University Press.

Shelley, M. (1831). *Frankenstein, or the Modern Prometheus* [Ebook, 42324]. Retrieved from https://www.gutenberg.org/files/42324/42324-h/42324-h.htm.

Shorter, B. (1987). *An Image Darkly Forming*. London, England: Routledge.

Chapter 11

Do you want to be 'Daddy's girl'?

'The little girl found'
Rising from unrest,
The trembling woman pressed
With feet of weary woe;
She could no further go.

William Blake, *Songs of Innocence and Songs of Experience*, 1901

Each of us harbours within us a number of characters, parts of ourselves causing conflict and mental distress when not understood or used consciously. We might be relatively unacquainted with these players and their roles, and yet they are constantly seeking a stage on which to perform their tragedies and comedies both personally and collectively.

> But what if I should discover that the least amongst them all, the poorest of all beggars, the most impudent of all offenders yea the very fiend himself – that these are within me, and that I myself stand in need of the alms of my own kindness, that I myself am the enemy who must be loved – what then?
>
> (Jung, 1969, para. 520)

In Jungian parlance one of these characters is *puella,* a term referring to an archetype describing the modern daddy's girl.

Conceptually 'daddy's girl' has had relatively little attention in Jungian literature. There is so much shadow around her that the term *puella* is actually absent from Jung's *Collected Works* (noted by P. Harvey in personal communication, October 2005). Although puella has been addressed somewhat by Jungian theorists such as James Hillman and Marie-Louise von Franz, she is usually deemed the *female puer*, relegating her to the shadows and the feminine neither substantial nor significant in her own right.

Although taking different forms in each culture, the puella shares the descriptors of youth – virginal, energetic and idealistic. In Greek mythology, puella is likened to the maidens Kore and Echo. Kore as the daughter is sometimes aligned with Persephone, a daughter intimately connected with her mother, Demeter. As maiden she represents purity and innocence. And she is associated with the Greek goddess Hera, within whom existed three forms of the feminine, from maiden to fulfilled woman to woman of sorrows. Tracing these interrelations illustrates how each figure unfolds into the others with a similar patterning replicated in many other cultures. The puella, like all archetypal figures, is not singular and contains a spectrum of possibilities.

To explain the concept of the puella as maiden

> points to ... one's own origin but which is at the same time the ... count-
> less beings before and after oneself and by virtue of which the individual
> is endowed with infinity already *in the germ* ... it is a kind of immersion in
> ourselves that leads to the living germ of our wholeness.
>
> (Jung & Kerenyi, 1963, p. 8, original emphasis)

In this description puella represents the foundations and the grounding to one's self. 'Knowing and being are blended into a unity ... that indicates continuity and also an opening to enlarge and also to not fully understand' (pp. 154–55).

Puella is associated with the new moon, the slim, dawning light while emerging into the life stages represented by the moon's cycles. Also, she is aligned with the Greek goddess Artemis who was the youngest manifestation of the triple moon goddess. And she is the maiden becoming the heroine in fairy tales.

Although representing the young, her roots are deep, as the etymology of the name *puella* reminds us. For instance, Roman interpretations from the first century BCE are broader than those used today, which limit her to the eternal child, naive and immature. Then she carried the association with

> women who were thought of as disreputable; also used for young married women,
> sometimes was virgin, sexually mature, amorously regarded and then referred
> to as the sexually inexperienced maidens performing religious rites ... a word
> used to express pathos ... the standard term for a woman as a potential for love,
> engaging in sexual acts, sometimes for payment ... designating an affectionately
> regarded, erotically desired female not the wife or paid sexual partner of the male.
>
> (Hallett, 2013, pp. 203–205)

Puella symbolizes the preconscious childhood aspect of the collective unconscious. She is the child heroine with the strength to defy tradition while seeking freedom. As Jung said:

> In every adult there lurks a child – an eternal child, something that is always
> becoming, is never completed, and calls for unceasing care, attention and
> education. That is the part of the personality which wants to develop and
> become whole
>
> (Jung, 1954, para. 286).

Puella appears in the psyches of men with qualities similar to those described here. She appears in their dreams and relationships to self and others. Puella is identified as the young spirit, full of hope and ideals. Yet she can be thoughtless, with an innocence marked by a wandering nature, invention, idealism and fantasy. She aims high, will push and wonder and dream to make happen what seems impossible. Although ostensibly taking risks in what appears to be an untethered existence, she actually resists change. Her repetition of the familiar entails going from place to place and person to person. In this pattern she could remain psychologically removed and unknown, skimming the surface.

The joyous, intense energy of puella, although appealing, can also mask a fragile personality, sometimes unrealistic, brittle and easily dissembled. Self-abandonment, a cornerstone of the puella, is a barrier to individuation. She has not yet used the psychological function of reflection to ferret out her personality. Rather she flees the unconscious, hesitates and avoids. The puella is a girl, and if she remains only in that role, her conscious and unconscious cannot integrate, making it hard for her to proceed through the stages of life.

She is passionate, the spark within ignited but compromised when her creations are assessed as less than the fantasies about what they could or should be. She gets discouraged and avoids the hard work necessary to get there (von Franz, 2000, p. 30). Such attitudes reflect the psychological wounds of the puella, resulting from loss, rejection and insufficient attention, here focused on the absence of father. Without an inner anchor, she is anxious about delving within. With no father guidance for attaining maturity, her ego remains unsure of how to dignify her feelings. Significantly, the paternal way overwhelms the girl, the puella.

von Franz speaks about dropping the illusions as being difficult when a person is pushed out of childhood too soon and then crashes into reality, which is the case for the puella (2000, p. 38). She lives on the edge, superficial, removed from her nature. She seems to have a fierce independence, but it is actually a cover for the helplessness and dependency that keep her in an emotionally infantile state (Seligman, 1985, p. 82). She feels small, without enough ballast or body, and the personality can neither grow nor can she really survive. Life is like an infertile wasteland as the girl cannot give birth to herself.

It is as if she has forfeited her development to the father, and she does not yet recognize the ramifications. The puella as a daddy's girl is identified with and in thrall to the male. She wants to be most special to him, the light in his eye. Maybe she experienced some attention as a child, but it long ago disappeared so she holds on to a fantasy father. She clings to her childhood longings to believe he was good and the need to defend him and disguise the hurt from his lack of attention, presence or expressions of love.

In the role of daddy's girl she pays an exorbitant price for her dutiful and compliant accommodations. They conflict with her desires, the Eros within for creating and loving. Jung noted:

> as long as a woman is content to be a *femme à homme*, she has no feminine individuality. She is empty and merely glitters – a vessel for masculine projections. Woman as a personality, however, is a very different thing: here

illusion no longer works. So that when the question of personality arises, which is as a rule the painful fact of the second half of life, the childish form of the self disappears too.

(Jung, 1967, para. 355)

Because of the underdeveloped feminine aspects of the puella, she is left unaware of how much she repeats the father and other masculine parts personally, culturally and relationally. Idolizing the father adversely affects her confidence and promotes idealization of others as she internally cycles through inflation and deflation, inferiority and superiority.

The personal and cultural pressures that lead to her worshipping unattainable, unrealistic and inhuman youthful ideals can impatiently push her to make something happen. She is also portrayed as attractive, fascinating and innovative. Yet she feels disembodied, taken with a psychological distancing that can be disarming (Chalquist, 2009, p. 170). She relies on rituals based on the superficial such as cosmetics, body reshaping, shopping and other compulsive thoughts and behaviours. She does not deeply partake, be it food, love, emotion or anything to do with life because the basic instincts to body and psyche remain static. In a state of perpetual youth, not only is this false but also a stable sense of personal identity is hard to attain (Sherwood, 1994, p. 55).

The puella personality is prominent in Western youth-oriented cultures. She embodies a veneration of the adolescent qualities, the perpetuation of youth and denial of aging. The pressure to live 'as if', bolstered by persona adaptation belies her felt emptiness and does not address the narcissistic wounds. Attachment problems, divorce from the body, a distorted and split self-image and difficulty with intimacy and commitment are some of the hallmarks of this personality. There is a fear of being pinned down, of entering space and time completely.

The puella represents one end of an archetypal spectrum where the person cannot ground themselves into life or face reality. The entire spectrum includes the tension of opposites and, as such, becomes the structural precondition for change. But the puella can turn into a tragedy of changelessness, stuck and unmovable, limiting advancement from here to there, from past to future. Split from her roots, she experiences arrested development as the eternal child. The puella has difficulty recognizing when stasis and perfection abound.

Patience to move methodically, to listen to the world quietly, to engage with reverie, to contemplate the silence and the self are foreign. The redemption of the puella in the personality calls for reflection, a new spirit to recover from its wounds to release joy, play and spontaneity in living. The luxury of relaxing into just being is not easy for the puella, as she requires much stimulation and challenge. To avoid the underlying emptiness and the narcissistic wounds focus remains on the façade, the past, yet to be developed, the future with its flight from the present and disconnection from the physical. The puella character is not easy to pin down because elusiveness is reinforced as part of her charm. She attempts to evoke the illusion of unity.

Her romanticized ideals lauding youth make time a nonissue because it is unreal. Taking time is a precondition for reflection and change; however, our technological world can reflect a lack of balance with its roots in avoidance of the real (Gosling, 2009, p. 148). These attitudes are challenged by aging, the realization of time passing and the pressure of what remains undone. Life changes startle the puella. As a child, inhabiting one side of the spectrum, the puella cannot tolerate the beauty in ageing, leaving no space for maturing or adapting with flexibility. The negation of ageing signifies a denial of death and resistance to life. Sadly, puella women age without compassion or grace and with much sorrow. Age impatiently presents itself to her like a disaster, not a celebration. She stares in disbelief at what she considers cruel mirrors signalling loss and estrangement. Many women are still looking in these mirrors demanding impossible perfection, leaving them disillusioned and disappointed. Either existence becomes a continual search or she spends her life waiting for the moment, not yet here, when real life will begin.

Puella also represents new psychic contents arising from the unconscious into conscious life and the release from rote fixations and complexes. This process occurs not only through the mind or intellect but also from listening interiorly. The problem is that the sensitivity exists but not the internal psychology, because that is slow to develop. Then, quite suddenly, the meaning of it all becomes dust (Hillman, 1989, pp. 25–26). Because turning inwards takes time, she turns outwards. Impatient, she lives an ethereal existence, perpetually moving and striving for immediate satisfaction or achievement. The inner drive comes not only from the 'oral hunger and omnipotent fantasies but also from the frustration that the world can never satisfy' (Hillman, 1989, p. 26).

A hallmark of puella is the provisional life; she's always ready to leave, anticipating the future. She thinks about the pounds she wants to lose, the book she wants to write, or the picture she's going to paint or the garden she'll plant. She will do these things when ready, but too often it is tomorrow when she will be better prepared, not today. The focus on possibilities and perfection can turn each life into moments to be gotten through but without much pleasure or presence.

There is also the complication of boredom. The puella is impatient, demands everything now; time drags. What to do? But boredom, as von Franz noted, is the feeling of not being in life (2000, p. 66). The puella does not get into reality as she considers it too mundane and too much work. Nor does she know how to access the inner resources needed for personal fulfilment. The puella often does not bloom until midlife or later, as she does not realize until then she has value.

Persona

The puella relies on the persona. In Jungian psychology the persona is the face turned to the world as either a true reflection of the personality or an adaptation at the sacrifice of the real person. For the puella the persona is often denoted as superficial, focused on fitting in with others.

The word *persona* derives from the huge masks behind which actors spoke in ancient Greek plays. Psychologically, puella wears a mask to hide the real behind layers of actions and images to garner approval and success. Analytical psychologist James Hillman described this type of person as unable to find a sense of belonging, their place in the world, or the right niche, feeling precarious, lacking internal solidity (1989, p. 25). There is an insistent and often frantic emphasis on the persona and ego as if these superficial aspects will compensate for perceived lack, self-doubt and unease. Overidentification with the persona can become constrictive, one-sided and suffocating. As Jung said:

> The persona is a complicated system of relations between the individual consciousness and society, fittingly enough a kind of mask, designed on the one hand to make a definite impression upon others, and, on the other, to conceal the true nature of the individual.

> (1966, para. 305)

The puella personality can be further defined as the woman who is fascinating, has a free and child-like vitality, lights up a room and performs for the adulation of others. The persona that the puella wears is part of her unusual charm as she stands out and innovates. She seems made of ivory – beautiful, unblemished and complex. Her carefully manicured and controlled social self reflects strictly internalized standards for achievement and adulation. She does not like being restrained, enslaved to outer rules or convention or stopped short in any way, mostly by reality. In her flights of grandiosity she lives in an enchanting and paradisiacal world where she will be treated as a princess, adored and above it all.

Combined with this, as von Franz noted, this person is caught in a 'childish state of constant dissatisfaction with themselves and the whole of reality' (2000, p. 87). Although often highly creative, the puella can be deficient in her interior support system, and, without confidence, she is run by a hungry, empty self with little enjoyment. As Adam Phillips notes:

> Our passionate selves are our best selves: and a passionate life is only possible, by definition, if we can make our passions known: to ourselves … There can be no passion … – without representation. … Passion entails circulation and exchange.

> (1999, p. 166)

Shadow

Inordinate identification with the persona signals susceptibility to shadow formation, suggesting a significant part of the personality lies below the surface.

The shadow represents a coming to earth that is necessary for actualizing creativity and life (von Franz, 2000, p. 128). And the discomfiting but necessary awareness of the shadow implies individuation unfolding. The shadow can produce chaos and melancholy and feel like the darkest time. It means facing oneself without cover and accepting the imperfect. Acknowledging these personality parts is required for self-fruition whereas subverting the shadow can halt creativity and expressiveness. However, the puella tries to escape the shadow aspects and emotions that take her inwards. But when the potentiality of the psyche is not used, it becomes perverted (Leonard, 1983, p. 89). When wrapped in denial, the puella is obstructed from accessing her natural aggression and desires – two components necessary for self-knowledge and development of talent and intimacy.

The shadow exerts itself in the puella woman who looks the part and, according to others, functions outstandingly. Yet she often feels nothing is meaningful, and without meaning life is reduced to nothing (von Franz, 2000, p. 148). The antidote requires descending into the shadows and abandoning the false self for the real, something difficult for the puella type. The shadowy recesses reveal the parts calling for recognition, addressing her yearning and melancholy. 'Closer examination of the dark characteristics – that is, the inferiorities constituting the shadow – reveals that they have an *emotional* nature, a kind of autonomy, and accordingly an obsessive, or, better, possessive quality' (Campbell, 1971, p. 145, original emphasis).

So involved in her own strivings, the puella does not see anyone else even as she needs their approval, quite desperately. She has trouble giving genuinely and emotionally or responding flexibly and adaptively to another's behaviour. Her wandering nature seemingly denies the need for attachments, as life with others provokes anxiety. To hide this internal state, she attaches through insisting on sameness, a fusion without differences. Relationship means taking the other in, being seen and vulnerable, but for her this can be overlaid with shame (Rosenfeld, 1987, p. 274). Her shame might come from having needs, desiring love and closeness.

In defence against exposing herself, she may present a rude or cold and harsh façade; she avoids reciprocity in relationships. Behind the mask to please, howls a vortex of self-doubt. Without an acceptable image of herself, she feels she has nothing worthwhile to offer. She remains wounded, a child fenced off from others. She is curbed by the attitude she must not threaten or surpass anyone, as she does not want to be hated or excluded. Jung commented: '[Some are] overflowing with feelings of their own importance ... others ... give up all sense of responsibility, overcome by a sense of ... powerlessness' (Jung, 1966, para. 222). Although desiring closeness, she is a performer, assuming she must always be 'on'.

She feels unreal, and even though she may look the part, she does not know how to be a woman. The puella is the woman who struggles to feel confident in her body, to be constructive with her energy and to manifest strength. The puella problem is a rejection of the instinctual and a disconnection from the physical – a lack of feeling and self-compassion and an inner coldness. This is part of the absent father experience. The puella lives on uneasy foundations and no matter how her life looks from the outside, inside she is unsure of her stance or solidity.

Case example

Zoe called herself a daddy's girl. But what did this mean? She had no answer. In therapy, after recounting her mother's shortcomings and how she found women inferior, she described her father as flawless. This father was apparently so good that Zoe wanted to exist solely in his enveloping presence. The more she identified with her father and the male way the more difficulty she had establishing a separate identity (Murdock, 2005, p. xiii). 'Love is a profound attachment to another separate life, as a center of movement and choice, not being engulfed or fused' (Nussbaum, 1994, p. 91). And she insisted on disavowing the mother and anything maternal.

She adored her father and his voice reverberated in her head, insisting she do life his way. She wanted to be approved of by him, or even to be him (Murdock, 2005, p. 5). He was the authority, not her. She could not leave the identification with him, could not separate from being only a daughter, which limited other aspects of her personality. Father took up so much space in her mind she hardly existed. A daughter who senses that the father cannot tolerate any psychological separateness will attempt to create a state of mental fusion, a projective identification as a means of communication (Knox, 2003, p. 141).

She tried to please him as the adored darling. She remained in service to the masculine, and whether these figures were inner or outer, she operated as if she was less than. The split from her roots resulted in arrested development, an attitude that rejected the instinctual, the physical and the earth. She felt like a ghost, unseen, without substance.

In analysis, Zoe had a habit of rubbing her eyes and pushing the hair from her face. She had a vague dreamy look. Self-described as 'half-baked', her actions seemed like an attempt to clear a psychological fog or banish a spell. An internalized phantom father based on the absolute marvel of her own father reigned supreme and ruled her psyche; she was absent to herself (Murdock, 2005, p. 119). In each area of her life Zoe had let her father dictate what she should do as her independency and passions remained unformed.

Zoe was in her mid-thirties, married, but dismayed at how it was turning out. She was deeply unhappy and could hardly fend off the drag of impotence. She knew something was wrong, yet she strongly believed the inner negative voices that drained her and sapped her confidence. She was obsessed with her looks and the passing of time, panicked, convinced she should not be as she was yet not knowing how to be otherwise. She had a persistent feeling her life was a dream;

she didn't know how any of it had happened. Had she been numb all these years? What had she missed? She was shocked at contemplating these realizations.

Although an accomplished violinist, Zoe had let her career lapse in deference to her musician husband. She explained he played a 'feminine' instrument and she a 'masculine' one. He was employed but she was not, and without performing on stage, she felt her spark disappearing. Inhibiting tendencies had taken over, dissolving her desire, and she felt nothing without performing. A series of her dreams, with their symbols and images, were compensatory to the denied talents she could no longer neglect. These dream images appeared to loosen the psychological constrictions.

She dreamt: *I am looking at houses. There is a big house that is mine. My husband takes me into a room with a high ceiling, a piano and a beautiful rose-coloured tapestry. I notice there is one small seam in the tapestry that is undone.* As Zoe talked about the dream, she focused anxiously on the small tear, saying it represented the perfection she could not attain. Zoe assumed the dream husband was accusing her of imperfections by showing her the marred tapestry. Actually, her reaction illustrated the state of her inner world populated by criticism and flaws. It also replicated her husband's daily irritating interruptions whenever she was practicing. The house in the dream, appearing like a castle with the grandeur of high ceilings, piano and tapestry, symbolized the immensity and beauty of Zoe's self, but much was vacant and uninhabited. Zoe focused on the small rip in the tapestry, signifying the insufficient or damaged pieces of her personality. Although the rose colour in the tapestry could stand for passion, beauty, love and the feminine, her obsession on the flaw blinded her to the use of these qualities. The tapestry was also analogous to the process of therapy, as it takes time to bring the life strands together, including those in need of repair.

Zoe recounted a party after a musical performance, frantically escaping to the bathroom, sitting on the floor crying, hating herself for what she considered her poor performance, not knowing what to say or how to act with others. This behaviour was based on her felt sense of shame for not being perfect enough, and it usually followed anything good, destroying the beauty of an occasion that should be a celebration.

Along a similar theme and a bit later, Zoe dreamt: *I have a silk bag. I want to show my mother who will appreciate its value. But because my father is present, my mother will not approve.* The dream portrayed Zoe's father interfering in the relationship with her mother and gave a different perspective on the relationship than Zoe originally presented. It repeated the relationship she had developed with her husband extant within, as she diminished herself and he took precedence. She agreed to this arrangement; but why?

The problems began in childhood when Zoe recoiled from her mother's criticism, feeling nothing she did was good enough. Mother was associated with harsh edges and unempathetic responses, and Zoe turned from the maternal with disdain and disregard. The dream pictured Zoe seeking approval and closeness from her mother, yet the triangulation and loyalty to her father got in the way. In her loyalty to the father and alienation from her mother, she developed ambivalence about love and intimate relationships. She could not be angry with her father because with him she did not have to grow up, or so she thought. All the anger transferred to mother, but at the same time looped back to Zoe. According to Verena Kast, Swiss Jungian analyst, those daughters who are controlled and guided by a father need the admiration of men to maintain self-esteem as they are easily steered off course (1997, p. 113).

In further associating to the dream Zoe explained the silk bag was a container of small items, designed in a style that would appeal to her mother. She commented that she knew silk was made through a time-consuming and expensive process and, in this way, was similar to the tapestry in the earlier dream. Both are processes typically associated with the feminine and creativity as well as metaphors for the interweaving process of therapy. Historically these processes are passed from mother to daughter. They appeared in the dreams to compensate for what Zoe was not yet able to access.

Zoe wistfully spoke about her father's protection and his all-encompassing love. She said he was different from her cold mother who was the problem and the reason Zoe derided the maternal. She sarcastically joked hers was a typical Oedipal family – she emotionally aligned with her father and her brother with her mother. She liked being preferred by her father and having his attention rather than him giving it to the mother. The joke was no doubt a defence to hide her anxiety about the sexual implications and the psychologically incestuous feelings revealed in the dream and in the family. She did not see the disaster in the joke and what she sacrificed to remain attached to her father – to do so meant betraying herself to stay 'Daddy's girl'. Because she could not cope with the power of mother and her threat as the other female, she avoided the whole situation by leaning into the father (Perelberg, 2018, p. 45).

She could not bear to grow away from her father or disappoint him, so at a quite young age she secretly decided to negate her sexuality. Little did she realize this would affect her ability to leave the paternal way, detach from the ostensibly loving father and love anyone else. Father power as conveyed through his overwhelming presence kept her dependent on him. Zoe had a dream that spoke to the ramifications of the decision to remain loyal to her father and what she perceived as his need for her to stay young and psychologically attached. *A woman is going to commit suicide in a rubbish bin because she needs to be right for once. The importance of being right equals her very life.* The dream figure, the rubbish (her dream said trash so will you change it back?) and the rubbish bin all symbolize the shadow, the desire to be seen, heard and acknowledged, but all are thrown way. The dream showed how little empathy Zoe had for the self she assessed as rubbish. To survive and thrive, she would have to recognize the unconscious agreement made with this father, redeem her identity and reclaim what she had given over to him. All these tasks remained unknown at the time but were aspects of why she entered therapy.

Until this dream Zoe did not take seriously the extent of her denied self-interest, including the denigrated relationship to her body. Zoe admitted she felt a disturbing shock each time she realized this body was indeed hers. Life had been narrowed into the number of calories she consumed, how her skin looked, her inner rules tightly and unconsciously binding her to the patriarchal tradition and to her desire for perfection. Zoe remained at a remove from herself and described feeling like a mannequin. She constructed a false body-self, an illusionary perfect body and clung to this obsessively and desperately to keep the deadening sensations at bay. She made sure her body was hidden because she said her breasts sagged and her hips had cellulite, and yet she was secretly sexual. Zoe avoided being naked with her husband and physical displays, like emotional exposure, threatened her fragile makeup. She was so disconnected from her body that even when having sex, she thought about how much she weighed. This separation from body meant she was not present to the most basic experiences of life.

For Zoe, the daughter–father union grew as a result of the missed attachment with mother, but the intimacy with father excluded mother and set up more internal conflict. This created a sterile male attitude within Zoe combined with negating mother images. Her feminine side remained undeveloped and the father took on an almost archetypal significance and a fascinating influence (Adler, 1961, p. 114). Remaining with father interfered in her development. This father, although seemingly involved, was unable to engage with her at the correct level of erotic playback (Samuels, 1985, p. 31). Instead, Zoe developed as outwardly compliant, childlike and submissive. And she denied her energy and talent.

Zoe had a dream that had reoccurred throughout her life, but she had been unable to grasp it before, although she knew it was important. *I am about ten years old and am with a girlfriend playing music in the hall of our apartment. My mother is in a white diaphanous dress but is really a witch blocking the way out. We have to leave and go downstairs to the car in order to get out. My father is in the next room and not helping me. I fear my mother is the witch who will not let me out of the house in time.* Zoe wistfully commented:

> I remember playing and performing for my father because he loved it and encouraged me. We had a special relationship. I felt unsafe with my mother when he was gone. As a child I worried he would die, as he was the one I depended on. Yet I also suspected that he would, in the end, side with my mother against me. Now I wonder even more who will protect me.

Immediately Zoe associated the witch-mother in the dream to her mother. Although difficult to admit, she realized she had the same negative, demanding and denigrating attitudes, the very characteristics she abhorred in her mother. After the dream, Zoe expressed surprise and relief they had something in common. The identification is what she desired but could not previously accept.

Although Zoe loved performing, it was not for her mother, anticipating her biting criticism or that she would be told she was self-centred. On the other hand, the predictable praise from her father kept her wrapped in his soft circle. She learned to be protected by her father, not by herself, at the cost of remaining undeveloped.

The dream dynamics indicated the problems that prevented her from leaving home, the psychological betrayal by her father bringing into question their unconscious bond. His lack of support, which was repeated in both dreams, forced Zoe to remove the veils of illusion about their triangle.

After what seemed to Zoe a long time in therapy, she began using her musical talents again. A dream came when she was contemplating a job audition and felt ready to succeed in her career. To her amazement *in the dream a conductor repeated the phrase from the first dream she brought to psychotherapy many months previously.* In that initial dream the conductor said: *Your playing is special and from the heart, but your technique is sometimes lacking.* Zoe explained that for her the masculine, or the technique, was associated with the instrument she played and the feminine, or the heart, with the one her husband played. This meant she was now using the feminine to her advantage, whereas the masculine needed more attention. Zoe, stunned at the synchronicity of the dream with life, was, in fact, offered the musical position and accepted it. She was coming to realize she was equipped with the right instrument and with the ability to play.

The virgin girl

Never able to be young enough, thin enough, smart enough, the puella is caught by pressures promoting the unattainable. Metaphorically, the puella falls into the problem by keeping her makeup on, remaining superficial and impenetrable. Her nature has a virginal quality, representing a deep interiority and freedom from external contamination – an intactness of the psyche that protects what is immature and unripe (Hillman, 1989, p. 190). On the one hand, this quality could support the solitude necessary for self-growth and creative reflection. On the other, although open, radical and often outside the social norm, she can be enclosed within, leaving little room for engagement outside herself. This side of it indicates narcissism in the sense that her singularity lets in nothing and no one.

The puella woman feels undeserving of love and that it is not safe to trust those who offer love. After all, love can be painful, as it means entering into the heart of her wounds. So she stops, refusing to live through these experiences to the instinctual level (von Franz, 2000, p. 39). She always has an excuse when each situation is for the short term and relationships are met with similar noncommittal modes. It is no surprise the puella type feels inner emptiness, adding to her outer cravings for acceptance and adoration.

The puella is driven by the desire to be seen, to be the best and most loved. Her fantasy is of one day making it and becoming someone, yet at the same time she cannot get there if she flees the present (Hillman, 1989, p. 29). At her core she stops, fades before the fruit ripens, becoming only possibility, unable to carry through to the end. She exudes brittleness, an aura of aloofness and stiff veneer behind which she exists in a lofty and untouchable domain where the world is observed. But she lives in a bubble, not knowing how unaware she remains.

The puella's wounds are caused by early losses, rejections and an insufficient holding environment, in part associated with an absent or overarching father, leaving behind the feeling of insufficiency. The emotional arrest keeps her behind glass, removed. She lives tragically within her walls for protection. She sidesteps the dark aspects of the self, which threaten her fragile sense of identity (Schwartz-Salant, 1982, p. 22).

The puella is a stage in the development of the feminine, but when this is as far as it goes, a woman is working against accessing her complete self. She is an aspect of the psyche that needs love and attention yet engages in deception of self and others by putting on a performance and acting 'as if' (Solomon, 2004, p. 639). For instance, a woman says she wants to be the 'empress of the world'. This phrase expresses an aloofness, the need to remain untouchable to avoid hurt. Her lack of connectedness, her coldness and guardedness distances her from others and, although off-putting, comes from a sense of fragility. The denial of need for others often is misinterpreted as self-adoration.

At the same time, the puella represents the instinctive, preconscious, original, potentially redemptive and future promise (Gosling, 2009, p. 147). Judged on outer appearances, those identified with the puella are often regarded as successful performers and high achievers while their inner life remains hidden, its tumult often split from awareness. When preserved in a state of suspended animation, the puella cannot be present. The self-denial renounces identity, eating her up from within and cutting off her spirit from its innermost recesses. She engages in an unending war between the internal voices, sadistic, demanding, wanting and needing. The negative side is an arrogance, insistence on false fronts and a clinging to façade, retaining a black-and-white attitude, not only rebellious but also static in remaining young (p. 139).

Operating in the tradition of feminine passivity, many women stay dependent, immature and unaware, not knowing what they want or do not want and unable to express themselves. Many women remark about these inner forces replicating the sexual stereotypes, the social and family cultural pressures. Here are some of the voices interceding in the psyche of puella: 'I do not like the physical reality of getting older with my dry and wrinkly skin'; 'I hate what I see in the mirror'; 'I cannot accept the fact that I am who I am'; 'My work is not good enough'; 'I do not remember what I did, felt or thought yesterday'. Even though it hurts, she returns to these denigrating self-images day after day. In relation to this, Jung commented:

Whoever looks into the mirror of the water will see first of all his own face. Whoever goes to himself risks a confrontation with himself. The mirror does not flatter, it faithfully shows whatever looks into it; namely, the face we never show to the world because we cover it with the *persona*, the mask of the actor. But the mirror lies behind the mask and shows the true face.

(1959, para. 43)

For years she hardly notices who or what she is, preoccupied, floating through life with her head in the clouds. In viewing herself she selects a part, the effect or an image set for the occasion. Even sex can be a performance for approval, rather than a way to express and receive love. A punishing core of 'I am not enough' creates an ever-present tension, negating any pleasure in both mental and physical activities. In lacking a capacity for realistic self-reflection, adulthood is avoided, the ego narrowly narcissistic and the self hindered from individuating.

The puella represents a type of personality reflecting the current era. She does not breathe deeply and fears being touched emotionally; the lack of attention to her depth is a defence. The task of the puella is to be present, which is no small task. She can no longer simply rely on outer adulation or putting on masks, but is called to access the spark within, according to her own particular, real rather than ideal, standards.

Quite a bit later in therapy Zoe dreamt *she was alone onstage asking, 'What will happen next?'* The dream reflected the analytical process, recounting the memories and unravelling of old patterns to extend the capacity to think, feel and explore. By constructing something other than what was known, personally and collectively, she could become whole in the areas that were fallow, vacated by her father's lack of correct presence. By resolving these dilemmas, the father no longer blocked the way. She found her sources of strength and inspiration, free from enclosure with him and into herself. 'Woman … today … gives expression to … the urge to live a completer life, a longing for meaning and fulfillment, a growing disgust with senseless one-sidedness, with unconscious instinctuality and blind contingency' (Jung, 1970, para. 269).

References

Adler, G. (1961). *The Living Symbol*. London, England: Routledge & Kegan Paul.

Blake, W. (1901). The little girl lost. In: *Songs of Innocence and Songs of Experience* [Etext 1934]. Retrieved from https://www.gutenberg.org/files/1934/1934-h/1934-h .htm#page42.

Campbell, J. (1971). *The Portable Jung*. New York, NY: Penguin Books.

Chalquist, C. (2009). Insanity by the numbers, knowings from the ground. In: S. Porterfield, K. Polette & T.F. Baumlin (Eds.), *Perpetual Adolescence* (pp. 169–86). Albany: State University of New York Press.

Gosling, J. (2009). 'Protracted Adolescence': Reflections on forces informing the American collective. In: S. Porterfield, K. Polette & T.F. Baumlin (Eds.), *Perpetual Adolescence* (pp. 137–54). Albany: State University of New York Press.

Hallett, J. (2013). Intersections of gender and genre: Sexualizing the *Puella* in Roman comedy, lyric and elegy. *EuGeStA* - n°3. Retrieved from https://pdfs.semanticscholar.o rg/4762/6944ce031fa0d2326dda3ef2be626f19674e.pdf.

Hillman, J. (1989). *Puer Papers*. Dallas, TX: Spring Publications.

Jung, C.G. (1954). *The Development of Personality*, Vol. 17. Princeton, NJ: Princeton University Press.

Jung, C.G. (1959). *The Archetypes and the Collective Unconscious*. New York, NY: Pantheon Books.

Jung, C.G. (1966). *Two Essays on Analytical Psychology*, Vol. 7. New York, NY: Pantheon Books.

Jung, C.G. (1967). *Alchemical Studies*, Vol. 13. Princeton, NJ: Princeton University Press.

Jung, C.G. (1969). *Psychology and Religion*, Vol. 11. New York, NY: Pantheon Books.

Jung, C.G. (1970). *Civilization in Transition*, Vol. 10. Princeton, NJ: Princeton University Press.

Jung, C.G. & Kerenyi, C. (1963). *Essays on a Science of Mythology*. New York, NY: Harper & Row.

Kast, V. (1997). *Father, Daughter, Mother, Son*. Zurich, Switzerland: Element Books.

Knox, J. (2003). *Archetype, Attachment, Analysis*. London, England: Routledge.

Leonard, L.S. (1983). *The Wounded Woman: Healing the Father/Daughter Relationship*. Boston, MA: Shambhala.

Murdock, M. (2005). *Father's Daughters: Breaking the Ties That Bind*. Dallas: Spring Publications.

Nussbaum, M. (1994). *The Therapy of Desire: Theory and Practice in Hellenistic Ethics*. Princeton, NJ: Princeton University Press.

Perelberg, R. (Ed.) (2018). *The Psychic Bisexuality: A British-French Dialogue*. London, England: Routledge.

Phillips, A. (1999). Taking aims: André Green and the pragmatics of passion. In: G. Kohon (Ed.), *The Dead Mother: The Work of André Green* (pp. 165–74). London, England: Routledge.

Rosenfeld, H. (1987). *Impasse and Interpretation*. London, England: Tavistock.

Samuels, A. (Ed.), (1985). *The Father*. New York, NY: New York University Press.

Schwartz-Salant, N. (1982). *On Narcissism*. Toronto, Canada: Inner City Books.

Seligman, E. (1985). The half-alive ones. In: A. Samuels (Ed.), *The Father* (pp. 69–94). New York, NY: New York University Press.

Sherwood, V. (1994). *Psychotherapy of the Quiet Borderline Patient: The As-If Personality Revisited*. Lanham, MD: Jason Aronson.

Solomon, H. (2004). Self creation and the limitless void of dissociation: The 'as if' personality. *Journal of Analytical Psychology*, *49*(5): 635–56.

von Franz, M.-L. (2000). *The Problem of the Puer Aeternus*. Toronto, Canada: Inner City Books.

Chapter 12

Behind the mask and the glitter – a narcissistic response

> It is not that we have so little time but that we lose so much. ... The life we receive is not short but we make it so; we are not ill provided but use what we have wastefully.
>
> Lucius Annaeus Seneca, *On the Shortness of Life* (1.i)

The modern prevalence of narcissism illustrates how difficult it is to discover oneself in Western culture (Jacoby, 2016, p. 27). Narcissism includes the problem of impenetrability and distancing from self and others with personal and cultural effects. This chapter addresses the paternal absence exacerbating these issues. Narcissism has to do, not with self-love, but self-hate (Schwartz-Salant, 1982, p. 24). This chapter explores it from the viewpoint of Jungian psychology along with several other psychoanalytic perspectives. Narcissism includes envy, entitlement and betrayal, anger and weighty internal disappointments. The loss of self prevails.

In Ovid's story of Narcissus, Cephissus, the river-god, forces the gorgeous nymph Liriope into coitus under the waves. She gets pregnant by him and gives birth to a beautiful child that she names Narcissus. 'Being consulted concerning him, whether he was destined to see the distant season of mature old age; the prophet, expounding destiny, said, "If he never recognizes himself"' (Ovid, 1893, Book III, 342–71).

The Greek myth of Narcissus illustrates the love of his reflection, a fascination leading to his death. Transfixed, Narcissus cannot take in anyone or anything separate from himself (Jacoby, 2016, p. 21). So absorbed in his surface image, he is unable to access his inner world. Even when he realizes his beloved is none other than himself, this form of self can only tolerate replication with an identical other (Jacoby, 2016, p. 22). *Narcissism* seeks mirroring in sameness and singularity while avoiding difference, which is challenging to the fragile ego of the narcissist.

Love is transformative. Yet the narcissist who does not easily adapt to change or difference fears transformation. Anything touching on the area of love and relationship forces the narcissist's unknown and avoided issues to become apparent. The search for love borders on the edge between a precipice into which one might fall and a dark cave from which one might emerge.

In the myth, Echo, who by gender is not the same as Narcissus, wants to be with him, but he refuses her along with any others, either male or female. In the tale and its interpretations Echo recedes out of sight while Narcissus gathers attention. A forgotten figure, Echo also feels the pangs of longing for the other she cannot have. As the myth unfolds, both lose their bodies and remain separate from each other and from anyone else. Narcissus only belongs to his image and can be with no other. Echo desires to be only with the one who refuses her.

Becoming whole complex human beings, according to Jungian analytical psychology, means accepting the different, unknown shadows beyond the surface presentation. Narcissism connotes an isolated place of interior aloneness as the narcissist neither sees nor acknowledges the existence of the other or their own depths. To comprehend the psychological, we must explore differences, the lack of belonging, loneliness and our sense of isolation (Singer & Kimbles, 2004, p. 125). The narcissist is self-absorbed but without connection, and the foundations of the self remain unknown.

Like today's diagnosed narcissist, in the myth Narcissus sees an idealized likeness, one without warts and blemishes. Yet he is unaware of himself as the source of his reflection. There is failure in the self-experience and inadequate access to inner resources. Underneath there rumbles the restless, dissatisfied yearning while Narcissus's self-identity is inflated, unrealistic, incomplete, refusing relatedness to any other. 'Depression is the hidden face of Narcissus, the face that is to bear him away into death, but of which he is unaware while he admires himself in a mirage' (Kristeva, 1992, p. 5).

Developing a perfected and idealized surface or persona hides the fissures underneath. A central question is: Can the narcissist learn to engage with the other? 'Relationship to the self is at once relationship to our fellow man, and no one can be related to the latter until he is related to himself' (Jung, 1966, para. 445). Narcissism is a portrayal of a psychic state of oneness. This mirror reflects the singular rather than the multiple subjectivities of the world and its complexities as all narrows to eliminate otherness.

The myth continues.

> He knows not what he sees, but what he sees, by it is he inflamed; and the same mistake that deceives his eyes, provokes them. Why, credulous youth, dost thou vainly catch at the flying image? What thou art seeking is nowhere . . .
>
> (Ovid, 1893, Book III, lines 420–50)

Like Narcissus, who apparently had no contact with his father, the failure of a daughter to recognize herself is, in part, due to paternal absence. A father's emotional distance forms a vacuum. When a daughter feels unlovable, she becomes alienated from herself, which escalates into various forms of psychological and physical numbing. When alienated from a father, she may become alienated from others. The narcissistic search for the ideal rather than the real is fuelled by the frantic inability to be present. Narcissism is characterized by possessiveness, the drive to prestige, discontent, a sense of being trapped, envy and difficulty accepting average and natural limitations (Jacoby, 2016, p. 26).

There are many reasons narcissists have challenges in love and difficulty in relationships, including with themselves. Underneath is tenderness so raw it does not trust opening to any other. The superficial and illusionary is part of the avoidance of being seen. The overriding question within the narcissistic personality is: If I am not exceptional, what am I? This person circles around but does not get into intimacy, feelings or emotions of love, appearing as a distant, shiny and idealized object.

In the myth, Echo,

> rushing from the woods, is going to throw her arms around the neck she has so longed for. He flies; and as he flies, he exclaims, 'Remove thy hands from thus embracing me; I will die first, before thou shalt have the enjoyment of me'. She answers nothing but 'Have the enjoyment of me'. Thus rejected, she hides her blushing face with green leaves, and from that time lives in lonely caves; but yet her love remains, and increases from the mortification of her refusal. Watchful cares waste away her miserable body; leanness shrivels her skin, and all the juices of her body fly off in air ... they say that her bones received the form of stones. ... It is her voice alone which remains alive in her.
>
> (Ovid, 1893, Book III, lines 385–401)

Narcissism has been described as a grandiose sense of self, as exhibitionism with disturbed object-relationships as predominant symptoms. Behind the seeming omnipotence lies impotence, pessimism and resignation of failure (Jacoby, 2016, p. 85). Although healthy narcissism can contain self-esteem and a good and loving feeling towards oneself, it becomes disturbed when fraught with inferiority, fear of vulnerability and self-deprecation. These issues cause the narcissist to recoil from others when there is the least sign of critique or perceived unacceptability. The narcissistic personality is precarious, and plummets from grandiose to absolute worthlessness, oscillating wildly between these extremes (p. 83).

British psychoanalyst Herbert Rosenfeld contended that one type of narcissism was what he called 'thick-skinned' and insensitive to deeper feelings while the 'thin-skinned' type was hypersensitive and easily hurt by the smallest slight (Rosenfeld, 1987, p. 274). He further went on to attest that each contained the other. In other words, both types of narcissist have difficulty letting others in. The problem is finding the real person within the web of the image.

Further, narcissism is marked by difficulty establishing an integrated sense of 'I'. André Green also described two attitudes applicable to the absent father and what is passed on to his daughter. He called one type 'death narcissism', or the person experiencing void, emptiness, self-contempt, destructive withdrawal and permanent self-depreciation with a masochistic quality. The pull to dissolve in the fantasy of oneness, to act out the romantic illusion of paradise also is accompanied by difficulty with reality or an inability to bear life's burdens. In Narcissus's fantasy the longing to find the one in order to feel complete is followed by death as his desire fails to be realized.

Green called another attitude 'life narcissism', a way of living – sometimes parasitically, sometimes self-sufficiently – with an impoverished ego that is limited to illusory relationships and without any involvement with living objects (Green, 2002, p. 644). Neither brings the daughter into life as the love of self has been damaged, partially due to the absent father. Green went on to note disappointment lay at the root of depression, especially when either or both parents were disillusioning, unreliable and deceptive.

A secret image

> She looks at herself instead of looking at you, and so doesn't know you. During the two or three little outbursts of passion she has allowed herself in your favor, she has, by a great effort of imagination, seen in you the hero of her dreams, and not yourself as you really are.
>
> Stendhal, *The Red and the Black* (1916, p. 401)

Evie, a composite of many with similar experiences, harboured memories of not being acknowledged by her father who was tyrannical and unavailable. The father's militaristic need for control and obedience was roughly exercised on his children. He never once said he loved her, was wrapped up in his own world, often drinking too much, and yet the family had to cater to him. Moreover, he continually made comments about women and their physical looks in a leering and lecherous manner. Anxiety ruled her internally, but Evie learned to keep everything bottled within. Her unapproachable father was an emotionless, rude man.

Evie developed a secret image of herself as a heroine, alone, able to save and help others. The need and the secret both derived from the father around whom she felt helpless, depressed, sorrowful. She was envious of those who had it easier. Early in life her inner world became the only place of self-preservation, not an uncommon occurrence when the father world is lacking in protection or guidance. Safety of the self initially depends on a loving experience with another, a father. But since this did not occur, she was left without trust. Even into the present day, she still worried her inner spaces would be broken into.

Evie dreamt, *I am on a co-ed high school tennis team, at practice, hitting balls with a teammate. The male coach is watching. He is macho and demanding. Even though I am playing very well and am a dependable, high-quality player, he is critical of me, left and right. He even calls out one of my shots that is clearly in. It makes no sense. He never offers praise or compliments. It makes me wonder why I'm there. I am so frustrated and angry but would not dare challenge him. All I can do is persevere, try to hold on to myself, fight back tears and rely on my strengths to get through.*

Who was this coach? Immediately she said it was obviously her father who could not ever be supportive or let her shine. He bullied and argued, challenging and diminishing whatever she did. He had to be the one who was correct. As an adult she suspected this attitude derived from his envy of her abilities and his low self-worth, but as a child she just felt defeated by his harangues to not be so smart. She often perceived judgement from others, similar to how her father acted towards her. Both his envy and hers indicated the extent of lack (Colman, 1991, p. 356). Evie took on the father's life frustration at being unacknowledged, unappreciated and too small.

As a child Evie reacted by staying clear of him but was unaware how much terror was denied. Yet she sought his approval, trying, trying and still unable to quell the disappointment at getting nothing no matter how well she performed. His voice of inferiority rang in her head. It said she should have done better, and any applause she received was phony. Everything had to be just so, perfect, controlled. In reference to this type of situation, French psychoanalyst Julia Kristeva has written:

> The self – wounded, incomplete, empty, is felt to have a fundamental flaw, a congenital deficiency ... a complex dialectic of idealization and devalorization, both of self and other. It is an identification with the loved/hated other – through incorporation, introjection, projection – that is effected by the taking into oneself of an ideal, sublime, part or trait of the other and that becomes the tyrannical inner judge.
>
> (Kristeva, 1992, p. 6)

If a father has been mercurial, inconsistent or downright hostile, the daughter's attachments and trust in others become disturbed. This rendition of narcissistic suffering can arise as a consequence of missing sufficient attachment with a father. A type of object hunger develops, a need to fill the emptiness with people, places and things to compensate for being unsafe and uncared for. Yet even when she gets what she craves, she can't shake off the uneasy anticipation it can be summarily removed. As a result, she becomes a talented actress ready to perform, but never really believing in her role or the stage on which she finds herself. She withdraws from psychological distress, standing outside herself, gazing from a distance, unaware, sleepwalking through life.

'Narcissican melancholy is fundamental sadness bound with immemorial loss' (Kristeva, 1992, p. 129). Detrimental effects occur when the daughter has to please or save the father to obtain a semblance of parenting. The absence of the father's love develops into a loss of meaning in life. This psychological constellation feeds her internalized paternal neglect, abandonment and emotional rigidity, making it difficult to love or care for herself. In effect, there is a paralysis of the self, limiting the capacity for integration and individuation.

On closer observation, at the heart of narcissism is a lack of warmth. As with Narcissus staring into the pool and not recognizing himself, a genuine inner experience is missing. Julia Kristeva refers to the notion of alienation, or splitting off of the self from the repression of feelings. These secret and unknown wounds could drive one to wander (1992, p. 267). When instinct turns self-destructive, the ego, from early in life, lacks cohesion and falls into bits (p. 19).

Narcissism in its singularity occludes relationship to the unconscious, which also represents the other. Oneness does not integrate or expand to include twoness. This insistence on sameness becomes a defence against feelings of inferiority and shame. As Jung said: 'Your vision will become clear only when you can look into your own heart. Who looks outside dreams; who looks inside awakes' (1973, p. 33). In the myth of Narcissus, the seer said that Narcissus would not live if he got to know himself. The message in this myth is present in the unconscious of us all, to some extent. Knowing oneself involves knowing and opening to the other.

Insufficient paternal experiences impact the formation of the self.

> The [parent's] adaptation … is … *not good enough*. The process that leads to the capacity for symbol-usage does not get started (or else it becomes broken up) … in practice the infant lives, but lives falsely … Through this False Self the infant builds up a false set of relationships, and . . . even attains a show of being real.
>
> (Winnicott, 1995, p. 146, original emphasis)

Narcissism becomes a defence against replicating the earlier and painful object losses and internalizations that have left the daughter with feelings of misery, lack of satisfaction and despair.

No wonder the need is for never-failing narcissistic gratification (Jacoby, 2016, p. 159). The demand for love indicates the needy psyche, and narcissism paradoxically protects against these very needs. Evie said she had imaginary conversations in her mind with the one who saw, admired and wanted her. She imagined this other looking at her, seeing how well she was doing, applauding her. She was never alone in this space and, in fact, could hardly stand to be alone. She had to be reflected, the other recognizing and praising her as looking good and being outstanding. No matter what she did, there was a need for the other to approve and think well of her and continuously feed her with adulation and praise.

Not being responded to or threatened triggered the wounds, vulnerability and imperfections she tried to hide. Evie hid from herself and others to avoid the expected negation. She did not understand the basis of her shame and rage, not realizing she had assumed her father's language of destruction, denigration, failure and inadequacy. After all, she told herself, she shut him out and hated him so he could not affect her. Meanwhile her soul cried out and she did not know how to listen or respond.

Such a daughter is out of touch with herself due to the absence of father and lacks the means to establish good internal resonance (Kohon, 1999, p. 36). Life becomes filled with unease. The accompanying fantasy is of self-sufficiency, of needing no one. In this state, struggling to contain herself, she cannot find value in being herself. Her self-image is distorted, reflecting little of her true being (Jacoby, 2016, p. 158).

Evie would hold back, apprehending rejection, and she experienced a thick blanket smothering any memory of feeling otherwise. This internal structure operated against the self, attacking and destroying good experiences (Colman, 1991, p. 360). The rage turned inward as she experienced impotence and frustration in the desire to engage. There remained within a mixture of despair tied to the desire for reciprocal exchange (Meredith-Owens, 2008, p. 462).

This is not a simple story; a complexity of intricate challenges confronts the narcissist. The psyche and body are bombarded with the defeating thoughts that there is no point anyway – because nothing will ever be perfect enough. No matter how it seems, the narcissist has no natural relation to the body. It is something to make over, to objectify, to distance from. She focuses on outer appearance, food, behaviours, all kept in rigid scrutiny. Hers is a story of loneliness with little access to the affective/emotional life, as she feels only half-alive. She withdraws, defeated and feeling deficient. Easily hurt, she reacts aggressively in defence of her personal sphere (Jacoby, 2016, p. 161).

The shield of aloofness is an attempt to make up for what should be alive and genuine but she comes across as inauthentic. Her words might be right, but the feeling is off. The shell is attractive and fascinating, but something is missing. Moving closer to her, the essence becomes more elusive, the real hidden. This cover remains solidly in place, especially because the encounter with another puts her face to face with feelings of vulnerability (Kristeva, 1992, p. 55). Defensive fear and denial cause the narcissist to ignore, project and even exploit the vulnerability of others. Again, all this deflects from anyone getting close.

Envy

The narcissistic experience of being separate and different from others comes out as envy, idealization, competitiveness, low self-esteem and inadequacy along with the wish and apprehension of being the object of envy. This belief system serves as a safety net against intimacy and as a remedy against the underlying chaos and void (Britton, 1998, p. 181). Experiences of shame, embarrassment, smallness and fear are all reactions indicating envy. These are also acquired from the envious father, absent in his ability to give.

Evie had a dream illustrating this emotional impasse associated with the disappearing, ungraspable, unsupportive and envious father. *I am in high school, a senior. I have great news to share with my family that I've been accepted to a top-tier East Coast college and earned a scholarship to pay for school. They don't respond much. My dad was in another room, so I am not sure he heard. I watch him retreat to another split-level house they have across and up the hill. I follow him there to tell him the news. I hear him slam a door and know I cannot talk to him. Then I am back at the main house, holding my youngest brother on my lap. He is about three to four years old, tired and wanting to be nurtured. As I hold him, I recall a trail that leads from the second house where my dad was, up into a wooded area towards the mountains. It is a spiritual place that reminds me of the*

Elvin world of Middle Earth in Lord of the Rings. *There, I thought, there is hope, answers, and a new life. I burst out to my Mom, 'C'mon, let's go'.*

In the dream the refusal of the father, his turning away and leaving, reminded her of a higher road she could take. It was beyond where he went and connected to aspects of life Evie knew her father could not acknowledge. There lay hope and a better life away from him but this life could include the mother. Evie would not be alone, although she would be without a father.

A sense of lack is at the heart of envy, which is associated with neediness and emptiness. Jung stated an antidote:

> If you will contemplate your lack of fantasy, of inspiration and inner aliveness, which you feel as sheer stagnation and a barren wilderness, and impregnate it with the interest born of alarm at your inner death, then something can take shape in you, for your inner emptiness conceals just as great a fulness if only you will allow it to penetrate into you.
>
> (1963, p. 190)

Envy disturbs relationships. Its destructive aspects include the erasure of inner space to think and reflect. Such a daughter feels inadequate around the father and, as a consequence, around others, making the display of emotions perilous. The distressing ravages of envy and jealousy foster unconscious projective identifications, and its corrosive nature denudes the inner world (Stein, 2017). Envy is rampant for the narcissist as part of the internal tendency to destructiveness, despair and feelings of separation from others. The outer arrogance and omnipotence hide the very real feelings of emptiness, formless terror and dread (Fordham, 1974).

The narcissist does not take in good experiences, and little builds due to the lack of a containing environment within. There is an inability to mourn, accept happiness or trust. American analyst Schwartz-Salant describes envy as the ego's rejection of the self (1982, p. 105). This daughter neither lets herself feel the grief, the loss, nor even fully realize the deep longing for connection. Doing so will require turning inward and facing the emotions thus far avoided.

An attack of envy is an attempt to redress the sense that internally I have little or nothing and the other person seems to have it all. In other words, I so want it, and for the other person to not have it, I will destroy what that person has. Interestingly enough, *invidia,* the Latin for *envy*, translates as 'nonsight'. 'The Inferno', Italian for *hell,* is the first part of Italian writer Dante Alighieri's fourteenth-century epic poem *The Divine Comedy.* In hell, Dante depicts the envious plodding along under cloaks of lead with their eyes sewn shut with leaden wire. Blind to what they have and wanting what others have, they can only look inward.

Accompanying envy, a daughter's fragile inner cohesion makes her unable to fully empathize with others.

> The world is empty only to him who does not know how to direct his libido towards things and people, and to render them alive and beautiful. What

compels us to create a substitute from within ourselves is not an external lack, but our own inability to include anything outside ourselves in our love.

(Jung, 1969, para. 253)

The surface and ego remain primary while the inner life stays undeveloped. Such a daughter too often feels disintegrated, so the hurt, or its anticipation, becomes devastating. Therefore, she does not really risk much and holds back emotionally (Hillman, 1989, p. 69).

The crime

XIV: How the days draw in
What meaneth nature by these diverse laws.

Baron Brooke Fulke Greville, 'Chorus
Sacerdotum' (1798, Line 147)

For many years Evie had a recurring dream *that she committed a crime*. The dream bothered her, especially because she did not know what the crime was or what she had done. In time the dream *escalated from her being an accomplice to her being the main robber or killer*. The reasons for this were never given in the dream. The shock upon awakening was the acknowledgement she had, indeed, done the crime. 'Oh, no', she would exclaim in dismay. She was unconscious the crime was still going on and that she was upset by the dream's message. She was not yet aware the crime was a commentary about her falsity. She was grandiose and considered most people inferior. The dream image repeating over and over portrayed the unknown act and its unconscious self-betrayal so she would begin to address the damage to herself.

However, rather than listening and reflecting, she tried to escape the dream and its insistent message, often not talking in therapy about its recurrence and her emotional disturbance. She resisted, not listening to the voices within. Not paying attention was also the crime referenced in the dream. And then the dream stopped. Now Evie associated the dream to the harshness of her work, the secretive nature of it, the deception and high-powered force she had to muster, but she also said this was not all of her personality. The false self she put on at work had been covering the real self of her heart. When she stopped being under the gun of this part, the dreams desisted. Over time she became what she called softer, more open, more a yoga person and less the politico. She liked the yoga part but said it didn't make money or manifest in the aggressive push needed for her high-stress position, even though the yoga aspects were better for relationships. Although separated from love, she needed control.

When in a relationship, Evie was subject to losing the psyche or soul side of herself. Eros, referencing the love related to intimacy and sex, turned into the solely erotic, and as a narcissist, she demanded attention. She was aware enough to realize love became a loss of self as she was overpowered by her feelings. As her anxiety gathered, she ended up being possessive and manipulative with whomever she was dating. Turning distrustful, she sent repeated and frantic texts as appeals for attention and reassurance.

These actions are typical of someone who fears yet desires love. For Evie, once her feelings were aroused, she reacted with vulnerability. The feeling was so uncomfortable and panicky she avoided it and would begin to back off. Here is part of the significance of the crime dream. Evie did not like who she became in a love relationship, as she could not manage the intensity of intimacy. Unable to give up control, she killed the connection between self and other. In the absence of a secure self she became obsessive and clinging, so no matter what kind of attention she received, it never satisfied the gnawing insecurity. Confidence and trust, Psyche and Eros, Narcissus and Echo remained disparate.

The failure in the paternal holding environment can result in the narcissistic response. This response is often based on insecurity. Evie was maladapted to life's trials and tribulations. Intimacy exposed what she felt as the tattered shards of her personality and endangered the safety of her insulated world. She described a vacuous space at the centre, as if nothing was there. Life with others was uneasy, as without foundations she felt flawed. '[She] started out in the world with averted face … And all the while the world and life pass her by like a dream – an annoying source of illusions, disappointments, and irritations' (Jung, 1959, para. 185).

Through therapy and the therapeutic relationship Evie kept pursing the intimacy she had desired for so very long. She found internet dating too stiff and set up for the falsity she could so easily slip into. She decided to just follow her interests and let life become more natural. The crime dream stayed with her as a reminder to be true to herself. She continued to record other dreams and began a journal as she began to honour her thoughts and ideas. She was finally taking her whole self seriously. She did not repair the relationship with her father, deciding it was not worth it.

One-sided attention devoted solely to the pathology of narcissism runs the risk of neglecting or obscuring the deeper individuation urge embedded in this personality type. It is too simple to merely say the narcissistic person seems only self-involved and beyond reach. This negates the considerable effect therapeutic work can bring. The wider relevance of the narcissist's suffering and disillusionment refers to the conundrum of relatedness involving anything outside one's self. This is addressed in the therapeutic relationship. And these are the very human situations that open the narcissist to self-discovery.

> The conditions of a true critique and a true creation are the same: the destruction of an image of thought which presupposes itself and the genesis of the act of thinking in thought itself. Something in the world forces us to think. This something is an object not of recognition but of a fundamental *encounter*.
>
> (Deleuze, 2004, p. 176, original emphasis)

References

Britton, R. (1998). *Belief and Imagination*. London, England: Routledge.

Colman, W. (1991). Envy, self-esteem, and the fear of separateness. *Journal of Analytical Psychology*, 7(4), 356–67.

Deleuze, G. (2004). *Difference and Repetition*. Paul Patton (Trans.). London, England: Continuum.

Fordham, M. (1974). Defenses of the self. *Journal of Analytical Psychology*, 19(2), 192–99.

Green, A. (2002). A dual conception of narcissism: Positive and negative organizations. *The Psychoanalytic Quarterly*, LXXI(4), 631–49.

Hillman, J. (1989). *Puer Papers*. Dallas, TX: Spring Publications.

Jacoby, M. (2016). *Individuation and Narcissism*. London, England: Routledge.

Jung, C.G. (1959). *The Archetypes and the Collective Unconscious*. New York, NY: Pantheon Books.

Jung, C.G. (1963). *Memories, Dreams, Reflections*. New York, NY: Vintage.

Jung, C.G. (1966). *The Practice of Psychotherapy*, Vol. 16. New York, NY: Pantheon Books.

Jung, C.G. (1966). *Two Essays on Analytical Psychology*, Vol. 7. New York, NY: Pantheon Books.

Jung, C.G. (1969). *Symbols of Transformation*, Vol. 5. New York, NY: Pantheon Books.

Jung, C.G. (1973). *Letters, Vol. 1: 1906–1950*. Princeton, NJ: Princeton University Press.

Kohon, G. (Ed.) (1999). *The Dead Mother: The Work of André Green*. London, England: Routledge.

Kristeva, J. (1992). *Black Sun: Depression and Melancholia*. Leon Roudiez (Trans.). New York, NY: Columbia University Press.

Meredith-Owens, W. (2008). 'Go! Sterilise the fertile with they rage': Envy as embittered desire. *Journal of Analytical Psychology*, 53(4), 459–80.

Ovid. (1893). *The Metamorphoses of Ovid* [Ebook, 21765]. Retrieved from https://www.gutenberg.org/files/21765/21765-h/files/Met_I-III.html#bookIII.

Rosenfeld, H. (1987). *Impasse and Interpretation*. London, England: Tavistock.

Schwartz-Salant, N. (1982). *On Narcissism*. Toronto, Canada: Inner City Books.

Singer, T. & Kimbles, S. (Eds.) (2004). *The Cultural Complex*. London, England: Routledge.

Stein, M. (2017). Where east meets west in the house of individuation. *Journal of Analytical Psychology*, 62(1), 67–87.

Stendhal (1916). *The Red and the Black: A Chronicle of 1830* [Ebook, 44747]. http://www.gutenberg.org/ebooks/44747.

Winnicott, D.W. (1995). Ego distortion in terms of true and false self. In: *The Maturational Process and the Facilitating Environment*. London, England: Karnac Books.

Wordsworth, W. (1798). *The Poetical Works of William Wordsworth, Vol. II* [Ebook 12145]. Retrieved from http://www.gutenberg.org/files/12145/12145-h/12145-h.htm.

Chapter 13

The body in shadow

She could see what she lacked. It was not beauty; it was not mind. It was something central which permeated; something warm which broke up surfaces and
rippled the cold contact of man and woman, or of women together.

Virginia Woolf, *Mrs. Dalloway* (1990, p. 31)

Integration of the personality begins with the throes of despair, confusion and dissociation in a delicate interweaving between body and mind. This can be discerned
in the eruption of autoimmune disease representing the body–psyche collapse. Of
those affected by autoimmune disease, 78.8 per cent are women (Fairweather
& Rose, 2004, p. 2005). For this and for many other reasons the body must be
addressed in the psychological process. The composite clinical example in this
chapter emphasizes the relationship a daughter has to her body when a father is
absent, neglectful or inappropriate.

In addition, the diverse yet aligned perspectives of Julia Kristeva, French psychoanalyst, and Jungian analytical psychology bridge the border between self and
other. They both describe the defences of the self appearing in psyche and soma.
Jung said: 'The body is a most doubtful friend because it produces things we do
not like; there are too many things about the body which cannot be mentioned.
The body is very often the personification of this shadow of the ego' (Jung, 1976,
para. 40). Kristeva, with her concept of the abject, describes opening to the areas
that hide the unexpected: 'The danger ... from within the identity ... threatens'
(1982, p. 71).

What kind of damage results from the exclusion of physicality from the
father–daughter relationship? ... [h]er father's inhibition ... in handling ...
her cannot help in the formation of a positive attitude toward her own body,
a sense of its 'rightness', beauty, power and integrity.

(Samuels, 1993, pp. 149–50)

When absent, obviously no father is there to impart self-care. When the daughter
does not hear about her body from her father in a healthy way, she stops listening.

Rana had no emotional care from her father, no way to feel loved, no memory of hugs or touch, no Eros. There were almost no pictures taken of her as a child and few verbal snapshots conveyed about her childhood. Mostly her childhood was spent alone and hiding, and to this day Rana has difficulty receiving attention or being physically touched. Rana felt nothing about her body as she ceased experiencing it long ago as a worthy part of herself. Her body became a distant object, subjected over many years to various forms of self-violence and betrayal. She did not consider ignoring good care as particularly negating because she simply forgot to do so. These reactions affected her somatic responses. She carried images of herself as ugly, useless and insignificant, old and ignored. No matter how painful, these feelings did not disappear. Finally, an illness in psyche and body pushed Rana into Jungian therapeutic work to access her ability to survive and find meaning.

The body does not forget. Like the psyche it is a symbolic communicator of the traumas, dissociations and messages from the unconscious. As Julia Kristeva commented: 'We shall be concerned with the shadow cast over the fragile ego, barely dissociable from the other: a shadow cast, precisely, by the loss of this necessary other – a shadow of despair' (1992, p. 5). The lack of an attentive father creates emotionally wounded areas that often appear later in life in physical responses.

In autoimmune disease the misidentification of threat from within leads the immune system to raise antibodies to its own cells, misperceiving them as 'not part of the self' in what is called an autoimmune response. If the body learns from the mistake quickly, there may be little harm. However, with autoimmune disease, the immune system goes to war with the very body it is charged to protect. The ability to distinguish self from other is impaired and attempts at self-protection may create the painful and damaging conditions the immune system attempts to avoid in the first place. The absence of a stable self is narrated in autoimmunity as a loss of self. The body destroys rather than guards against the aggressions and intrusions in a self-refusal that gathers force through life. 'It is just as if that particular complex had a body of its own . . . [with a] certain amount of its own physiology' (Jung, 1976, para. 148, 149).

Rana was a psychological and physical portrait of a daughter's unprocessed wounds and repressed mourning. The traumas she suffered as an adult most likely replicated events in childhood that she could no longer remember. She registered feeling unloved, abandoned, emotionally paralyzed, displaced. She learned these attitudes, actions, affects, assumptions, rituals and culture early in life (Kimbles, 2004, p. 200). The wounded areas live on in the psyche as unassimilated material.

In the midst of a successful career Rana's physical system collapsed with an autoimmune illness, and she was in despair. She tried to push through it, demanding she continue when it was not possible. For Rana, her self turned on itself, the shadow insisting on attention as the repressed memories returned. She faced the unaddressed losses she had defended against her whole life. She began to hear the hollowness within and the yearning for attachment. Something vital had been missing. Her numerous accomplishments and awards did not fix the absent internal places. Jung commented: 'The spirit is the life of the body seen from within, and the body the outward manifestation of the life of the spirit – the two being really one' (1970, para. 195).

For her, the illness seemed to re-create the isolation and abandonment of paternal care she experienced in childhood. A psychic void arose from the outer loss of the father and was experienced depressively as an inner void (Kristeva, 1992, p. 82). Rana described a father poorly attuned, unable to empathize with her internal experiences, only recognizing her mind. Her longing to get close enough or feel securely accepted went unmet; disappointed, she neither found comfort nor learned self-soothing from him.

'There is a huge gap or silence over the part played by the father's body in an early direct relationship with a baby' (Samuels, 1993, p. 137). The quality of connection between father and daughter shapes her awareness, satisfaction and care of her body throughout life. The more he withdraws his love and rejects her, both physically and emotionally, the more she becomes abandoning and anxious towards her body. When the father's supportive attitudes are absent, she runs the risk of feeling negativity towards all bodies, mostly her own.

Distress occurs when the outer positions meant to shore up the personality become exhausted and her inner reserves collapse, as they are no longer sustainable. Kristeva called this a lost mirage of the past, leaving in its wake absence, depression, self-loathing and ennui (1994, p. 271). Always uneasy, this woman is subsumed with obsessive drives and persecutory impulses like anxious overeating when not hungry, the oppressive weight of mindlessness, binge-watching the internet and television. This daughter is assailed with fears of driving, both literally and symbolically in Rana's case, and she often feels no motivation to live.

Confronted with memories untranslatable until now, Rana expressed the loss of not belonging to herself. She tried to keep on reinforcing the competency façade to hide increasing desperation, ineffectiveness, inertness and malaise. She felt she could tell no one and had to pretend she was still able, but these efforts became more difficult to maintain. *In a dream she is up high and eating a zebra with knife and fork. Others are around and watching. She is upset at the dream because zebras are showy, and they cannot hide. They are black and white, and she wants to be grey. That is why she needs to eat the zebra.* She lost her self-definition in exhaustion, weight gain, unable to go to yoga. Gradually, her body's hormones, thyroid and adrenals stopped functioning.

> Part of the sluggishness and carelessness of everyday life … is its failure to grasp its own experiences …, its failure … to recognize and take stock of itself . . . the mind … learns to repossess its experiences from the fog of habit, convention, and forgetfulness.
>
> (Nussbaum, 1994, p. 340)

She was in the situation Julia Kristeva described as the feeling of 'falling into pieces [that] may be caused either by … *nonintegration* impeding the cohesion of the self, or by a disintegration accompanied by anxieties and provoking the schizoid splitting' (1992, p. 18, original emphasis). Through the development of an autoimmune illness, the psyche–soma exposed her denied fragility, the cracked and dissociated parts of herself. The rift in the constitution of her identity marked a split between a demonic persecuting double and an invisible, disappearing, ghost-like self. Silence surrounds women's capacity to talk about their bodies, yet this silence also has gone unaddressed. Women go to war with their bodies and inflict punitive requirements of unattainable perfection with distress and shame as the result. Sometimes even in therapy Rana maintained a silence about her body.

The body is problematic for women who do not feel physically connected. They mistreat their bodies, perversely desiring to transcend them altogether. So many women do not eat what they want, wear what they want or express what they want – because nothing will be perfect enough. Compulsive negative thoughts and behaviours kill off desires and bring about dissociation from self and others. The acts of satisfying hungers, taking things in, indulging in pleasures become distorted and various obsessions take over. The body is disembodied, subject to denial. 'Don't run away and make yourself unconscious of bodily facts, for they keep you in real life and help you not to lose your real way in the world of mere possibilities where you are simply blindfolded' (Jung, 1998, p. 48). The emotional wounds that appear physically are actually a protective mechanism to permit the ego to survive.

Trauma/wounds

Psychic trauma occurs when reality overwhelms with a brutality and speed exceeding the capacity to manage the experience. The word *traumatic* is from the Greek, referring to a piercing of the skin, a breaking of the psychological and physical envelope. It intrudes through the protecting shield and overwhelms the defences against anxiety. Trauma is the story of a wound that cries out in the attempt to remember and to tell.

Rana described feeling a self that was other than what she knew. In a dream she related: *I am lost on a street. Where do I belong? I wander around. Where is the place? I have to go up and down. But, yes, now I remember I was here before and this time I have to find the exit.* The dream illustrated the various delays, hesitations and questions that arose when she lacked a sense of cohesion. It denoted a feeling of being rudderless, without guidance, direction or connection. The dream ended with her determination to find the way out.

What remained unknown and unconscious were the strangers within. Rana wrote in her journal:

This morning I once again glanced over what I had written a few years ago and it made me shiver. Something in this piece terrifies me. I feel it may open up some venues to the discovery of my own self-selves.

Jung referred to these as the shadow comprised of the parts resisted, the others awaiting integration, the unconscious where empathy for self and other reside. Julia Kristeva contended what is foreign to one's self is actually part of oneself. Autoimmunity demonstrates a double movement: protection and destruction and threat and chance. It is not just poison but also a possible medicine that, when made conscious, opens up opportunities and hope. In relation to this Julia Kristeva links psychoanalysis with the unconscious as a place of transition and transformation. Jung interpreted the dissociation between body and psyche, ego and shadow, ideal and real as material not only for dissolution but also for personality construction.

The development of an autoimmune disease opened a descent into the ashes. This was Rana's psychological and physical experience of the alchemical stage called the *nigredo* – a darkness, decomposition and painful loss of bearings. She described it as black, unpleasant, bewildering, disorienting, a sickness of spirit. Rana graphically depicted feeling lost in the dissolution, the *massa confuse*, or the chaos necessary in order to reform. Her consciously held values and former self-image had become outmoded. Yet, now at a crossroads, she was understandably ambivalent. Ego and body consciousness had yet to work out a new relationship with the unconscious.

The abject

Abjection is a 'sickness at one's own body' (Elizabeth Grosz, 1994, p. 78). Abjection is about what has been repressed. 'The abjection of self would be ... that experience of the subject to which it is revealed that all its objects are based merely on the inaugural *loss* that laid the foundations of its own being' (Oliver, 2002, p. 232, original emphasis). The foundations referred to include the loss for the daughter not only of a father but also of her self. Rana did not notice what was lacking, as these were the unattended places that her father deemed unimportant.

Rana, overcome with exhaustion and no longer able to continue as before, is typical of many who develop an autoimmune disease. The way forward as planned is halted. The rejected pieces have to be picked up and integrated. As Kristeva denotes, the abject is located in a liminal space, on the margins between the conscious and unconscious, reflecting the places of transition and transformation. The abject disturbs conventional identity by affecting the body. It is likened to the shadow in Jungian psychology, also representing the negated, submerged and denied aspects of physical and emotional life. Both shadow and abject are destabilizing and disruptive, unfamiliar and unsettling.

The abject is the rejected from which we cannot part. For Rana, a lifelong attitude of distance from her body and a denial of its needs could no longer suffice. Now locked in internal combat Rana felt chaotic and uncontrolled. Another way of saying this is her self-disappearance and disinvolvement indicated destructive withdrawal and self-depreciation.

The daily sabotage to her system reflected something crucial was not being fed, held or seen. The body instincts were injured as she repudiated or rebelled against herself. She faced disconnection from the body, or not being fully 'embodied': the presence of an idealized, dynamic and potent – but elusive – self; and of a weaker, passive version of self, which was disregarded in a shadow sense, or even despised (Goss, 2006, p. 681). In therapy Rana phrased it as being controlled by a part of her personality that felt strange. This fed the internalized cycle of depression and paternal neglect of her feelings, making it difficult to love or care for herself. Julia Kristeva describes psychoanalysis as an apprenticeship in living beyond despair and accessing the helpful others within (1992, p. 17).

However, Rana lived outside her skin. She often did not feel ownership of her body. British Jungian analyst Michael Fordham said: '[T]here is a need for … "defenses against what is not-self [as] essential to health" … directed against foreign bodies, i.e. those coming from sources external to the self and internally as auto-immune reactions' (Fordham, 1985, p. 167).

Rana's sleep became disturbed, her food imbalanced and digestion off, signifying the basics of body and psyche were out of sync. This reflected an accumulation of internal violence and hostility split off from the loving communication towards the self. Again, care is subverted when there is no modelling of it from a father.

Disembodiment was manifested by lack of vitality and emptiness. She feared if she removed the body-mask there would be nothing behind it. The old stresses and new crises combined with the dissociation between her body and psyche became apparent with the development of the autoimmune disease. This suggested that feelings of not really being alive were linked to the fact that she had no inner representation of her face or body (Connelly, 2013, pp. 636–56).

The cultural lack of favourable feminine images throughout life fosters the inability to facilitate nurturing attitudes towards self. As a woman ages, the looks she relied upon alter and age itself becomes abject. If she feels age is without beauty, she ends up despising the arc of life. The American poet and writer Adrienne Rich commented, 'But the fear and hatred of our bodies has often crippled our brains. We have tended either to become our bodies – blindly, slavishly, in obedience to male theories about us – or to try to exist in spite of them' (1976, pp. 284–85). Self-hatred is at work in the desire to be rid of the body – because it is female. She feels insignificant, rejected, disgusted, trapped. Denying the body leaves a woman without desire and the dispossession of her body means her energy is partially blocked.

Body experiences bring one into the here and now; 'the striving to transcend the present level of consciousness through acceptance of the unconscious must give the body its due' (Jung, 1970, para. 195). The body can become a catalyst for deeper reflection, investigation and imagination. Julia Kristeva speaks about the notion of the stranger and suggests we touch this otherness, escape its hatred and burden though accepting the differences it implies (1994, p. 3).

However, Rana's inner system was obstructed with misconnections between mind, body and soul harkening back to the misconnections with her father. The autoimmune disease presented the realization of her early denied vulnerability. She described melancholia, a noncommunicable grief about the sadness, aloneness and a sense of 'offness' with others (Kristeva, 1992, pp. 12–13). In flight from her body, she lived in her head. The abject and the shadow elements created within her the idea that no one cared and her life made no difference. This replicated how she felt with her father, an intellect who only valued her mind.

Identity is concerned with the notion of strangeness within and a person's conscious idea of self as distinct from outer appearances. Julia Kristeva includes the double of the inner self, making analysis simultaneously a journey into the strangeness of the other and also oneself (Kristeva, 1994, p. 182). The theory of abjection recognizes there is a zone of disgust inside where otherness resides, locked away as the conscious mind represses what it considers the horrors. 'The very material that is being repressed, the things we never knew or no longer know, that creates anxiety of different degrees' (Meier, 1986, p. 223). The foreign within has the capacity to give birth both to what is best and what is worst in us, depending on how we react.

Rana learned to collude with the father influence and other masculine aspects personally, culturally and relationally. The perceptions of women as inferior reflected the limiting and fragmented psychological parts reflected from culture.

> The daughters of such fathers often arrive in analysis with a façade of self-sufficiency. They despair of earning their father's attention except temporarily and unconsciously, often as a sexual object, and they are caught in having to defend themselves while trying to prove themselves equal and worthy of their father's praise. They split off their sensuousness, capture men and/ or accomplishments, but feel no tenderness and little self-regard. They are focused forever on seeking the father's blessing and personal attention.
>
> (Perera, 1981, p. 66)

The personality seeks self-regulation as the therapeutic process collects the dissociated fragments and brings them into relationship. The self becomes more complete as the abject is accepted and integrated. Both the abject and the shadow bring engagement with the foreign, the repressed and the projected material separating self from others. In therapy Rana developed a dialogue between psyche and body, as her psychic history was slowly constructed. Dreams emerged that aroused her self-curiosity along with emotions and memories. The autoimmune illness helped slow the rhythm of her life, opening her to quieter and more fulfilled self-expression:

> Illness is the means by which an organism sheds what is foreign to it; all that needs to be done is to assist it in being sick, to have the complete illness, and then to escape from it, for that constitutes its progress.
>
> (Rilke, 2005, p. 98)

References

Connolly, A. (2013). Out of the body: Embodiment and its vicissitudes. *Journal of Analytical Psychology*, *55*(5), 636–56.

Fairweather, D. & Rose, N. (2004). Women and autoimmune diseases. *Emerging Infectious Diseases*, *10*(11), 2005–11.

Fordham, M. (1985). *Explorations into the Self*. London, England: Karnac Books.

Goss, P. (2006). Discontinuities in the male psyche: Waiting, deadness and disembodiment. Archetypal and clinical approaches. *Journal of Analytical Psychology*, *51*(5), 681–99.

Grosz, E. (1994). *Volatile Bodies: Toward a Corporeal Feminism*. Crow's Nest, Australia: Allen & Unwin, p. 78.

Jung, C.G. (1970). *Civilization in Transition*, Vol. 10. Princeton, NJ: Princeton University Press.

Jung, C.G. (1976). *The Symbolic Life*, Vol. 18. New York, NY: Pantheon Books.

Jung, C.G. (1998). *Jung's Seminar on Nietzsche's Zarathustra*. Princeton, NJ: Princeton University Press.

Kimbles, S. (2004). A cultural complex operating in the overlap of clinical and cultural space. In: T. Singer & S. Kimbles (Eds.), *The Cultural Complex* (pp. 199–211). Hove: Routledge.

Kristeva, J. (1982). *Powers of Horror*. New York, NY: Columbia University Press.

Kristeva, J. (1992). *Black Sun: Depression and Melancholia*. Leon Roudiez (Trans.). New York, NY: Columbia University Press.

Kristeva, J. (1992). *Black Sun*. New York, NY: Columbia University Press.

Kristeva, J. (1994). *Strangers to Ourselves*. New York, NY: Columbia University Press.

Meier, C.A. (1986). *Soul and Body: Essays on the Theories of C.G. Jung*. Culver City, CA: Lapis Press.

Nussbaum, M. (1994). *The Therapy of Desire: Theory and Practice in Hellenistic Ethics*. Princeton, NJ: Princeton University Press.

Oliver, K. (2002). *The Portable Kristeva*. New York, NY: Columbia University Press.

Perera, S. (1981). *Descent to the Goddess: A Way of Initiation for Women*. Toronto, Canada: Inner City Books.

Rich, A. (1976). *Of Woman Born*. New York, NY: W.W. Norton & Co.

Rilke, R.M. (2005). *The Poet's Guide to Life: The Wisdom of Rilke*. Ulrich Baer (Ed. and Trans.). New York, NY: Random House.

Samuels, A. (1993). *The Political Psyche*. London, England: Routledge.

Woolf, V. (1990). *Mrs. Dalloway*. New York, NY: Houghton, Mifflen, Harcourt.

Chapter 14

Sylvia Plath's 'Daddy'

Mirroring numerous scenarios, literature and psychology express similar journeys about life dramas, emotional reactions and events. Both render the psyche visible through metaphor, image and the symbolic, detailing the intricate dynamics of what it is to be human. The dance between conscious and unconscious elements is of the moment while simultaneously addressing the universal and timeless.

Through Sylvia Plath's life, poetry and dreams, the issues of the absent father are blatantly expressed. The pathos depicted in them conscripts us to gain consciousness of our feelings. Plath delineated the psychological reactions of many current women who likewise bear the effects of an absent father. Her writings reverberate with the paradoxes of hate, desire and deprivation, rage, longing, self-destruction and creation. They describe the anguish of the unresolved, ambivalent attachment with her father as it was composed of unconscious strands and blurred boundaries. Her discontent, disequilibrium and inner tension were also noted to be the sources of her artistic productivity.

She wrote, dramatizing significant intimate matters, translating her private hurts into public images. In explicating her truths, she expressed the break with the paternal tradition of being a dutiful, sweet daughter. She angrily articulated protest against the masculine domination she keenly felt. Her knife-edged words expressed the psyche rife with images and symbols aimed at release and freedom. While both yearning for a father and his affection, recognition and security, Sylvia Plath's writing also portrayed the female serving a male torturer yet rebelling against the woman as a sacrificial object. 'Poetry is a form of self-discovery as well as redefinition for both poet and her audience and that its refigured images can help assimilate into consciousness new definitions of the feminine' (Jung, 1960, para. 355). Her poems display themes of insecurity, masks, lack of love, death and loss as well as rebirth.

Her father, a university professor of Austrian descent and a classically authoritarian patriarch, was emotionally absent, strict and remote from family life, regulating play with children to a half hour a day. He died when she was eight years old. She wrote in the second person in her journal about the image of her father in childhood:

> You remember that you were his favorite when you were little, and you used to make up dances to do for him as he lay on the living room couch after supper. You wonder if the absence of an older man in the house has anything to do with your intense craving for male company.
>
> (Kukil, 2000, p. 64)

In a connection between mourning and creativity, her writing can be viewed as compensation for the loss of the good object, focusing here on the father. Along these lines, the following describes Plath. 'The personality is rooted in lack, estrangement or disintegration of selfhood; the personal narrative organized around a lost moment of origin, which, though endlessly reconstructed, was not recovered' (Britzolakis, 1999, p. 40). The passion of her creativity arose from attempts to transform in life the psychological forces pulling her to unite with her father in death. This highly wired tension gave her work its continuing emotional appeal.

Suicide

Sylvia Plath was an American poet of the mid-twentieth century who took her own life at the age of 30. She was living in London after her husband Ted Hughes, later to become Poet Laureate of Britain, left her for another woman who took her own life in a similar manner.

Intensity fuelled her work, as she tried to extricate herself from psychological agony and break the narrow cultural scripts of the daughter/woman who was to be sweet and pretty on the arm of a man. She wrote to slough off these ill-fitting roles, to release herself from being a girl-toy of the man. Her language was inflamed against males and the patriarchal exclusionary cultural attitudes, angrily pricking at the unquestioned adoration of women towards men.

Her language expressed feminine repression, binding sexual differences and cultural alienation. In Sylvia Plath's era, intelligent women were channelled towards menial roles, their futures perceived as satellites to men, a pernicious societal attitude with disastrous effects on both women and men. One of her dreams said this in another way:

> How many times in my dreams have I met my dark marauder on the stairs, at a turning of the street, waiting on my bright yellow bed, knocking at the door, sitting only in his coat and hat with a small smile on a park bench; already he has split into many men; even while we hope, the blind is drawn down and the people turned to shadows acting in a private room beyond our view.
>
> (Kukil, 2000, p. 459)

The dream identified the marauders as males, many of them, appearing everywhere. There was fear aroused in the dream by these figures deemed as menacing and dark forms of the negative male and also with unsettling sexual implications. The following comment about her referred to this: 'It is this sense of threat, as though she were continually menaced by something she could see only out of the corners of her eyes, that gives her work its distinction' (Alvarez, 1971, p. 10).

In the poem 'Purdah' she wrote:

> I am his.
> Even in his
> Absence, I
> Revolve in my
> sheath of impossibles ...

(Plath, 1981, p. 243)

These words illustrate Sylvia Plath's psychological state affected by the absent father. In her journal she wrote, 'crying and crying with this terrible pain; it hurts, father, it hurts, oh father I have never known; a father, even, they took from me' (Kukil, 2000, p. 223).

Her poems used various symbols for the father, from the colour black to larger-than-life mythological figures. This father was a phantom, shrouded in mystery, like the Greek stone statue of the Colossus, a figure of huge and awesome proportions. It was erected at the entrance to ancient Athens, signifying patriarchal power and its overriding law. The stone also symbolized the non-responsive father, impenetrable and oblique, with an unyielding hardness. There is no change to him and there is no life in his world for her. The Colossus represented an inner frozen place, inert, cold. She desired an oracle of large proportions, able to give love and worthy of receiving her love. Yet she appropriated the power of the Colossus, using the name as the title of a poem in her book of poems of the same name.

In Sylvia Plath's poetry and prose, the father was potent as a symbol of absence, a target of anger signifying the impossibility of love and the pull towards death. In fact, the father is usually, for her, associated with death and deadness rather than life. Trying to empty out the inner conflict through her poetry suffused it with repetitive actions, words, themes and circularity of movement. This psychic activity, like her rhymed words, attempted to integrate the personality and establish a coherent sense of identity. From a symbolic perspective, it represented the circularity that we die in order to begin again (Bollas, 1995, p. 190).

The biographical fact of her father's death and its detritus haunted her childhood prior to the natural separation between daughter and father. Father became a point of reference, the psychological introjection of negative self-images. This aspect of the dead father created the internal and external negative male energy:

> Me, I never knew the love of a father, the love of a steady blood-related man after the age of eight ... He was an ogre. But I miss him. ... I hated men

because they didn't stay around and love me like a father: I could prick holes in them & show they were not father material.

(Kukil, 2000, p. 431)

She described a father/master demanding the identification he both held yet refused in 'the paternal perversion of an impossible paternal ideal' (Rose, 1991, p. 231). The childhood father became an object of vengeance through her poetic imagery, articulating the depth of loss. The spectre of her father appearing everywhere became a way to mourn the internalized dead father who ruled her life (Kroll, 1976, p. 109).

In her writings the father was unapproachable, black, absent, dead and oppressively influential. She coped with the internalized destructive forces arising from this situation by 'deadening herself due to the deadened object [the father] within' (Bollas, 1995, p. 74). Devotion to him became a type of depersonalization – a mechanism derived from his emotional deadness and physical absence. Enchantment with him constellated her petrifaction and has been conjectured as contributing to her suicide. 'She is sentenced to live her daughterhood as a father's priestess, votary, bride, and queen' (Kroll, 1976, p. 83).

Her poetry, especially the poem 'Daddy', her dreams and journals reverberate with distress and anger at males, the masculine, her husband and father. In them she exposed the anguish of their incomplete, disappointing, ambivalent attachment. The father who was absent became a strong actor in her writing, although she, holding the power of the word as a symbol of the father, gave him no words to speak.

Much of her work also described the lack of connection to her mother who followed the patriarchal tradition by agreeing to submerge the feminine. In several of her works Plath uses imagery evoking the Electra Complex. In the Greek myth Electra was the daughter who helped her brother and his friend murder their mother and her lover for killing their father. The first line of her poem, 'Electra on Azalea Path' implies she, as the speaker of the poem, is dead and therefore dead to her father, a mysterious and absent figure she wants to love but cannot. The poem reports that the death of the father kills off his daughter, and her love remains unmet. She wrote: 'You have had chances; you have not taken them, you are wallowing in original sin; your limitations ... You have lost all delight in life. You cannot love, even if you knew how to begin to love' (Kukil, 2000, p. 154).

Sylvia Plath's life and writing have attracted commentary from various disciplines and psychological approaches but little from the Jungian perspective. This is surprising as her writings illustrate her interest in Jung, especially in the concepts of the collective unconscious, the archetypes and the use of symbolism. Drawn to the depths of the psyche, Sylvia Plath read Jung and the mythologist Robert Graves who both recognized the symbolic and the mythic with their psychological applications. About this, Jung commented: 'The images of the unconscious place a great responsibility upon a man. Failure to understand them, or a shirking of ethical responsibility, deprives him of his wholeness and imposes a painful fragmentariness on his life' (1963, p. 193).

Sylvia Plath's search for self-knowledge was graphically connected to her intense inner and outer conflicts. Her anger and rage at 'Daddy', society and the patriarchal establishments were basic themes, and similar psychological, cultural and collective positions resonate to this day. She used archetypal narratives, patterns of action and motifs in her writings referring to the death–rebirth cycle, the stages of dis-memberment and re-memberment, the search for the parent, the sacrifice, the meeting with the other and so on. As Jung commented:

> The artist is not a person endowed with free will who seeks his own ends, but one who allows art to realize its purposes through him. As a human being he may have moods and a will and personal aims, but as an artist he is 'man' in a higher sense – he is 'collective man', a vehicle and moulder of the unconscious psychic life of mankind.
>
> (1955, para. 157, p. 101)

Masks

Drawing a singular image of Sylvia Plath is not possible, as she inhabited so many. This woman of many masks carefully revealed only selected facets of herself. The veils and guises succeeded in forestalling anyone from knowing who she really was, despite her quest to discover the answer. The layers seemed to form a kind of carapace – a shell masking a gap, a persistent and agonizing hollowness at the core. 'Look at that ugly dead mask here and do not forget it. It is a chalk mask with dead dry poison behind it, like the death angel' (Kukil, 2000, p. 155). She announced through many of her works an absence at the centre of her being (Bollas, 1995, p. 180).

Her poetic images show confrontations of old selves looking at the new, the doubles, the mirror images and the complex relationships between all these selves. They present self-loss, alienation bringing about extreme self-involvement, the self as fragmented, dissipated and obsolescent with their many masks and positions (O'Reilly, 2004, p. 360). In her journal she wrote:

> Transmuting the objective reality into something quite personal (like the death of My Father) tears, sorrow, weeping, dolorous tints, numbing of certain areas of sensation and perception about the stream of life moving about one … Something freezes me from my real spirit: is it fear of failure, fear of being vulnerable.
>
> (Kukil, 2000, p. 121, 476)

Sylvia Plath was described as intelligent, attractive and sexual, but in her lifetime women were discouraged from displaying all these qualities. When a woman's combination of physical appeal and intellect are disallowed her instincts have to be overtly ignored but remain in internal conflict. As such, Plath's writing can be read for its multiplicity, subtexts of ambiguity and fantasy and the ways she has become the object of critical fantasies and debates about femininity, violence and contemporary culture (Rose, 2002, p. 13).

Behind the masks were the sorrows and hurts from the lack of father. Her writing was a form of identity-making as she was wrapped in this emotionally and psychologically disturbing internal material. Even as commentary about Sylvia Plath has continued to proliferate, what is noticeable is that none has succeeded in creating an integrated portrait. 'I was overreacting to the initial brutality of the verse without understanding its weird elegance ... In all this time the evidence of the poems and the evidence of the person were utterly different' (Alvarez, 1971, p. 17).

Critics continue to make various projections onto Sylvia Plath, and since her death the portrayals of her have become more intricate, sometimes pathologized, entangled. She is someone onto whom a script is written, as if this would answer the question of who she really was. Have they now superseded her definition? Sylvia Plath was described in so many ways – as fragile, brilliant, driven, scarred by her father's early death; trying to shrug off the limiting culturally prescribed roles for women; a perfectionist; a woman shattered by her idealized husband's betrayals. The disparate psychological elements and personal and collective wounds fuelled both her creation and destruction.

Her allure is an enticing mix of poison and passion, making her poetry gripping, as she flirts close to the fire of burning feelings. 'The poet becomes an instrument destined to give expression and form to those yet unformed ideas that lie dormant in our soul' (Jacoby, 1992, p. 66). Her writing is filled with filiation, paternal heritage and injunction, stressing the wounding nature of love derived in part from the early loss and absence of her father. Sylvia Plath wrote in her journal: 'Why are we conditioned into the smooth strawberry-and-cream Mother-Goose-world, Alice-in-Wonderland fable, only to be broken on the wheel as we grow older and become aware of ourselves as individuals with a dull responsibility in life?' (Kukil, 2000, p. 35).

Melancholia

'If the pain of loss is evaded and left unprocessed, one is increasingly melancholic, the ego fragmented. Melancholy names that condition whereby the grief and pain of loss remain unmetabolized and trapped inside the self' (Frankel, 2013, p. 9). Plath's writing articulated the mourning of the absent father and its psychological ramifications, making her experiences intelligible. It was fraught with difficult psychological struggles; her use of myths and personal and social events depicted a spiralling back as death and ending was followed by rebirth and renewal. Her use of metaphor worked along circuitous lines, following the psyche with its non-linear and poetic bent. 'Artistic sublimation is a process that gives form to love and loss' (Kristeva, 1991, p. 128).

Especially depicted in Plath's later poems is the melancholic, the bereft and abandoned female subject. The identification with the dead and lost father drew her to the inner malign things and its tangle of frustrated needs and fury. These she described in the short story, 'Johnny Panic and the Bible of Dreams':

> 'Father', she said in a small pleading voice. 'Father'. But he did not hear, withdrawn as he was into the core of himself, insulated against the sound of her supplicant voice. Lost and betrayed, she slowly turned away and left the room.
>
> (Plath, 1979, p. 312)

The father is silent and withdrawn, suggesting the character's sadness and inability to reach him. The story reveals the complex psychological experiences and their effects on daughters whose fathers are absent emotionally and/or physically. The sad discoveries that love was not as she assumed and the unbearable nature of this and its emotions went into her poetry. As André Green said, 'the work of writing presupposes a wound and a loss, a work of mourning, of which the text is the transformation' (1986, p. 322).

Split selves

Sylvia Plath's poems have been read either as dark wastelands of expression or as survival in a phoenix-like psychological recovery. In her search for identity, forays into the past merged into the present, quite like what happens in therapeutic depth work. For Plath the psychological conflict consisted of a grieving, empty, sad self, separated from the image presented to the world as gay and happy. It was 'as if' she was the image taking prominence over the real.

The outward reflections of her strife obfuscated the distress plaguing her – the death of her father; self-defeating perfectionism not allowing failure; her relationship with her husband, Ted Hughes, and his adulterous affairs; her inability to control the world around her and her illnesses. There is a trauma or paradox internal to identification with the father (Rose, 2011, p. 266). In another dream of Plath's: 'Dreamed last night I was beginning my novel ... to "set" the scene: a girl's search for her dead father – for an outside authority which must be developed, instead, from the inside' (Kukil, 2000, p. 416).

Self-loathing vied with perfection and her prolific creativity; failures were devastating, and she fell into despair. Sylvia Plath addressed the demon within her that wouldn't allow her to succeed, to be human; the murderous part that scolded her, calling her stupid and weak. Her poetic imagery of dismemberment suggests physical alienation and fragmentation as well as the psychological struggle to reconnect the pieces of her personality. She recounted image after image of selves devoured, hollowing out or abstracting the living matter from which it was initially composed. Disunion and union, colours shifting, meanings morphing into passionate expression dramatized the war in her soul. For Sylvia Plath, as well as for many daughters with absent, neglectful or oppressive fathers, the mirroring without a father unveils his negativity and rejection projected onto her.

She noted the effects of a negative father complex in her journal, writing: 'God, is this all it is, the ricocheting down the corridor of laughter and tears? Of self-worship and self-loathing? Of glory and disgust? ... I sit here without identity: faceless (Kukil, 2000, p. 17, 26).

'Daddy'

Jung stated about poetry: 'The unsatisfied yearning of the artist reaches back to the primordial image in the unconscious which is best fitted to compensate the inadequacy and one-sidedness of the present' (Jung, 1960, para. 130). Sylvia Plath wrote especially about the impact of the negative father complex in her vitriolic poem, 'Daddy'. There she exploded with rage, dis-enchantment, dis-illusion and dis-solution. In this drama the father has to be killed, although he is already dead (Rose, 2011, p. 261). In the poem she proceeded from victim to vengeance, released from the role of dutiful daughter or sweet female. No more will she take it, surrender or give in.

This poem, startling with its overt hatred and brash rage, is a tirade against the father. It is a drama in which the speaker resurrects her vampire-like father only to kill him again and efface a source of her psychological pain. In the poem he is described as the godhead, origin of the country and the word (Rose, 2011, p. 261). For Sylvia Plath, the early love for her father turned into violent rejection. In the poem she killed the father, but the inner persecutory forces eventually killed her. 'Daddy' portrays the violence caused by a father not there and parallels the complex alchemical and psychological themes for becoming one's self.

Arousing controversy, Sylvia Plath wrote beyond the personal, identifying with social and politically violent and persecutory situations. Although this has been noted, especially with the virulent reaction to her Holocaust references in the poem, there is general trauma or paradox in identification with the father (Rose, 2011, p. 266). She experienced difficulty studying the father's German language, and in the poem, she cannot speak to him.

> I could never talk to you.
> The tongue stuck in my jaw ...
> I could hardly speak.
> I thought every German was you.
> And the language was obscene ...
>
> (Plath, 1981, p. 224)

The poem's speaker has come to the end of the line with this father, unable to speak or be understood. The poem tears apart the myth of a father's right to dominate. As he is both feared and desired, her identity and language are lost with the father who is oppressive in his absence. Ubiquitous and invisible, finding him nowhere, he is everywhere (Rose, 2011, p. 263).

The emotionally laden staccato rhythm in the poem 'Daddy' describes the anguish of her reactions both interpersonally and intrapsychically. Rage from the melancholic daughter is directed against the seductive paternal oppressor (Britzolakis, 1999, p. 213). It is like the beating of a heart that is crying out, shrieking to be heard. The poem protests a lost father; his spectre is black, authoritarian, overpowering. She vacillates between love for him, guilt for this love and the wish to kill him. About Sylvia Plath's words of violence, British writer Jacqueline Rose commented: 'Writing is as much a place to explore what did not happen but is – say – most feared or desired as what did' (Malcolm, 1994, p. 187).

> I was ten when they buried you.
> At twenty I tried to die
> and get back, back, back to you.
>
> (Plath, 1981, p. 224)

'Daddy' also addresses the betrayals and loss of love with her husband, Ted Hughes, enacting a doubling of similar emotions when her father died. Both men left her with grief, rage, masochism and revenge. The poem recounts that she married a husband who was like her father, and both took her blood. The synchronous link is that she knew her father for eight years before he died and her husband for eight years before she killed herself. In her journal Plath recounted:

> I dreamed the other night of running after Ted through a huge hospital, knowing he was with another woman, going into mad wards and looking for him everywhere: what makes you think it was Ted? It had his face but it was my father, my mother. I identify him with my father at certain times, and these times take on great importance: e.g., that one fight at the end of the school year when I found him not-there on the special day ... Isn't this an image of what I feel my father did to me? ... Images of his (Ted's) faithlessness with women echo my fear of my father's relation with my mother and Lady Death.
>
> (Kukil, 2000, p. 447)

The dream illustrates the negative father complex personified by the elusive, death-dealing, rejecting and changing males who are also associated with Lady Death. Here is re-enacted the internal strife and triangulation between herself, her parents and husband.

Bitterness appears in the first line, 'You do not do, you do not do / Anymore, black shoe', where the speaker identifies herself as the foot restricted by the shoe (Plath, 1981, p. 222). Symbolically she is held within the phallic shoes implying repression from a confining father. A shoe suggests following a particular identity, so perhaps the speaker is acknowledging she cannot follow the father's path but must pursue her own. The fact that the shoe is black could also represent the father's shadow that she can now identify rather than assume (Rose, 2002, p.

12). This makes the poem a means of separation managed by expressing intense emotion.

The narrator declares, 'Daddy, I have had to kill you. / You died before I had time –'. These lines reveal the frustration at not being able to kill the father image before now. 'Daddy' is sarcastically named 'a bag full of God'. The line 'I made a model of you' indicates her seeking similar achievements to get his approval even as he is associated with a blackboard. In another line, 'A father bites his daughter's heart in two' represents the cognition of his presence as a hostile reality, vicious and unmerciful to her heart. The desire for father love instead proves to be torturous on 'the rack and the screw'. The father is compared to a swastika, 'so black no sky could squeak through'. The speaker refers to herself 'like a Jew' several times, reinforcing being a victim to the Nazi father: 'Daddy, you can lie back now. // There's a stake in your fat black heart' (Plath, 1981, p. 224).

As the poem progresses, its tone seeps into disdain directed at herself and his image, before erupting into triumphant fury with the line, 'Daddy, you bastard …'. 'Daddy' called a bastard means a father who has no father (Rose, 1991, p. 269). Here she was not only cursing him but also releasing his hold on her personality, identity and destiny as he was determined to be illegitimate. In the poem after seven years she amassed the strength to defeat him. This is the same length of time appearing in fairy tales when the maiden is ensconced in a forest, a castle or underground. The maiden's emergence, like the poem's end, signifies the years of fear, hiding and pain are over. Ultimately, Sylvia Plath attained power not by following the dream of marrying a prince and subsuming herself in him, but through appropriating the male energy herself. The poem is an emotional catharsis at the father, transforming the voice of the young female into the one who can obliterate him. She resists enclosure with the father in a partial psychological victory of the daughter triumphing over him. The true self emerges from entrapment in the false self by overthrowing repression and oppression. She is no longer paralyzed and has broken out of being man's prey.

'The vampire of primal hate … silences her if she does not use the energy' (Van Dyne, 1993, p. 54). Filled with his blood, tainted by his identity, is the daughter like the father in the very ways she abhors? Daddy is vampirish, and vampires make their victims into what they are. If this applies to the description of him as aggressor, she has the power to kill. In its discomfiting portrayals, the speaker in 'Daddy' extricates herself from the father's psychological hold, yet who is she without him? Driving the stake in his heart might not really free her and instead could be an example of psychological splitting. Is she now free to use the aggression against herself?

'Sylvia Plath occupied a place of the crisis of representation in the place of the father' (Rose, 1991, p. 227). She wanted to get back to him. Is this to her childhood? Is this to be dead with him, as it is often interpreted? Is this the ambivalent back and forth dynamics of giving up old patterns? The popularity of this poem is juxtaposed with more of her poetry presenting the female protagonists as objects in the male-inscribed text. There, the themes and images abound of physical dismemberment through mutilation, torture and victimization, gruesomely describing the tragedy of what happens to the overpowered feminine. The woman is portrayed as vulnerable, erased and unable to forge her own image. The power of her writing and the tragedy of her story as well as the dismay at how she was pathologized by male criticism to a psychological or mentally ill case with her psychic pain lost in the process (Rose, 2011, 345).

Inconsolable

The father constellated her petrifaction and maybe even her suicide. Sylvia Plath did not escape the early childhood wounds associated with her father. Her writings on the father express complex feelings with which many readers still identify. The conflict she carried psychologically demonstrated aspects of the struggles of many daughters – the psychological and the personal and collective wounds continuing from generation to generation. She described women in situations where the self is distorted, disguised and in shards, selves that are petrified, cracked, patched up, disillusioned and divided (Ekmekçioğlu, 2008, p. 96). Emerging from the images in her poems of plastic dolls, mannequins, robots and idols of the male imagination, the body is an object, a stony possession becoming one of carnal vengeance – and ultimately denied.

Her life represented the extremes of tragedy mixed with accomplishment. Yet her words live on, reflecting a disturbing netherworld shaped by her father's influence and the destructive effects of the physically and emotionally absent father. The psychological oppression, desire for release and vengeful reactions that are central to her poetry are also infused with death and rebirth. Jung wrote that:

> Conflict consists in the fact that two forces are at war within him: on the one hand the justified longing of the ordinary man for happiness, satisfaction and security, and on the other a ruthless passion for creation which may go so far as to override every personal desire … . He usually must pay dearly for the divine gifts of creative fire.
>
> (1960, p. 102)

Sylvia Plath's life, death and writings have been interpreted in many ways. Her poetry was laden with rejection, isolation, frustration, internal division, self-alienation and a restless dynamism trying to escape the deadening enclosures. She described protagonists in search of identity and truth, as women demanding sacrifice, hinting at her eventual suicide. Her creative work was rooted in traumatic experiences existing in the psyche. Although emotional wounds can lack language and cognition, her words expressed the concomitant necessity of recounting losses and working through the painful areas. She wrote: 'Writing breaks open the vaults of the dead' (Kukil, 2000, p. 286), and it has been conjectured that 'She remained broken where she should be whole' (Kroll, 1976, p. 110). Yet, true to the paradox and ambivalence of the psyche as it seeks regulation, she also included the possibility of rebirth.

'The father remains artificially present, but not internally included in any set of relationships. It is as if the mind of the child remains completely out of touch with him as an existing person' (Kohon, 1999, p. 36). Her father's life and death left her bereft, unable to be consoled in an absence that became a devouring aggression against herself. In the disturbing netherworld shaped by his influence. If she had remained muted, she would have avoided both self-knowledge and the sharing of it.

Although the incorporation of destructive forces took her life, her struggle remains inviolable through her words, charging future generations to continue efforts to access their souls. She used her self-agency to deal with the absence oppressing her. Sylvia Plath's quest, her personal myth as expressed in her poetry, explored the contemporary, psychological and social imbalances propelling her quest. Grappling with the ordeals of feminine identity and estrangement, discordance and unity, her poetry during the last year of her life underwent transformations, reinventions and increased authority. Her words illustrated reversals and inversions of meaning and the poetic parallax inherent in the creative process. This parallels the therapeutic process for psychological repair. Jung said about the poet and her task: 'The primordial experiences rend from top to bottom the curtain upon which is painted the picture of an ordered world, and allow a glimpse into the unfathomable abyss of the unborn and of things yet to be' (1960, para. 141).

References

Alverez, A. (1971). *The Savage God: A Study of Suicide.* New York, NY: W.W. Norton & Company.
Bollas, C. (1995). *Cracking Up: The Work of Unconscious Experience.* New York, NY: Hill & Wang.
Britzolakis, C. (1999). *Sylvia Plath and the Theatre of Mourning.* London, England: Clarendon Press.
Ekmekçioğlu, N. (2008). Sylvia Plath's mirrors reflecting various guises of self. *Plath Profiles, 1*, 92–102.
Frankel, R. (2013). Digital melancholy. *Jung Journal: Culture & Psyche, 7*(4), 9–20.
Green, A. (1986). *On Private Madness.* London, England: The Hogarth Press.
Jacoby, M. (1992). The analytical psychology of C.G. Jung and the problem of literary evaluation. In: R. Sugg (Ed.), *Jungian Literary Criticism* (pp. 59–74). Evanston, IL: Northwestern University Press.
Jung, C.G. (1955). *Modern Man in Search of a Soul.* New York, NY: Harcourt Brace.
Jung, C.G. (1960). *The Spirit in Man, Art, and Literature*, Vol 15. Princeton, NJ: Princeton University Press.
Jung, C.G. (1963). *Memories, Dreams, Reflections.* New York, NY: Vintage.
Kohon, G. (Ed.) (1999). *The Dead Mother: The Work of André Green.* London, England: Routledge.
Kristeva, J. (1991) *Strangers to Ourselves.* Leon Roudiez (Trans.). London, England: Harvester Wheatsheaf.

Kroll, J. (1976). *Chapters in a Mythology: The Poetry of Sylvia Plath*. New York, NY: Harper and Row.

Kukil, K. (Ed.) (2000). *The Unabridged Journals of Sylvia Plath*. New York, NY: Anchor.

Malcolm, J. (1994). *The Silent Woman*. New York, NY: Knopf.

O'Reilly, C. (2004). Sylvia Plath. In: J. Parini (Ed.), *The Oxford Encyclopedia of American Literature*, Vol 3 (pp. 355–62). Oxford, England: Oxford University Press.

Plath, S. (1979). *Johnny Panic and the Bible of Dreams*. London, England: Faber and Faber.

Plath, S. (1981). *Collected Poems*. New York, NY: HarperCollins.

Rose, J. (1991). *The Haunting of Sylvia Plath*. London, England: Virago Press.

Rose, J. (2002). This is not biography. *London Review of Books*, *24*(16), 12–15.

Rose, J. (2011). *The Jacqueline Rose Reader*. Durham, NC: Duke University Press.

Van Dyne, S. (1993). *Revising Life: Sylvia Plath's Ariel Poems*. Chapel Hill, NC: University of North Carolina Press.

Chapter 15

Filling the absence

What fills absence? Despair, defeat, depression, joy, pleasure, new ways? Absence of father is an area to explore, to understand, to gain release from and to become oneself. Without the good and present father, a daughter's life can slant to disappointment, discouragement and expectations sadly unmet, as she is burdened by the memory of his absence. The lack gives point and necessity to the pursuit. It becomes the pursuit of self and the value of changing from what was into what can be.

The emphasis is on how to stay conscious of the hurt, cynicism, denial or avoidance and use her experiences for development out of the absent space. It means emerging from the ashes into the creative. It means recognizing the pain in the lack, the spaces unrepaired and missing. But it also means that by doing so the daughter realises her own self-expression. Jung wrote in an essay entitled 'Women in Europe' that it was up to women to move the story onwards. In doing that, this book attempts to expand from absence and lack to knowledge and assertion, so the daughter of an absent father can take her place as she sees fit. The relationship with the absent father constitutes both a context of loss, rage, longing, wounds, despair and emptiness as well as a significant entry gate to transformation.

Gaining corroboration for the emotional effects of absence is not so easy when there is a powerful cultural overlay and history of denial. With an absent father, the daughter's story is made inconsequential. Father was in charge, and she was told for so many years to accept it. Psychologically, the two opposites contain not only what is being shed or left behind but also what is being discovered and gained. The absent father remains a presence and representation within the psyche even when experience has been lacking; positive and expansive representation can be created, encouraging a daughter's individuality. Because the father archetype implies qualities residing or possible in all people, the daughter can develop a beneficial and supportive father of impetus and energy for her well-being without the physical father (Kast, 1997, p. 123). The hope here is that through inner psychological work the daughter finds the way into herself. This applies personally and culturally, consciously and unconsciously.

Even at the crossroads of change, we carry the memory and influence of the father/patriarchy, a time denoting the too-central masculine and less-central feminine. These are the issues for the daughter to unravel and the material from which to re-create her life, her hopes, and her self. 'From the idea that the self is not given to us, I think that there is only one practical consequence: we have to create ourselves as a work of art' (Foucault, 1997, p. 262). Psychologically daughters lacking the father figure have the need, opportunity and responsibility to fill the gap, as it is a space still too empty.

> Pain has an element of blank;
> It cannot recollect
> When it began, or if there were
> A day when it was not.
>
> (Dickinson, n.d., XIX, p. 47)

Rather than engage in a return to what was the traditional pattern, the Jungian process of individuation, the process of personality becoming, recognizes the responsibility to understand what is lacking and move beyond it. As Jung put it: 'Personality is the supreme realization of the innate idiosyncrasy of a living being. It is an act of high courage flung in the face of life, the absolute affirmation of all that constitutes the individual' (Jung, 1954, para. 289). As the stories told in this book illustrate, the quandary of the daughter becoming her complete self entails transgressing beyond the father into the passions of life as they define her. The journey towards embracing a more embodied self, although fraught with uncertainty, leads to conscious repair and a greater sense of solidity and internal soul connection. It may not, however, lead to an actual relationship between father and daughter. To merely forgive is an insufficient answer; accepting the fact that there are some unredeemable situations is also part of becoming conscious.

The psychological work includes grieving the absent, emotionally dead father, processing the losses and mourning the suffering. The wounds are addressed through attention to the unconscious and its connections to conscious life. The effort is to explicate the damages and discover what can be transformed. As the energy shifts, a daughter establishes authenticity when she no longer either accedes to or rebels against the father. She has her own feet firmly planted, but not in the father tradition.

An absent father does not teach love, respect or affirm the daughter's personal choices. The daughter might become defiant, compliant or adopt various iterations of these conscious or unconscious responses. Any of them can lock her in protest against a father not there, perpetuating the continuation of negative and demeaning patterns. The gilded ideal of paternal traditions imprisons daughters, does not affirm personal choices and holds her in stasis. The search for the father, the lost love object, and feelings about herself as a result of his absence, maltreatment, emotional lack and damage are the dominant psychological themes. These are what she can repair, as can he.

André Green described 'the colors of mourning [as] black or white. Black as in severe depression, or blank as in states of emptiness' (Green, 1986, p. 146).

From black to white, this is the range a daughter contends with, as what has been repressed and ignored leaves holes in the psyche. According to Green, absence is not absent, as it leaves a presence. Absence seeks to be filled, to realize what has been unconscious and references how we do or do not cope. Recognizing what was *not there* is necessary for new things to become possible. To accept the reality of lack opens the door to new experiences. As traced through the many narratives here, filling the absence means going into and through the feelings and emotions playing havoc with the daughter's mind, body and soul.

The daughter walks a long road from illusions and wishes towards authenticity and reality. Integration occurs through encountering the oppositions between 'as-if' and the real and accepting the shadow and the abject in psyche and body. To do this, she has to betray the collusion with the roles detrimental to her individual style and find supportive ones. It takes time, often more time than imagined, to acknowledge the personal and collective historical memories marked by unrequited desires and losses. Here is the psychological work to be done, part of which is consciously feeling the hurt in order to move through it. The process requires examining the past, finding ways for self-care and rebuilding related inner father images. The daughter uses the acquired psychological flexibility and elasticity to carve out the new, to educate, to solve issues and find potentials beyond the previous and conventional. This process redefines traditions formerly dictated by the father way as she differentiates into her own way.

The emotional gaps from father absence do matter. The daughter's hurt is real and the emotional deprivation a problem. Dreams are often crushed and the daughter demoralized. Yet the absence also motivates the impulses to unravel complicated truths, hurt and despair. The process of self-awareness is like walking a labyrinth. This work pierces the psychological complexes. It means becoming conscious of the past to move into the present and future with awareness, developing an independent self and reigniting desires and passions.

The daughter without a father learned to put on masks to please but behind this lay his legacy imposing on her self-doubt and impotency, lack of focus or grounding. She might have feigned confidence and composure, creating façades, feeling the need to protect, all the while metaphorically locking herself alone in her room. But there remains little safety or security when isolated within as it causes outer isolation as well.

The more unconsciously destructive a father is, the more likely a daughter will acquire a similar behaviour. She might seem unreal, artificial to herself and at odds with the world. With little sense of personal constancy or cohesiveness, she wavers. American poet Adrienne Rich commented: 'It is an extremely painful and dangerous way to live – split between a publicly acceptable persona, and a part of yourself that you perceive as the essential, the creative and powerful self, yet also as possibly unacceptable, perhaps even monstrous' (1979, p. 175).

Psychological development is marred by a father's absence. He has been a mystery, and this arouses strong feelings, misconceptions and unresolved longing. The non-presence of the father can tenaciously occupy a central position in the daughter's psyche. Common themes in my work with such a daughter are feelings of being half in life, being uncommitted, unsure, faltering although talented. She manifests anxiety about relationships and intimacy. She might retain anger or be susceptible to developing somatic symptoms from a shaken sense of identity and poor self-image.

Without a nurturing paternal figure, this daughter can be susceptible to invasion by negative images. She might identify with an insufficient father or a completely absent one. He does not mirror a range of helpful masculine or feminine energies. Self-denigrating habits and moods abound when a father cannot fulfil his daughter's needs for love and affirmation. The internalized negative energy coagulates, as did his neglect, humiliation, abandonment and emotional or physical assaults, making it difficult for her to love or care for herself. Showing him adoration and idealization, even when turning her back on him, she can become buried in his skin and act against herself. As the emotionally, physically, psychically missing or, in some cases, dead father becomes idealised, there is a concomitant repression of negative feelings towards him. Both the daughter's idealization and her warding off of anything negative are attempts to compensate, betraying the fact he was just not there. In reality this daughter lives under wraps, her desires ignored; she is confused and distracted with destructiveness lurking beneath the façade and going along with the idealization of him – but not of herself.

The memories can no longer be held back. From her experiences with an absent father, the child and later the adult are affected. She carries the scars of refusal and rejection. The absent father can become an inner unsatisfied and unapproachable judge. She feels forever pushed about, examined, futile, trapped, disintegrated and hopeless. What goes on between the father and daughter, or does not, is an important determinant of whether she will become an adult capable of living her whole self. Or will she be ashamed, dragged back by his abandonment? If so, she does not breathe deeply, fears being hurt and struggles to make her creativity come alive. An uncomfortable, aimless and searching nature defines those devoid of sufficient fathering. Psychological attitudes can only change through letting go of idealized images and acknowledging the insufficient and even dangerous father.

Betraying the traditional father is a way to recall herself. Remaining faithful to old images and his authority devalues her existence. All this is more intricate and complex because the feminine and masculine, as inner and outer concepts and realities, are more fluid. As humans, we have many identifications and pluralities of choices. Hence, we do not only have to unconsciously repeat tradition or engage in a conventional return as that merely succeeds in propping up what was ailing. Through feeling the absence, the daughter has a responsibility to listen to herself and express her thoughts. Although she is privy to the absence of a father, this lack can push her to her true self. This betrayal sets her on the journey to encountering so she can move beyond what has formerly been merely accepted.

Many daughters have a story of hurt and sadness. She might not yet realize how the repression and denial set in and over time mushroomed. From lack and the pain of absence, she might have become a starving self. This takes time to address. As her awareness opens and she gains insight, she is able to move beyond the abandonment, resentments and betrayals. Jung wrote at the end of his essay, 'The significance of the father in the destiny of the individual': 'It is to be hoped that experience in the years to come will sink deeper shafts into this obscure territory, on which I have been able to shed but a fleeting light' (1961, p. 301).

In the process of addressing the absence, the daughter proceeds to be conscious of fulfilling her existence. Meaning comes after the experiences, after the loss, and often evolves with time passing. It takes a while to realize the impact of the father absence, as this absence has to be acknowledged and the loss mourned. She transforms through psychological examination of memory. Linking experiences and finding meaning brings release and healing. It moves the status quo. To look back and yet grow beyond the old daughter–father patterns, the conscious and unconscious must come together. It also means no longer remaining a copy of the female model built on outmoded patriarchal concepts.

Paternal dynamics, too often loaded with deprivations and/or distortions, influence the reasons that a daughter enters therapeutic treatment. Women may present with a variety of issues such as narcissism, the 'as-if' personality, the dead father effect, problems with intimacy, identity, the mix of masculine and feminine – with their roots in either the direct father–daughter relationship or its absence. Their paths open for psychological understanding and knowledge traverse both psyche and body. The process means staying aware, learning to hold while releasing the destructive attachment, opting for voice rather than silence. Various perspectives on father abandonments, neglect, lack of nurturing and general absence come from French psychoanalysts André Green and Julia Kristeva, the negative father complex in Jungian analytical psychology, the 'as-if' personality, excerpts from the life and poetry of Sylvia Plath, the puella archetype, narcissism and the composite examples of patients seen.

By breaking down the ideal a daughter can reclaim her life rather than be swayed by denial. She then can access the spark within according to her own particular real rather than false standards. To name the pain from the father absence both validates and simultaneously separates her from the father way. This involves engaging with the wounds, reclaiming the damaged parts and integrating the shadow aspects. When a daughter can dream into her own life and walk through the experience of the absent father, she finds she is able to do so (Rose, 2011, p. 341). What opens is a sense of wonderment and freshness, a space of fluidity and flux, creativity expressed. It is a space of richness, complexity and establishing her voice.

Yet, there is a brutal aspect to what has happened in the daughter–father dynamics even as its recognition is a move in the direction of growth. André Green called this the negative instinct, and like destruction it involves the killing or elimination of the father image (Kalinich & Taylor, 2009, p. 192). Often, this is what it takes to alter what has been. There is something intensely seductive about the negative father complex with its repetition of past thoughts, feelings and actions. These are aspects from the ancestry of the absent father bankrupt of attention and sufficient expression of love and care. Through therapy the daughter learns to negotiate what were the blank and empty cycles, to leave the illusions behind. Getting in touch with the complex reality brings a capacity to discover and sustain nourishing internal dialogue as well as relationships with others.

Consciousness of self is the basic goal of the process Jung termed individuation. 'Individuation means becoming a single, homogeneous being, and, in so far as "individuality" embraces our innermost, last, and incomparable uniqueness, it also implies becoming one's own self. We could therefore translate individuation as ... "self-realization"' (Jung, 1966, para. 266). Individuation is the development of the capacity to realize and to experience one's separateness, one's wholeness, one's uniqueness (Jung, 1959, para. 490). Inner work encourages us to remain engaged in the challenge of making sense of and space for the analytic and therapeutic relationship to enrich life. The psychological search requires being exposed and also distraught, stripped to the core. Past wounds and hurts are examined to attain flexibility of thought and affect. And, again, the reality of the damage does not always lead to love and relatedness. The situation goes beyond acceptance and might mean that although the daughter can be restored, the father relationship cannot. The journey is not aimed at happiness per se but has a wider perspective.

The personality continues to search. Internal examination brings the conscious and unconscious into alignment, helps break the old traps, betrayals, abandonments and losses. Analysis is an attempt to articulate a problem that is, or should be, preoccupying in our times. The hope is that from lack and absence both daughters and fathers can emerge as more related, connected and consciously understood. Admittedly, many daughters are left to deal with the damage, but they can recover their lives. Therapy helps create something other than the usual self-defeating ideology and brings her into an internal resilience she did not previously know or own. Becoming active in self-expression leads to an integrated personality and releases the creative spaces where a daughter can realize her potential rather than ignore or misuse it.

Fathers can also learn about growing a more complete relationship with their daughters. The absence of fathers affects them as well as their daughters. The absence is to be filled by both but in diverse ways. The process will be similar to that of the daughter in recognizing the lack and how it has composed their personalities, depriving them both who are now seeking other solutions. Fathers no longer have to go along with this lack. They also can participate in the changes leading from imbalances to entering uncharted and challenging territories. Fathers can take the information about their daughters and apply it consciously to their own selves, creating honest, fuller and more satisfying and conscious relationships.

The way out is to re-open to the 'deconstruction of old constructions' (Phillips, 2001, p. 205). Analysis disturbs the enclosure in old narratives and upsets the former balance that was imbalance. The purpose, therefore, is not to reconstruct what was but to regain another synthesis of the psychological elements. New forms open ways to retranslate and discover what is now possible. It is a re-centring and claiming of representation. This brings receptivity to other stories, the others within, a personality able to surprise and expand. The messages from absence, the pain and deep hurt are inescapable but also open the daughter to the core of who she is. By conscious gathering of the psyche, she is found and able to fill the absence.

Encounters can then occur based on the real rather than the imagined. Rather than wishing for the past to have been better, she listens to the present situation, entering into a dialogue of thought, rather than the predictable old complexes. She takes charge of her speech. As Luce Irigaray, French psychoanalyst, said, 'We have to listen to the present speaking of the other in its irreducible difference with a view to the way through which we could correspond to it in faithfulness to ourselves' (2002, p. xi).

The psyche is trying to balance, expand, emerge and alter the energy for new horizons to open. The imaginal world of the psyche contains healing properties and through imaginative projections these daughters can entertain possibilities and be potentialized (Krampe, 2003, p. 132). Rather than only suffering absence and lack, she is weaving the tapestry of her life. She begins to honour feelings and listen to her own self. She can hear the unconscious rather than be overrun by anxieties, compulsions, losses and the sorrows of frustrated desires. Her heart can begin to blossom by going to the dregs of her experiences rather than defending against them.

There is a purposive element at work within, a phenomenon Jung referred to as the self. This core aspect of the psyche restores her psychology by getting inside herself and beyond the prescribed scripts of a dutiful daughter. Jungian analysis includes working with the defences and resistances in the distorted and stuck areas. And all this applies as well to fathers who are more involved in the family and emotional life and thereby honouring their psyches.

Jungian depth work means being uncertain and respecting the uniqueness of the personality. The mystery of the human psyche keeps us managing the not knowing while searching for meaning. Elucidating this process Victoria dreamt: *I am sitting on one of many rocks surrounding a well. I am swaying from side to side as I play. With each movement toward the well I draw out a dream on a gossamer streamer and give it to one of the people gathered there.* The dream was significant to Victoria as she realized it connected her to increased possibilities and to the depth and breadth of life. By following her heart she was dipping into the well of personality parts formerly rejected, neglected and relegated to the shadows.

The love relationship with father serves many functions. 'Psychic structure evolves through the interaction of internal and external worlds' (Benjamin, 1995, p. 121). The absent father is a powerful inner agent in the emotional life of a daughter. Absence means that the offer of recognition and the experience of being wanted for her individuality are also absent. The wish and desire to be seen derives, in part, from healthy and wide-ranging identifications with a father. The father qualities and dynamics with the daughter affect relationships to self and other, body and psyche, conscious and unconscious.

Absence of father confronts the daughter with both vulnerability and the resilience to thrive. Exploring the absence of father draws out the creativity to make life worthwhile. The problematic symptoms turn towards a gaining of strength. Reassembling the present from the shambles of the past and making sense of what happened is complex. It means confronting memories and bringing them into the new light of consciousness and hope. Nothing really goes away and the process means going back and embracing the vibrant self.

A woman dreamt that before her were many old books and also an iPad and iPhone, all mixed together, and she had an urge to explore each one. She could not wait to have the time for them all. She reflected the dream meant her continued enthusiasm to know more, to keep on in her late sixties; her thirst for learning had neither ended nor had it been quenched. She felt free to hope, and even though she could recognize huge chunks had been taken from her with an absent father, she had moved from despair and deprivation into being inquisitive and curious for more knowledge. A quote from the French feminist Simone de Beauvoir provides an answer to the absent father experience:

> I saw opening out before me a clearly marked field of activity, with all its problems, its hard work, its materials, its instruments, and its inflexibility. I no longer asked myself: what shall I do? There was everything to be done, everything I had formerly longed to do ... but everything was possible.
>
> (2005, p. 365)

Rainer Maria Rilke wrote a letter to a young poet over a century ago, in which he urged the young man to try to love the questions themselves, to live with them, not to try and obtain answers because it would be too soon, but some day if he really were able to live the questions themselves he might live his way into the answers (Rilke, 1986, p. 34).

> Love the world as your self; then you can care for all things.
>
> Lao Tzu, *Tao Te Ching* (Verse 13)

References

Benjamin, J. (1995). *Like Subjects, Love Objects: Essays on Recognition and Sexual Difference*. New Haven, CT: Yale University Press.
De Beauvoir, S. (2005). *Memoirs of a Dutiful Daughter*. New York, NY: Harper Collins.
Dickinson, E. (n.d.). *Poems by Emily Dickinson, Series One*. [Etext 2678]. Retrieved from https://www.gutenberg.org/files/12242/12242-h/12242-h.htm#Series_One.
Foucault, M. (1997). *Ethics, Subjectivity and Truth*. London, England: Allen Lane.
Green, A. (1986). *On Private Madness*. London, England: The Hogarth Press.
Irigaray, L. (2002). *The Way of Love*. London, England: Continuum.
Jung, C.G. (1954). *The Development of Personality*, Vol. 17. Princeton, NJ: Princeton University Press.

Jung, C.G. (1959). *The Archetypes and the Collective Unconscious*. New York, NY: Pantheon Books.

Jung, C.G. (1961). *Freud and Psychoanalysis*, Vol. 4. Princeton, NJ: Princeton University Press.

Jung, C.G. (1966). *Two Essays on Analytical Psychology*, Vol. 7. New York, NY: Pantheon Books.

Kalinich, L. & Taylor, S.W. (2009). *The Dead Father*. London, England: Routledge.

Kast, V. (1997). *Father, Daughter, Mother, Son*. Zurich, Switzerland: Element Books.

Krampe, E.M. (2003). The inner father. *Fathering, 1*(2), 131–48.

Phillips, A. (2001). *Promises, Promises*. New York, NY: Basic Books.

Rich, A. (1979). *Essential Essays: Culture, Politics, and the Art of Poetry*. S.M. Gilbert (Ed.). New York, NY: W.W. Norton.

Rilke, R.M. (1986). *Letters to a Young Poet*. S. Mitchell (Ed.). New York, NY: Random House.

Rose, J. (2011). *The Jacqueline Rose Reader*. Durham, NC: Duke University Press.

Index

Made in the USA
Las Vegas, NV
04 April 2024

88265258R00109